Ex Líbrís

Randy Manning

B212 © APCo

THE

ANTIETAM
CAMPAIGN

THE ANTIETAM CAMPAIGN

John Cannan

GALLERY BOOKS

An Imprint of W. H. Smith Publishers Inc.

112 Madison Avenue
New York City 10016

Acknowledgments

There are so many people who, knowingly or unknowingly, assisted me in the creation of this my first effort at a book and of course I would like to thank them all. Much thanks go to Robert Pigeon and Albert Nofi who gave me the chance in the first place. For assistance in preparing the research and writing, gratitude must be extended to the friendly people at the Falvey Library, Philadelphia Free Library, Civil War Library and Museum, Boston Public Library, Dartmouth College Library, University of Georgia Library, University of Maryland Library, Library of Congress, and IMS Department/Villanova University. Also thanks to Dr. Joseph Casino whose immense wisdom helped me deal with some of the many difficulties of trying to describe a battle and for getting me interested in the Civil War in the first place. And my gratitude to Gavin Spiers for being there for so many years, putting me up in Washington, and for driving me around most of Maryland. I am indebted to Bill Byrne whose advice, auspices as a good friend, and incredible patience about overdue library books contributed immensely to this volume. Other people who have helped with the many aspects of this work in their own special ways are; Carol Breedlove, Park Ranger David Fox, Erik Schmidth, Troy Lowry, Jim Weeks, Sam La, Gary Cywinski, Luisa Cywinski, Charles Desnoyers, Dave Chen, Charles Johnson, Joe Muscella, Fred Marcantonio, Team Bookstore (Rick Markham, Kevin McDonnell, Rod Jaballis, Jim Burnett, Joe Sigey), Jeff Middleton, Arthur Yao, Mike Hicks, and, of course, Alexandra, Edmund, Dan and John Owen.

To My Family: Mom, Pop, Edward, Jane, Gwynedd, Catherine, David, Celia, Clare, Teresa, Fran, Alice, Paul, and Marc.

Editorial development and design by Combined Books, Inc., 26 Summit Grove Avenue, Suite 207, Bryn Mawr, PA 19010.

Produced by Wieser and Wieser, Inc., 118 East 25th Street, New York, NY 10010.

This 1990 edition published by Gallery Books, and imprint of W.H.Smith, Publishers, Inc., 112 Madison Avenue, New York, NY 10016.

ISBN 0-8317-0379-2

Printed by Bertelsmann Printing & Manufacturing, Co., U.S.A.

CONTENTS

INTRODUCTION

The day 5 September 1862 was a glorious moment in the annals of the Army of Northern Virginia. As a regimental band happily played, the jubilant and victorious legions of Lee, Longstreet, and Jackson crossed the Potomac into Maryland in the first invasion of Northern territory in the East. This crossing was only the second stage of an offensive that had begun almost a month previous with the battle of Cedar Mountain. Since late June the fortunes of both the North and South had changed dramatically. The Confederacy seemed to be on the edge of collapse; McClellan was storming the gates of Richmond with a mighty host of almost a hundred thousand men while the embattled Rebels could only muster half that number. The Federals didn't know it yet but their fate had been sealed on 31 May when Robert E. Lee assumed command of the Army of Northern Virginia after the previous commander Joseph E. Johnston was wounded in the Battle of Seven Pines. On 26 June, a smashing attack was launched against the Army of the Potomac and in a week it was no longer a threat, blockaded up at Harrison's Landing on the James River. Shortly after Stonewall Jackson's victory at the Battle of Cedar Mountain, Lee was able to turn his attention north against the hated John Pope and his Army of Virginia, launching an incredi-

ble campaign that would lead to a spectacular victory on the fields of the old Manassas battlefield and later take him across the Potomac on that long and bloody road to the penultimate confrontation with his arch-nemesis McClellan near Sharpsburg, Maryland, on the banks of the Antietam. As Lee's star rose, so fell the fortunes of McClellan, the Federal soldiers that followed him and the entire Union war effort. For "Little Mac," the Virginia phase of the Antietam Campaign marked the period when he vied for control of the army in the Eastern Theatre with a rival, John Pope. Both men, embracing dissimilar conceptions as to how the war would be waged, embarked on a bitter relationship of hatred and jealousy that could only lead to the ultimate disaster. While McClellan would emerged victorious from the struggle, his loyalty and judgement would be forever tainted in the eyes of Lincoln and his cabinet.

As McClellan and Lee embarked on the epic Antietam Campaign, both men possessed the potential to win a victory that could have ended the war early and win the bloody struggle for their own faction. In the end neither accomplished their true military objectives. Instead, Lincoln found a victory which, in turn, became a triumph for the Union and human freedom; the Emancipation Proclamation.

CHAPTER I

PRELIMINARIES
26 June – 11 August, 1862

John Pope was on leave from his command of the Army of Mississippi in June of 1862 when he received a fateful telegram commanding him to travel to Washington D.C. to take command of an army being prepared for his use. Up to early summer of that year, Pope had enjoyed several military victories out west including his successful campaign against the Confederate garrisons at New Madrid and Island Number 10. While the imposing general from the West was the darling of several Republican politicians and well known to Lincoln, Pope had not managed to win much respect from his comrades in arms who, due to his penchant for bluster and bragging, contemptuously labeled him a "bag of wind." Amongst the ranks of Pope's civilian detractors was Lincoln's Postmaster General and confidant, Montgomery Blair. He probably summed up the General best, describing him as a "braggart and a liar, with some courage but not much capacity." Despite jibes from Pope's myriad of critics, he was still a hard fighter, a quality that was desperately needed for the Union war effort in the East that was plagued by military leaders either too timid or incompetent.

To get the gist of his new mission, Pope quickly traveled to the Union capital to meet with a haggard Secretary of War, Edwin M. Stanton, whom the General described as having "the appearance of a man that had lost much sleep and was tired in both body and mind." For all the pains the trials of government had wreaked upon him in the harrowing months of civil war, the Secretary's infamous dictatorial demeanor was hardly impaired as he detailed Pope's role to be assumed in the East: to take command of the various Union forces scattered across northern Virginia, concentrating them into a force that could threaten the Confederate capital at Richmond while protecting Washington and covering the Shenandoah Valley. The units which Pope would lead into the field were a depressed mass of soldiers embarrassed by the ineptitude of their own leaders and humiliated at the hands of Thomas J. "Stonewall" Jackson during his epic Shenandoah Valley Campaign in the spring of 1862. At present, these dispersed forces, under three commanders with Pope junior to them all, were idling away in little communication with each other. Major-General John C. Fremont had some 11,500 men at Cedar Creek in the Shenandoah Valley. Spread out along the Strasburg Turnpike up to Front Royal, were the 8,800 troops of Major-General Nathaniel P. Banks' Shenandoah Department. Holding the largest unit was Major-General Irvin McDowell with some 18,500 troops divided between Brigadier-General James Ricketts' division at Manassas and another under Brigadier-General Rufus King at Fredericksburg. This hodge-podge of various commands was reorganized into the Army of Virginia with Fremont's men comprising the I Corps and Banks' and McDowell's men forming the II and III Corps respectively. Almost immediately after Pope took command on 26 June, there followed a corps command change. An irate Fremont objected to being superseded in command by Pope, a move he regarded as tantamount to a humiliating demotion. In a fit of protest, he tendered his resignation allowing Major-General Franz Sigel to assume the vacated post.

After he had assumed command of the Army

The master of bluster, Major General John Pope. After he led successful campaigns out West, Pope came east to command the newly formed Army of Virginia.

George Brinton McClellan. As his Peninsular Campaign collapsed into failure, McClellan found Pope his rival for command.

of Virginia, Pope issued orders for the consolidation of his far flung units: Sigel and Banks were to withdraw from the Shenandoah Valley and concentrate outside Thorton's Gap. McDowell's corps remained split with King's division held at Fredericksburg to cover Federal lines of communication in northern Virginia while Ricketts' division advanced to the Waterloo Bridge on the Rappahannock. The troop movements were slow and dispirited, hardly giving much cause for enthusiasm in the coming campaign. To rally his men, Pope decided to issue a grand speech to boost their depressed morale:

> I have come to you from the West, where we have always seen the backs of our enemies; from an army whose business it has been to seek the adversary and to beat him when he was found; whose policy was attack and not defense. . . . I presume that I have been called here to pursue the same system and to lead you against the enemy. . . . Meantime I desire you to dismiss from your minds certain phrases, which I am sorry to find so much in vogue amongst you. I hear constantly of "taking strong positions and holding them," of "lines of retreat," and of "bases of supplies." Let us discard such ideas. . . . Let us study the probable lines of retreat of our opponents, and leave our own to take care of themselves. Let us look before us, and not behind. Success and glory are in the advance, disaster and shame lurk in the rear.

Pope's arrogant words, attacking the past failures of his troops, only antagonized his own men who mocked and sneered at their leader, calling him a "five cent Pope." One soldier wrote that " . . . every man in the army wondered if he were a weak and silly man. . . . " Still despite their growing dislike for their new leader, almost every soldier in the Army of Virginia had constantly suffered the bitter taste of defeat and were eager to redeem themselves on the field of battle, with or without John Pope.

As the Army of Virginia prepared for its operations, the "Young Napoleon," Major-General George Brinton McClellan, leading the Army of the Potomac, was slogging away through the swamps of the Peninsula, campaigning against the Confederate capital itself. Despite all the hopes and aspirations that had followed the Young Napoleon to the field, McClellan would ultimately fail due to essential flaws in his character. Too slow and cautious, he constantly refused to attack the enemy until conditions perfectly benefited him. Though he had created the Army of the Potomac by fashioning country and city boys, inexperienced in the ways of war, into the ultimate fighting force, his ability to use them effectively in combat was crippled by an overwhelming compassion for his men (an admirable yet extremely detrimental trait for a military leader). Haunted by the ghosts of possible failure and defeat, the General sabotaged his own plans by overestimating the force of the opposition by thousands of troops. Believing himself to be outnumbered by the enemy, he stalled his movements while calling for large numbers of reinforcements. Unfortunately for McClellan and the country, things were about to get worse before they could get better. On the very day that Pope took command of his Army of Virginia, Robert E. Lee initiated his illustrious Seven Days Campaign of battles and drove the Union foe back down the Peninsula to Harrison's Landing. There the Army of the Potomac waited either for a renewed offensive or a complete withdrawal.

While the Federals were defeated in battle, they had not been defeated in spirit. Despite his faults, McClellan had the uncanny knack to inspire the common soldiery no matter how glum the situation. In his address to the troops of the Army of the Potomac on July 4 (a stark contrast to Pope's embarrassing blunder), he uplifted his men by making it appear that they had won a spectacular victory:

> Your achievements during the last ten days have illustrated the valor and endurance of the American soldier! Attacked by vastly superior forces, and with hope of reinforcements, you have succeeded in changing your base of operations by a flank movement, always regarded as the most hazardous of military expedients. . . . Your conduct ranks you as among the celebrated armies of history. No one will now question that each of you may say with pride: "I belonged to the Army of the Potomac!"

The soldiers responded to their leader's acclaim with praise of their own, affectionately calling their leader "Little Mac" and blaming recent reverses on interfering politicians who had denied the necessary reinforcements to achieve victory. Responding to criticism of McClellan at home, Corporal Adam S. Bright of the 9th Pennsylvania Reserves wrote in a letter to his uncle:

> I see by the papers that a good many people about Pittsburgh and vicinity are giving McClellan hark. I would just like to say to such people that they know nothing and should keep quiet. If they would hang about one half of all the political office hunters about Washington they would do a great service. If McClellan had received reinforcements when he asked for them . . . Richmond and part of

the Rebel army would now be in our possession.

Not only had McClellan failed, but he was refusing to cooperate with Pope in any fashion dismissing him as a political office seeker, a tool of radical abolitionists, and a rival for command. Concomitantly, the General from the West maintained far from favorable opinions of the capabilities of Little Mac,; in his infamous address to his soldiers he had surreptitiously mocked such McClellanesque terms as "lines of retreat," "bases of supply" and "taking strong positions and holding them."

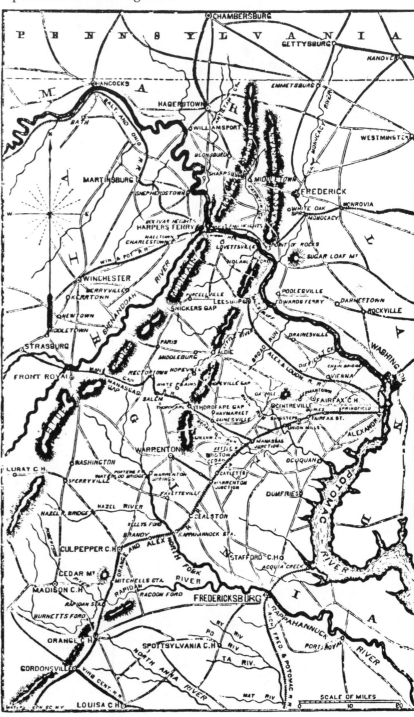

Yankee soldiers sing the praises of their commander Little Mac McClellan. Despite their commander's constant failure to attain victories, the common soldier admired McClellan and followed him loyally.

After receiving a sound beating by Lee and his Confederates, Federal troops of the VI Corps retreat down the Peninsula.

After McClellan's defeat, Lincoln came to the conclusion that another party would have to enforce and oversee cooperation between the Young Napoleon and the "five cent Pope" as well as to control the entire Union war effort which had been under the direction of the president and Stanton. To undertake this task, another general was imported from the West, Major-General Henry Wager Halleck to take the post of General-in-Chief of all the Armies, the position vacated by McClellan when he took to the field on the Peninsula. A military intellectual ill-suited for command, Halleck had talents of more use in bureaucratic affairs than in directing field armies. For the next few months, the befuddled Halleck would have the unenviable job of attempting to balance the animosities between Pope and McClellan that would ultimately threaten the Union war effort with disaster.

In early July, Pope had Sigel, Banks, and Ricketts move south to threaten the Confederate lines of communications for Richmond and Lee's army with the Shenandoah Valley and the rebellious states of the West. This objective was to be accomplished by assailing two vital rail links: Gordonsville and Charlottesville. In order to threaten these links, Brigadier Samuel Crawford's brigade of Banks' corps was advanced ahead of the main force to Culpeper on 14 July. At the same time, Brigadier-General John Hatch with the cavalry of that same corps was to disturb Rebel communications at Gordonsville.

Failing to get the operation underway before an enemy force occupied the town, Hatch was removed from command.

As the Army of Virginia proceeded through enemy territory, its mission was not only to attack the Confederate soldier, but the Confederate populace as well. General Pope had issued an infamous decree for his men to live off the fat of the land at the expense of its citizens. Worse still, the lives of all Virginians within Union lines would be fiercely regulated to ensure their obedience. All local citizens were to be forced to sign an oath of allegiance or be treated as possible spies and transported beyond Confederate lines if they refused. Violation of the sworn oath would be on penalty of death. Furthermore, citizens would be personally held responsible for guerrilla activities against the Union Army. If shots were fired from inside a house, the perpetrators would be executed and the house burned. Through such horrific threats, Pope anticipated the total war later embraced by Grant and Sherman.

While the harshest measures of Pope's cruel policies were never carried out, the troops of the Army of Virginia enjoyed their role as "wicked and demoralized robbers," seeing fit to strip anything of value from the farms and plantations in their wake as Joseph Gould, Quartermaster Sergeant of the 48th Pennsylvania, related:

> . . . General John Pope issued his celebrated order to the troops "to subsist on the country" and the troops took great liberties with it. But, oh, the turkeys, chickens, geese, sheep, pigs, calves, potatoes, and cabbage. Didn't the troops make them disappear? and then live "on the top of the heap." Some would think it strange that members of a regiment would be in favor of foraging, but we were none of those whose tender consciences (or tender sympathies for the rebels) make them think it wrong to live off the enemy. The soldiers thought in the discharge of their duty to the government, it was proper to take from the enemy everything that was of use to us as well as everything they could use against us.

The excessive liberties exercised by Federal soldiers under Pope's orders were such as to merit recriminations from the high command. Orders were issued to punish any soldiers who "entered the house or molested any citizen."

By early August, Halleck found himself in a strategic quandary: his forces were separated between Pope's Army of Virginia and McClellan's Army of the Potomac with Lee in between. Unless these units were united quickly, the Confederate General might fall upon one or the

Henry "Old Brains" Halleck, general in chief of the Federal armies from 1862- 1863.

other at his leisure. Still under the belief that the only chance for victory lay in another campaign on the Peninsula, McClellan argued that if he could only secure some 30,000 reinforcements, he could launch a successful attack. For such an endeavor Halleck promised 20,000 men. However, looking over the situation once more, McClellan increased his demands to 35,000 troops.

Unintentionally, Little Mac had overplayed his hand; the General-in-Chief had had enough of such hijinks. If the Army of the Potomac could not attack with the men it had, then it was in no position to stay on the Peninsula. On 3 August, McClellan was ordered to have his men board troop ships and head north to landing stations at Aquia Creek and Alexandria in order to join the Army of Virginia. After receiving the stunning order, a shocked Little Mac responded to Halleck, "I must confess that it has caused me the greatest pain I have experienced, for I am convinced that the order to withdraw this army to Aquia Creek will prove disastrous in the extreme to our cause—I fear it will be a fatal blow." Along with Pope's reinforcements from the Peninsula would come Major General Ambrose Burnside's IX Corps from a successful stint of campaigning on the coast of North Carolina.

While the Army of the Potomac was on the retreat, the Army of Virginia advanced. On 7 August, Pope finally had Sigel's and Banks' corps with Rickett's division, moving to Culpeper. On the next day, Federal cavalry probes reported the enemy crossing the Rapidan, moving simultaneously on Culpeper and Madison Courthouse. Believing the Rebel objective was to flank the Federal right, Pope sought to block their advance by placing his army to obstruct the fords of the Rappahannock. Crawford's brigade was ordered to take the advance position, this time at Cedar Mountain some eight miles southwest of Culpeper. In a position of support, Ricketts' division was moved just three miles to the north of the brigade. Within a day, the Yankees would have their chance for revenge upon the Confederates who had bested them so often—Stonewall Jackson's legion.

Not surprisingly, if Pope had managed to incur the contempt of his own men, his adversaries could hardly be expected to be in awe of the Western general. His blustering speeches and comments merely served as a source of entertainment for Confederate troops. After the commander of the Army of Virginia was quoted as saying he would sign his dispatches "Headquarters in the saddle," jokes began to spread around Rebel encampments such as: "Pope doesn't know his headquarters from his hind quarters" and "Pope puts his headquarters where his hind quarters should be." In response to Pope's intentions to drive the enemy before him many Johnny-Rebs were heard to say, "Just wait 'til old Jack gets a chance at him; he'll take some starch out of him."

In fact, old Jack or Major General Thomas J. Stonewall Jackson was going to have the chance to do just that. While the Army of Northern Virginia watched McClellan, Robert E. Lee was becoming increasingly disgusted with the violent activities that Pope and his army directed against the non-combatant citizens of Virginia. Desperately hoping to send his forces to the north, he yearned for the opportunity to "suppress" Pope as he told the President of the Confederacy, Jefferson Davis. When Pope began to threaten his communications at Gordonsville and Charlottesville, Lee was forced to respond by sending his most able lieutenant, Jackson, with some 15,000 men north to Gordonsville on 13 July, keeping the rest of the army under Major-General James Longstreet on the Peninsula. It was Stonewall's troops that beat Hatch to the railroad town. This was an incredible risk, for "Bobby" Lee had essentially divided his

The mastermind behind the Confederate victories on the Peninsula and Second Manassas as well as the invasion of Maryland was Robert E. Lee.

Thomas Jonathan Stonewall Jackson, the man who made a fool out of so many Federal generals.

army in the face of a larger army under McClellan, still an ostensible threat to the Confederate capital. However, among this Confederate general's innumerable gifts was the ability to correctly measure up his foe and take the necessary actions to whip him. Almost prophetically, Lee doubted the Army of the Potomac would move against him and, indeed, McClellan refused to budge.

Arriving at Gordonsville, Jackson uncharacteristically found himself unwilling to engage an enemy with larger numbers of troops. Thus, while waiting at his position he called for substantial reinforcements. On 27 July, Lee heeded this call by dispatching Major-General Ambrose Powell Hill's Light Division of around 10,000 men in a move that inaugurated a stormy relationship between the division commander and Jackson.

Upon learning from spies that the Federal advance force was in Culpeper on 7 August, Jackson, his courage bolstered by additional troops, opted to hit the unit while it remained invitingly in isolation. On the same day, his troops marched from Gordonsville to Orange Court House in the murderously stifling August weather with troops falling from the ranks from heat prostration. The next day, Jackson planned to move on Culpeper from Orange Court House while detaching a diversionary movement against Madison Court House to deceive the enemy into thinking he was moving there. The

Commander of the Light Division, Ambrose Powell Hill. His relationship with Jackson during the Antietam Campaign was not a friendly one.

Jackson's arch-nemesis, Major General Nathaniel Prentis Banks. Banks suffered numerous humiliating defeats at the hands of Stonewall in and out of the Shenandoah Valley.

initial movement degenerated into an embarrassing fiasco with Hill's orders getting confused and the entire Confederate column collapsing into a ridiculous jam. By the end of the day, Hill had advanced only one mile, while Major-General Richard Ewell's division managed to crawl along for about eight miles. Hill and Jackson both blamed each other for mistakes of that day, allowing bad feelings to arise. On the ninth, Jackson was to successfully resume his march against the Federals.

As the Confederates moved north, Pope relished the opportunity of a possible engagement. However, on 8 August, the Army of Virginia remained dangerously divided due to a major blunder on the part of the commander of the I Corps. Through befuddlement or stupidity, Sigel had lost his sense of direction on the turnpike to Culpeper and had to ask Pope for directions. For most of the day, the General, "remained like an ass between two bundles of hay in a state of perfect rest." Still Pope decided to act on the next day, sending Banks' corps of two divisions to reinforce Crawford at Cedar Mountain and hold off the advancing enemy while the rest of the army came up. Unfortunately, Banks interpreted Pope's orders to demand an all out attack against Jackson rather than the defensive operation the general commanding had intended. This was just as well for Banks, still smarting from his embarrassment in the Valley at Stonewall's hands, craving for a

Gunners of Captain Joseph Knapp's battery duel with the enemy during the Battle of Cedar Mountain.

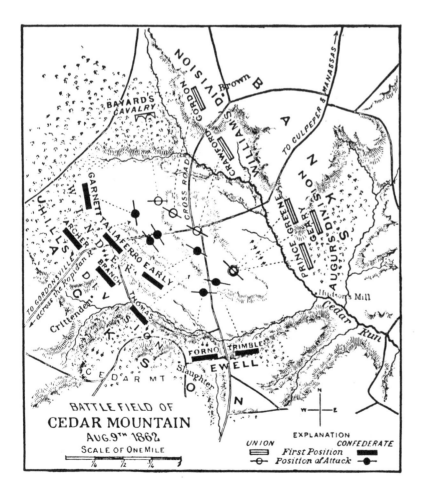

BATTLE FIELD OF
CEDAR MOUNTAIN
AUG. 9TH 1862
SCALE OF ONE MILE

EXPLANATION
UNION   CONFEDERATE
First Position
Position of Attack

chance at some form of retribution. Yet, he ignored the fact that his 8,000 troops were going to be up against a force twice its numbers. Worse still, reinforcements would be slow in coming: Sigel had finally arrived in Culpeper late on the ninth, but had failed to comply with Pope's orders for soldiers to keep two days of rations in their haversacks while campaigning. Thus, the I Corps tarried even longer to rest and draw supplies while Banks went on to Cedar Mountain on his own.

Eight miles southwest of Culpeper, running almost parallel to the Orange Culpeper Road was a broad ridge called Cedar Mountain or, more ominously, Slaughter Mountain after a local farmer. Below the mountain, to the south of the road, was a rolling valley interspersed with streams, wheat and corn fields, and clumps of trees. A forest ran astride the road near the base of the mountain, with the edge moving in an arc swinging to the north and then around to the south, surrounding a wheat field, then touching

Cedar Mountain (also known as Slaughter Mountain) ominously looms over the fields where Jackson's army defeated the Union corps commanded by Banks.

the pike again. Arriving on the field from the northwest, Banks set up his position before the valley of Cedar Mountain. The First Division under Brigadier General Alpheus S. Williams moved into the eastern portion of the woods to link up with Brigadier General Christopher Augur's Second Division running to the left through corn and wheat fields towards the mountain. Besides his artillery and Brigadier-General George D. Bayard's cavalry, this force was all Banks could count on. There was no reserve save Rickett's division in the near vicinity. But with no orders to assist the II Corps, it consequently remained removed from the battle.

Throughout the morning of the ninth, Jackson's army advanced north, skirmishing with Federal cavalry until it came under fire from Banks' cannons. Discovering the Federals in strength, Jackson decided to attack. Since he believed Cedar Mountain to be the strongest point from which to launch an all out assault,

Brigadier General Isaac A. Trimble's and Colonel Henry Forno's brigades of Richard S. Ewell's division were to advance over the mountain against the Federal left. Jubal Early of Ewell's division would march up the Culpeper road to meet the enemy center supported by Jackson's old division under Brigadier Charles A. Winder. After moving up the Culpeper road around 1400, Early took position on a small hill near a clump of cedars to the southeast of the road, unlimbering his three batteries of cannons, engaging in a fierce artillery duel with the Yankees in the cultivated fields ahead of him. An hour after Early went into position, Winder had put his Second and Third Brigades under Lieutenant Colonel Thomas S. Garnett and Brigadier-General William B. Taliaferro respectively into position in the woods along the Culpeper road at almost a ninety degree angle with Early's left in order to assault the Federal guns bombarding the Rebel center. Covering the left and center was the ever famous Stonewall Brigade.

Evidently little concerned with the force ahead of him, Jackson made moves on the ninth that were uncharacteristically poorly thought out; he failed to launch a proper reconnaissance and was on the attack even though the rest of his force, primarily his strongest division under Powell Hill, was not up with the rest of the army. Furthermore, only the divisional commanders had been notified of their leader's plans. These factors were to culminate in what could have led to an ultimate disaster beginning

A divisional commander under Jackson killed at Cedar Mountain, the unfortunate Brigadier General Charles S. Winder.

with the death of Charles Winder. While directing his guns, Winder was cruelly struck by an enemy shell that tore through the left side of his chest and arm and caused his mutilated body to crumble to the ground. Divisional command then fell upon the troubled brow of Taliaferro who had absolutely no idea of Jackson's intentions. He seemed to be in luck for the moment as the battle appeared to be merely a contest between the batteries of either side. For several hours, Napoleons and Parrott rifles blasted away creating a frightening cacophony of sound, the entire ground shuddering from the sharp thud of the firing guns while the air was pierced by screaming shells.

The real fighting was to begin around 1745 when Banks' troops surged forward on the attack. In the center, Early found himself in a sharp contest with Augur's division but solidly held his position and refused to give any ground. Taliaferro would not be so fortunate; he was still moving his men into position when he found himself caught by a rapid and vicious assault. All of a sudden, from the wheat field on his flank, the Yankees of Brigadier-General Samuel W. Crawford's brigade of Williams division gave a mighty yell, pouring forth on the

A Federal battery at rest before entering the fight at Cedar Mountain.

surprised Rebel left and flank. To meet the attackers, Taliaferro sent the Stonewall Brigade under Colonel Charles A. Ronald to the edge of the wheat field. The elite unit arrived at its destination just in time to meet a series of destructive volleys of Federal musketry at close quarters. Driving the Rebels before them, Crawford's brigade clambered through the trees and brush, losing all sense of formation in the tangled flora, inevitably collapsing into a charging mass in their mad rush. Moving to the left came Garnett and his men only to suffer tremendously from an intense cross fire on their front and left. Taliaferro's brigade fared no better with two rookie regiments, the 47th and 48th Alabama cracking under the pressure, scattering to the rear. With the left in an almost total state of collapse, Early's position became increasing threatened as well as the entire Confederate line.

In the Confederate rear, Jackson came to view a very rare sight, his men being routed from the field. Streaming from the woods in the wake of the enemy advance came hundreds of men running from battle, begrimed and bloodied from the awful carnage. Immediately, Old Stonewall rode to his defeated troops, attempting to draw his sword which stubbornly refused to budge from the scabbard. Waving his blade, sheath and all, in thick enemy fire, he pleaded above the din of whistling bullets, "Rally, brave men, and press forward! Your General shall lead you. Jackson will lead you. Follow me!" Almost immediately, his words displayed a telling effect as routed troops began to return to their retreating line to make a stand. Slowly, but surely the left began to reform and hold.

With Jackson narrowly averting disaster, the time came to respond to Banks' attack in kind. By 1800, Ronald and remnants of the Stonewall Brigade launched a smashing counterattack, wiping out Crawford's hard earned gains as the winded Yankees, lacking the necessary reinforcements, were forced back into the wheat field. Yet, Jackson could still be denied victory for Ronald had advanced unsupported with his flanks wide open. Seeking reinforcements, Jackson rode up to Hill's division, just arriving on

Members of Brigadier General Samuel W. Crawford's brigade launch a shattering assault against Jackson's left wing.

Ambrose Powell Hill (1825-1865)

Ambrose Hill was born into the Virginia aristocracy and embarked on a military career after graduating from West Point in 1847, a respectable third in his class. While serving in Mexico and the Third Seminole War, his most erstwhile fight was for the affections of the lovely Ellen "Nelly" Marcy, daughter of an eminent army officer. His prime competitor for her hand was the dashing George Brinton McClellan. After winning the woman's assent to marriage, her parents opposition to the affair forced the demise of the engagement, with Nelly going on to marry McClellan.

After resigning his commission, Powell Hill took up the standard of the Stars and Bars to serve as colonel of the 13th Virginia and eventually received command of a brigade. While inflicting heavy casualties on Joseph Hooker's command at the Battle of Williamsport on the Peninsula, Hill's heroics won him the rank of major

general. Supposedly, a reason for Hill's ferocity in combat, especially against the Army of the Potomac, was the grudge he maintained against McClellan over Ellen Marcy. While his troops were engaged against Little Mac's Yankees, one war weary Con-

federate was heard to exclaim, "For God's sake, Nelly—why didn't you marry him." During the Seven Days, Second Manassas, Antietam, Fredericksberg, and Chancellorsville, Hill consistently displayed his fighting prowess, playing an instrumental part in Confederate victories. Before Gettysburg, Hill took command of the III Corps of the Army of the Northern Virginia as a lieutenant general. Unfortunately, the Virginian's abilities seemed to decline with his increased responsibilities. At Gettysburg, Hill's performance was lackluster at best and at Bristoe Station disastrous: he lost 1300 men in an ill-advised assault.

After commanding troops in the Wilderness, Hill left the tribulations of warfare due to illness and returned to the ranks in 1865 during the autumn days of the Confederacy. At Petersburg, Hill was killed by Federal soldiers while he attempted to rally the broken troops of his command.

A site of misery and healing: a Confederate field hospital on the field of Cedar Mountain.

the field of battle, and directed them to join their fighting comrades. The subordinate responded by sending in Brigadier General L. O. Branch's brigade on the left and Brigadiers James J. Archer's and William D. Pender's brigades on the right. Spotting Branch delaying his attack in order to launch into some superfluous oratory before his troops, Jackson rode to the Brigadier with a faint smile, taking off his hat, and looking into the eyes of the troops. Interrupting Branch's speech, Stonewall then turned to the Brigadier, saying curtly, "Push forward, general, push forward." As the brigade pushed through the woods, they came on elements of the Stonewall Brigade falling back from the front. Scornfully recalling that moment, Branch wrote, "I had not gone 100 yards through the woods before we met the celebrated Stonewall Brigade, utterly routed and fleeing as fast as they could run." Waiting for the Confederates, Crawford grimly sat upon his mount, a musket across his saddle, with his worn and tired regiments preparing to make a stand in the wheat field. As the roar of the Rebel yell erupted in the Federal front and Branch's men arose from the woods, Banks sent Gordon up to brace Crawford's men. At first, both sides struggled desperately, refusing to give any ground. Finding the 27th Indiana withholding its fire, Gordon rode up to find the reason for their hesitance. The skipper of the Hoosier regiment responded

that there were Union troops in his front. The Brigadier shouted, "We have no men there, the enemy is there. Order your men to fire upon him." To prove his perception correct, Gordon rode in view of the enemy to attract fire to which the 27th then responded with fire of their own. The outnumbered Federals were only able to hang on until Pender added his strength with that of Branch to flank the enemy driving him back in disorder. At the same time that Branch had attacked, Early's brigade bolstered by Hill's reinforcements drove back the enemy left in retreat.

As night fell, Banks quickly withdrew to join the rest of the Army of Virginia. Jackson offered some pursuit, but, still unwilling to take on Pope's larger numbers, retreated to the battlefield. On the eleventh, both sides collected their wounded under a truce and buried their dead left before Slaughter Mountain. One soldier recalled the solemn sight of the field:

> Lying all around were dead men, mangled artillery horses, broken gun carriages, and accoutrements of war. . . . Everywhere were new made graves; all over the battle-field, by the roadside, in the fence corners, and under the trees,-every place

As night falls on the battlefield of Cedar Mountain, the outnumbered, battered and defeated forces of Banks prepare to withdraw.

A massive effusion of blood erupts at the base of Cedar Mountain as General Banks throws his outnumbered corps in a bloody charge against Jackson's army.

was dotted with the fresh earth turned over by some soldier who had fought his last battle and whose life blood had reddened the ground as he struggled in his agony to drag his mangled form to some place for shelter and relief. Within the Southern lines the graves were also numerous, no place without being full complement. Where the regiments stood the men fell in rows and heaps and were buried mostly where they fought and fell. In looking at these festering and bloated bodies, a soldier could truly realize what little value was placed upon that most precious gift, human life.

That evening, Jackson retreated across the Rapidan.

On that fateful day on 9 August, Banks suffered over 2,300 men lost and Jackson less than half that number. While Banks' had given Old Jack a run for his money, he could have hardly expected any fruitful result save large casualty figures in attempting to attack a larger enemy force in a good defensive position. On the Confederate side, Jackson wasted his men by throwing them into battle without taking a full stock of the situation and ensuring that all his men were brought up. Despite his failure at Cedar Mountain, Stonewall could claim one major advantage: Pope's march on Gordonsville and Charlottesville had been brought to a screeching halt. In Washington, Halleck decided it would be better to hold off such an advance with Pope maintaining a defensive position before the Rapidan until the Army of the Potomac could link up with him. Such a policy could only be a recipe for disaster. In biding his time before the likes of Robert E. Lee, the Union General-in-Chief had essentially given the Confederate mastermind the necessary time and opportunity to ultimately plan and effect Pope's downfall.

*On the balcony a few unlucky Rebels, captured
at Cedar Mountain, under guard
at Culpeper, Virginia.*

CHAPTER II

RETURNING TO MANASSAS
12 – 28 August, 1862

Throughout early August, McClellan continued to tarry on the Peninsula in the vain hope that Lee might do him the favor of offering battle. Upset over the orders from Halleck to abort his great campaign, the Young Napoleon hoped against hope that some enemy attack would somehow create the opportunity for a massive counteroffensive which would in effect force Washington to allow the Army of the Potomac to remain on the Peninsula. McClellan's hopes were not answered. Lee was not about to take on the Army of the Potomac safely entrenched at Harrison's Landing. Faced with no available tactical openings after eleven days of stalling, McClellan finally acquiesced to Halleck's decree, and put his troops on ships heading north to Aquia Creek. So ended the Peninsula Campaign in what turned out to be McClellan's first major offensive and greatest failure.

Informed by intelligence and rumor, Lee had already guessed that McClellan was going to retreat and thus was no threat for the time being. With the Army of the Potomac out of the way, the Rebel general was able to focus on other far more attractive and entertaining opportunities such as the long awaited "suppression" of John Pope. One day before McClellan was to begin his departure, Lee dispatched Longstreet north to join Jackson on the Rapidan in preparation for an offensive against Pope's Yankees. Longstreet's men took position at Gordonsville where they waited for their leaders' plans for their next move. Obviously the foremost obstacle that confronted the Confederate Army was the Rapidan River; as long as Pope held the banks of that river he was almost invulnerable to a frontal attack. However, Lee was able to perceive a dangerous weakness in

Two Federal generals with experience in defeat, Irvin McDowell and George "Little Mac" McClellan.

"Where's Your Hat?" Cavalry Antics with J.E.B. Stuart

While the jaunty J.E.B. Stuart awaited the appearance of Fitz Lee and his troopers at Verdiersville, Virginia, on 17 August, he lay down upon the porch of a local citizens house placing his prized plumed hat beside him. There has been some discrepancy as to where the hat actually came from, some historians claiming it was the present of a lady friend. A more lively account has Stuart meeting two old friends, Brigadier General Samuel W. Crawford and Brigadier General George D. Bayard on the battlefield of Cedar Mountain during a truce to collect the wounded. After a good natured conversation, the Rebel cavalryman made a wager with his friends that the Northern press would attempt to play up the recent fight as a victory for the Union. The Federals agreed with the stakes to be a hat. Sure enough, Stuart found he won the bet;

on 9 August a package was sent through the lines containing a fine plumed hat and a New York newspaper clipping claiming Cedar Mountain a Northern victory.

When Union cavalry troopers suddenly surprised Stuart and his men on that August afternoon at Verdiersville, the Confederates scattered, with the cavalry commander leaving his prized hat behind to become a trophy for the enemy. Although Stuart made a successful his getaway, he was forced to use a handkerchief to cover his head from the sun, creating an amusement for his comrades who called out with good humor, "Where's your hat?"

It was not long before Stuart managed to exact his revenge upon the Yankees and John Pope. After the raid on the Major General Pope's headquarters during the attack on Catlett's Station, his cavalry commanders set-

tled down to converse about some matters. All of a sudden, Fitz Lee appeared from behind a tree dressed in a Federal officer's hat, cloak, and dress coat, trophies taken from the raid on Pope's tent. While the sight brought laughter to all around, Stuart decided to bring his enemy in on the joke and sent a dispatch to Pope, "General. You have my hat and plume. I have your best coat. I have the honor to propose a cartel for a fair exchange of prisoners." Evidently the Federal commander did not think too much of this humor at his expense to deem it worthy of a reply.

Meanwhile, Stuart decided to have a little more fun at Pope's expense. Adding insult to injury, the major general's coat was sent as a gift to the governor of Virginia, John Letcher, who put it on exhibition at the State Library in Richmond.

The pride of the Confederacy, Confederate cavalry.

Pope's position. In the rear of the Army of Virginia ran another mighty waterway, the Rappahannock. To the east of the Federals, both the Rappahannock and the Rapidan joined as they flowed towards the Atlantic. Unknowingly, Pope had been so kind to his adversaries, managing to place himself in the jaws of perilous trap. If Lee could get a cavalry force in the Union rear to cut their supply and communication lines across the Rappahannock at Rappahannock Station, the rest of the Army could cross the Rapidan upstream, flank the enemy, and pin him helplessly against the confluence of the rivers.

Unfortunately, this plan contained a major difficulty; the Confederate cavalry was spread out across Virginia and would take some time to concentrate. So Lee bided his time, planning a crossing on 17 August. In the meantime, the commander of the Confederate cavalry, Major-General J.E.B. Stuart, waited at Verdiersville for the rest of his troopers to come up. While the General was resting leisurely on a porch, he and his men were taken completely by surprise by a detachment of Federal cavalry. Stuart's command quickly scattered, their leader leaving behind a prized plumed hat and his maps and plans of the coming movements of the Army of Northern Virginia. This unfortunate turn of events forced Lee to postpone his advance until the twentieth, only to find his tremendous opportunity had passed. Pope, supplied with information as to Lee's intentions, retired to safety across the Rappahannock on the eighteenth and nineteenth.

Discovering the enemy retreat Lee commented to Longstreet, "General, we little thought that the enemy would turn his back upon us this early in the campaign." Lee's troops were to follow the enemy a day later taking position along the Rappahannock.

The Confederate crossing of the Rapidan added another chapter to the unfolding feud between Jackson and A.P. Hill. Ordering Hill to

Site of one of Stuart's legendary cavalry raids, the Federal base at Catlett's Station, Virginia.

move as soon as the moon rose on the night of the twentieth, the divisional commander failed to get his troops going on time. Riding up, an incensed Jackson ordered Hill's troops on the move himself.

With Pope holding a strong position on the Rappahannock, Halleck directed him to stay there until reinforcements arrived from the Army of the Potomac. While the Army of Virginia passively waited, Lee was already planning another attack. With Pope's men vigilantly guarding the Rappahannock fords, Lee could hardly afford to attack directly, but instead had to find some available opening. In order to stir things up, Stuart, eager to repay the Yankees for the ignominy inflicted on him a few days earlier, offered to lead a raid against the railroad bridge at Catlett's Station over the Cedar Run to cut the enemy's lines of communications. With Lee giving the go ahead, on 22 August, the jubilant Stuart with 1500 troopers started off on his campaign for retribution by crossing some unguarded fords upstream. While he circled around the Federal right flank, storm clouds began to blanketed the night sky. As a torrential rain commenced, Stuart's cavalry diligently pressed on, through the pitch darkness, their path lit only by intermittent flashes of lightning. Charging into the Federal encampment at Catlett's Station, the Rebels took the enemy completely by surprise driving many Federals away in confusion and capturing several others. Still despite their success, the Rebels failed to successfully complete the actual purpose of their raid, for the rain had dampened the bridge over the Cedar Run making it impervious to all efforts to set it afire. Despite the disappointing results of this endeavor, some of Stuart's men had managed to raid Pope's headquarters and triumphantly returned with several trophies including a dispatch book containing orders from the previous days. Gleeful over their efforts, Stuart's men returned to their own lines confident that they had rebuked the insult tendered to them on the seventeenth.

On the same day, Jackson attempted to make a crossing in the vicinity of Sulphur Springs, sending Early's brigade across an old dam to probe the opposite bank. As Early made the crossing, the night's rain increased the flow blocking his retreat. Cut off from the rest of the force, his position became increasingly grim as enemy troops of Sigel's corps began to appear in the near vicinity. As a bridge was feverishly constructed to recover the exposed brigade, Jackson repeatedly sent dispatches urging Early

A constant thorn in the sides of Generals Pope and McClellan, J.E.B. Stuart. His daring cavalry raids flustered and embarrassed enemy commanders.

to hold on. The Brigadier irritably replied, "Oh! Well, old Jube can die if that's what he wants, but tell General Jackson I'll be damned if this position can be held." Fortunately for Jackson and his men, Sigel had major difficulties getting his men into position to attack. His delays allowed a relieved Early to cross the new, but flimsy, bridge to safety on 23 August.

For the past week Lee had tried in vain to take on Pope before reinforcements reached him. Time was already running out; Major-General Ambrose Burnside's IX Corps under Major-General Jesse L. Reno had already joined with the Army of Virginia shortly after Cedar Mountain. On 20 August Major General Fitz-John Porter's V Corps disembarked at Aquia Creek. In two more days, Major General Samuel P. Heintzelman's III Corps would arrive at Alexandria while Brigadier General John F. Reynolds' Pennsylvania Reserve Division joined Pope on

23 August form Aquia Creek. With these units, Pope's ranks would swell to some 70,000 men while the Army of Northern Virginia could only count on 55,000 men. On 24 August, Lee masterminded the plan to draw the Army of Virginia away from the banks of the Rappahannock; the army would be split into two with Longstreet holding the Rappahannock line with 33,000 troops while Jackson took his 23,000 men on a flanking maneuver around Pope striking the enemy's lines of communications somewhere in the rear. Once Pope removed himself from the Rappahannock, the rest of Lee's army would follow and rejoin Jackson. It was a tremendously risky maneuver once again dividing the Army of Northern Virginia in the face of a powerful enemy. Characteristically, Jackson rel-

ished the opportunity; it was his kind of campaign based on rapid mobility and complete surprise of the enemy.

On 25 August, Jackson left the Rappahannock in what was to become one of the most amazing marches in all of military history. Soldiers arose early in the day to cook three days of rations, all the food they would have as Jackson was leaving most of his supply wagons behind to not slow down or give away his movement. The troops went northwest towards Amissville, turned northeast as they crossed the Hedgeman

Federal troops at Catlett's Station. These gentlemen were completely surprised when J.E.B. Stuart and his troopers decided to pay a visit on 22 August.

One of Jackson's famous foot cavalry on the march yet again.

River to Orlean, putting them beyond the Rappahannock. Tired and hungry, the men trudged on their long dusty trek, many dressed in tatters or complete shreds. A significant number pitifully ambled along the scorching roads without shoes. A member of the 55th Virginia regiment of Hill's Light Division, Allen C. Redwood wrote of the march,

> The hot August sun rose, clouds of choking dust enveloped the hurrying column, but on and on the march was pushed without relenting. Knapsacks had been left behind in the wagons and haversacks were empty about noon; for the unsalted beef spoiled and was thrown away, and the column subsisted itself, without process of commissariat, upon green corn and apples from the fields and orchards upon the route, devoured while marching; for there were no stated meal times, and no systematic halts for rest.

A South Carolinian officer J.F.J. Caldwell recalled many locals came out to witness Jackson's moving column, "Our march filled the inhabitants with wonder. They crowded into the roads as we passed along, asking whence we came, how we came, wither we were going, and many other things which evinced their utter bewilderment at Jackson's great flanking march." Many brought the desperately needed gifts of food and water to their thankful defenders as they pressed along. Throughout the day, Jackson rode up and down his marching column, constantly giving orders for the ranks to be closed up as it pressed on to Salem. Near the town, Jackson paused by the roadside for a well needed rest. As his troops trudged on, they painfully mustered the strength to utter cheers for their beloved commander from their parched throats. Fearing the shouts might reveal the movement to the Federals, Stonewall implored his men to be quiet. They silenced themselves, instead raising their hats and caps in salute as they passed by. Immensely touched by the gesture, Jackson proudly stated, "Who could not conquer with men such as these." When orders finally came to halt a mile south of Salem, men fell to the ground and lapsed into slumber. After a few hours of sleep, they arose once more to continue their march in almost total silence, in no mood to speak even if their dry mouths would allow them.

Moving to cross the Bull Run Mountains at Thoroughfare Gap, Jackson was passed by Stuart's cavalry, which had mirrored his route towards the rear of the Army of Virginia, going forward to give the flanking movement a necessary screen. Passing through Haymarket and Gainesville, Stonewall decided to hit the Orange and Alexandria Rail Road line at Bristoe station. As the Confederates zeroed in on their target, the men, sensing that they were about to lay a nasty surprise on the hated Pope, excitedly picked up their pace.

Arriving at Bristoe Station, Jackson's troops easily scattered the Union defenders who were no doubt surprised to find the Rebels so far behind Federal lines. Several trains, the railroad, and the bridge were heartily destroyed there, effectively cutting Pope off from his communications with Washington and his supplies. However, despite their success the attackers' hearts fell when they found the post contained little in the way of supplies. Yet, Jackson had learned from the town's inhabitants that there was a huge stock of stores a few miles to the

Engineers from the Union army work to complete a bridge near Sulphur Springs, Virginia.

Jackson's troops on their famous trek into Pope's rear.

north at Manassas Junction. That night Briga-dier-General Isaac Trimble was sent with two North Carolina regiments to take the town with Hill following later. Ewell remained at Bristoe Station to block any enemy advance. Arriving at

Manassas Junction after the Confederates raided the Federal supply depot.

Manassas Junction on 27 August, Jackson's soldiers thought they had entered paradise: two tracks contained over 100 train cars packed with exotic food and drink, clothes, shoes, blankets, ammunition, guns and cannons. Nearby were warehouses stuffed to the brim with similar stores. Trimble's men were left to guard the loot, but they were not able to stop the upcoming ravenous troops from descending upon the objects of their desire. That day was remembered as on of the biggest parties of exquisite excess in the entire war. One soldier wrote:

> The quantity of booty was very great and the amount of luxuries absolutely incredible. It was amusing to see here a ragged fellow regaling himself with a box of pickled oysters or potted lobsters, there another cutting into a cheese of enormous size, or emptying a bottle of champagne;

while hundreds were engaged in opening packages of boots and shoes and other articles to replace their own tattered garments.

Another recalled,

> Twas a curious sight to see our ragged and famished men helping themselves to every imaginable article of luxury or necessity, whether of clothing, food, or what not. For my part, I got a toothbrush, a box of candles, a quantity of lobster salad, a barrel of coffee, and other things which I forget.

The fear that soldiers would become hopelessly inebriated on available spirits prompted

A locomotive derailed by Jackson's troops during their attack on the Federal base at Bristoe Station.

Yankee and Rebel

In viewing the prints of Louis Kurz and Alexander Allison (such as the one on the cover of this book), one is attracted by the romantic notion of war envisioned in the drawing. Soldiers in pristine uniforms pose in heroic stances as they engage in an almost bloodless conflict. It is a child's version of war, devoid of the grim realties of bloody strife, the terror of combat, the senseless death and cruel destruction. One wonders if veterans looked at these prints with grim amusement or hateful disgust at the misrepresentation of the way Kurz and Allison portrayed their exploits. Perhaps no better proof of the fallacies prevalent in these overly romantic paintings can be found than in the dress and equipage of both sides.

The ideal Union soldier was as he appears in the Kurz and Allison prints. The Yankee usually wore a dark blue jacket, with upturned collar, light blue pants, blue kepi with black visor, and unwieldy shoes called "gunboats" which must have been sheer murder to walk any long distance in. Dressed somewhat differently than their counterparts in the infantry, cavalry and artillery personnel wore shorter jackets and boots instead of shoes. Uniforms were usually trimmed with color to distinguish which branch of the service a soldier belonged to: red meaning artillery and yellow, cavalry.

Originally, as units were hastily organized across the North, soldiers arrived in camp with a variety of uniforms. In one instance, the 79th New York, comprised mainly of Americans of Scotch ancestry, wore kilts to display their heritage. They abandoned such dress when low-minded individuals taunted them. Some units even wore Confederate gray which tended to cause confusion on the battlefield. Perhaps the most fantastic uniforms belonged to the Zouaves who copied the dress of French troops engaged in North Africa. The attire usually consisted of bright red pantaloons, short blue jackets with braids, and fezzes instead of the usual kepi.

For the most part, uniforms were made out of wool and made marching in the intense heat of the Southern summer unbearable. Resulting heat exhaustion was common during the treks of the army; in many of the reports from the Battle of Cedar Mountain, officers tell of several soldiers falling dead from sun stroke. In the winter, long overcoats were available to protect soldiers from the elements.

Soldiers did not often find their military clothes comfortable in the heat or cold, as a good fit was rare. Yankees often made a series of trades with comrades to acquire outfits of proper size. Worse still, early in the war, when contracts were hastily awarded to companies to provide clothing for the masses of troops entering the army, seedy individuals provided shoddy goods which quickly fell apart after limited wear or after a rain storm, leaving soldiers almost completely naked.

At any rate, long campaigning reduced even well made uniform to tatters. After the battle of Antietam, a reporter wrote after a call on the 30th New York, "The most notable feature that I remember of this visit was the lack of clothing of the rank and file. I don't think that one man in the regiment had a full suit of clothes and many had scarcely sufficient to save them from the complaints of indecent exposure." Things weren't much better in the 88th Pennsylvania as the regimental historian noted while encamped on the fields near Sharpsburg a month after the battle, "The men were badly off for clothing and shoes, many being in rags and almost barefoot, and consequently suffering much these cool October nights."

Perhaps the most prized possession of the Yankee, like any soldier, was his primary instrument of death, the rifle. Many unfortunate soldiers got stuck with smoothbores and poor European rifles; the 118th Pennsylvania suffered severely when it was attacked by Confederate troops at Shepherdstown on 20 September, while armed with defective Belgian muskets. The more for-

tunate found themselves with British .57 calibre Enfield Rifles or .58 calibre Springfield rifles. The Springfield was usually the weapon of choice as it was somewhat lighter and easier to bear on a long march.

As for the rest of his load, the Federal infantryman usually carried a haversack, cap box, cartridge box, rubber or woolen blanket, bayonet with scabbard, canteen, and knapsack. All of a fighting man's possessions, which could include underwear, socks, knick-knacks from home, brush and soap, were placed in the knapsack. Usually, the total weight carried was some 50 pounds. More often than not, however, to lighten their loads, soldiers would rolled up their things in a blanket, tied both ends together and carried it over their shoulders.

Considering the state of the Confederate infantryman, he must have envied his Federal counterpart. Had the Southern government been able to provide proper dress for all of its soldiers, Johnny Reb's uniform should have consisted of a double-breasted gray coat, trousers of either light blue or gray, and a kepi. As the government lacked the proper facilities to clothe its troops, at first soldiers were required to furnish their own uniforms. In some cases the state would provide proper attire or companies would put together a collection from among members and even citizens to purchase what they needed. Of course, this led to a diverse variety of uniforms; the Louisiana Tigers were a Zouave outfit from New Orleans and wore red tasseled caps, short brown jackets with red trim and baggy white trousers with blue or red, white, and blue stripes. As the war progressed, the Confederacy tried to standardize the uniforms of its soldiers with little success.

By 1862 the government was issuing standard gray uniforms, sometimes with foreign contractors manufacturing the dress. But the South was still unable to provide for a significant number of its men. Thus, more often then not, a soldiers inability to get an outfit depended on his own ingenuity. Usually, a major source of supply was captured Federal stores. Jackson's men were notorious for supplying their needs from the Federal sources (at Manassas and Harper's Ferry during the Antietam Campaign), though in some cases, even the dead were deprived of their shirts, coats, and trousers to serve the needs of the living. Belt buckles obtained from Federals were like wise turned upside down to mark the allegiance of the wearer. At Antietam, the Confederates used captured Federal uniforms to some advantage with A.P. Hill's men confusing the Yankees on the Federal left, allowing the Rebels to get close and scatter the befuddled enemy. As the Federal blockade tightened and reduced the South's access to gray cloth, uniforms were usually dyed in an infusion of nutshells, resulting in a yellowish brown color called butternut.

Two important commodities to the Confederates were hats and shoes. During campaigns, some form of headgear was absolutely necessary for protection from both rain and sun. Most Rebels preferred the brimmed slouch hat which came in many sizes and varieties. In one instance at Hagerstown, some of Lee's troops bought a merchants total supply of beaver hats which gave the soldiers who wore them a certain resemblance to Daniel Boone. The supply of shoes was a desperate problem for the Confederates. Lacking them, many soldiers were forced to fall out of the ranks due to cut and scraped feet. The problem was especially endemic during the Antietam Campaign and a major cause of the disastrous plague of straggling which hampered Lee's effective strength. Of course, the lore of the Civil War records General Harry Heth's quest for shoes during the Confederate campaign in Pennsylvania that led him to the town of Gettysburg on 1 July 1863, thus inaugurating the fateful three-day battle there.

The Southerners also lacked the ability to provide their troops with the proper arms needed to wage war. Most troops used the common .69 calibre musket which fired buck and ball with an effective range of 100 yards and permitted its owners to get two to three shots off in a minute. Armed with Springfield and Enfields firing accurately at about ten times that distance, Yankees were often in a good position to deal heavy blows to their adversaries while receiving few casualties in return. The commander of the 3rd North Carolina suffered severely in such a manner at the end of the day at Antietam although his troops had used their buck and ball muskets with such effect earlier that some soldiers were asked, "What were your men armed with? We never saw so many men wounded in one battle."

Vessels to carry equipage were also lacking in the Rebel Army. Soldiers lugged their belongings in a rolled up blanket in the same manners as their Union counterparts. As tin canteens were scarce, jugs, bottles, and small wooden containers were often employed to carry desperately needed water on the march and into battle. A lucky few carried their food in haversacks and ammunition in cartridge boxes attached to the belt.

Federal participants in the Civil War.

The appearance of the Confederates in the Kurz and Allison prints is fanciful to say the least. An actual representation of their appearance during the Antietam Campaign is given by Private Alexander Hunter of the 17th Virginia in his description of some of the veterans of Longstreet's command:

What a set of ragamuffins the looked! It seemed as if every cornfield in Maryland had been robbed of its scarecrows. . . . None had any underclothing. My costume consisted of a ragged pair of trousers, a stained, dirty jacket; an old slouch hat, the brim pinned up with a thorn; a begrimed blanket over my shoulder, a grease-smeared cotton haversack full of apples and corn, a cartridge box full and a musket. I was barefooted and had a stone bruise on each foot. Some of my comrades were a little better dressed, some were worse. I was in average, but there was no one there who would not have been 'run in' by the police had he appeared on the streets of any populous city, and would have been fined the next day for undue exposure.

Sons of the South who fought for their homeland.

Jackson to order the destruction of hundreds of barrels of wine, whiskey and beer. Major Roy Mason recounted that, "I shall never forget the scene when this was done. Streams of spirits ran like water through the sands of Manassas, and the soldiers on their hands and knees drank it greedily from the ground as it ran."

The day's excitement wore along with only a minor annoyance provided by an attack by some green New Jersey troops that had disembarked up the railroad but were dispatched with ease.

While his troops stuffed themselves, Jackson turned his attention to his next possible move. The Federals would no doubt be on their way in great strength before long and could easily conquer his small command if he were not careful. Ewell was already skirmishing with Hooker's men at Bristoe Station. What was needed was a

Jackson's foot cavalry enjoy an orgy of excess as they gorge on food and other supplies at the expense of the Federal government.

good defensible hiding place where Stonewall and his men could hole up until the rest of Lee's army under Longstreet joined him coming through Thoroughfare Gap. Ultimately, Stonewall picked a wooded height, called Stony Ridge or Sudley Mountain, running almost parallel to the Warrenton Turnpike, prophetically, only a mile west from the old battlefield of Bull Run.

Taking what ever they could from the looted Federal supply depot and putting the rest to the torch, Jackson's men set off at 0300 the next morning. Despite the confidence of the Confederates, there was some concern as to whether Longstreet would reach them before the Army of Virginia. Speaking for this anxiety Major Mason boldly approached Jackson to ask, "General, we are all of us desperately uneasy about Longstreet and the situation, and I have come on my own account to ask the question: Has Longstreet passed through Thoroughfare Gap successfully?" A smile widened on Jackson's

lips as he responded, "Go back to your command and say, 'Longstreet is through, and we are going to whip in the next battle.'"

Pope had left his lines of communications to "mind themselves" and paid the price for it when Jackson hit Bristoe Station and Manassas Junction like a storm. No doubt suffering some irritating inconvenience from the flanking maneuver, Pope had decided to make the best of it. The Confederates were in his rear, but dangerously separated from the rest of their compatriots. If the Army of Virginia could just find them, the enemy could be easily crushed. Unfortunately, the good General had a erroneous sense of reality that would impair his ability to achieve this objective. Believing that only Jackson's advance force had reached Bristoe Station and the rest to be near Gainesville, on 27 August, Pope ordered his forces north: McDowell, Sigel, and Reynolds were to march directly for the town with Kearny's division of Heintzelman's corps and Reno going to Greenwich nearby. Porter

would come up in support while Banks, his men still winded from the fight at Cedar Mountain, protected the trains moving to Manassas Junction preceded by Major-General Joseph Hooker's division.

Irritably enough, finding Jackson not where he was supposed to be at Gainesville, at 0100 on 28 August Pope then had his forces concentrate in the vicinity of Manassas Junction. Having received disturbing reports that enemy troops were moving on the Thoroughfare Gap, Mcdowell left Ricketts' division to guard the pass while he moved on. After Pope had abandoned the Rappahannock line, Longstreet followed Jackson's route, descending on the pass by 1500 of 28 August. Kearny's division and

Former slaves follow Pope's army in search of freedom.

Desperately searching for Jackson's army, Pope's Yankees hike through the Virginia countryside.

Reno's corps were directed to the Manassas Junction as well leaving Porter's corps to move on Bristoe Station. Arriving in the town at 1200 that day, all Pope found were the charred remains of the millions of dollars of supplies looted by Jackson's men. With two strikes against him, the General reasoned that his quarry must be attempting to retreat to safety past Centreville through the Aldie Gap in the Bull Run Mountains. Thus the army was put on the road again, this time towards Centreville.

The Battle of Groveton rages as Gibbon's rookies engage Jackson's seasoned veterans. The contest ended in a draw.

While Federal troops chased ghosts around the Virginia countryside, the well entrenched and safely hidden Jackson himself was becoming concerned. He was not so much worried about being discovered, but rather that Pope might be in retreat to the north without offering any chance of an engagement. Learning that Lee and Longstreet were close by in the vicinity of Thoroughfare Gap behind the Bull Run Mountains, Stonewall and his men lusted for the opportunity to swoop down on vulnerable Yankee prey. On the afternoon of 28 August, just such a promising target presented itself; a brigade of King's division of McDowell's corps on the march northward up the Warrenton

Turnpike from Groveton towards Centreville. Jackson himself took the opportunity to observe the column firsthand, riding towards the enemy for a closeup look. The weary Yankees paid no mind to what appeared to be nothing more than a single Confederate cavalry trooper. Blackford described the Rebel encampment as the commander returned:

> Presently General Jackson pulled up suddenly, wheeled and galloped toward us. "Here he comes, by God," said several, and Jackson rode up to the assembled group as calm as a May morning and touching his hat in military salute, said as in as soft a voice as if he had been talking to a friend in ordinary conversation, "Bring out you men, Gentlemen!" Every officer whirled around and scurried back to the woods at full gallop. The men were watching their officers with as much interest as they had been watching Jackson, and when they wheeled and dashed towards them they knew what it meant, and from the woods arose a hoarse roar like that from cages of wild beasts at the scent of blood.

Licking their chops, expecting easy victory the Confederates went into position and advanced to a small rise before Stony Ridge on which the Brawner Farm was located. However, they soon found out that their adversary was not the usual Federal brigade, but a collection of rookie Western regiments soon to be known as the best fighting unit in the Army of the Potomac: The Iron Brigade of the Blackhat Brigade.

Their leader was a solid fighting Brigadier-General by the name of John Gibbon, a veteran artillery officer. While at the advance of his column, he saw off in the distance enemy guns going into battery. As Rebel shells came screaming down upon the Yankees, Gibbon got his men into a battle line supported by the fire of his own Battery B and set off to take the enemy's guns. As the rest of Jackson's men revealed themselves with a yell and sharp musket fire, the battle was on. The resulting action was a knockdown drag out fight with both sides standing out in the open, in parallel lines roughly 75 yards apart. Deadly volley after volley was fired in what Gibbon called, " . . . the most terrific musketry I have ever listened to. . . . " For a time, it appeared as though the outnumbered brigade might be flanked as Jackson threw more and more of his men into the fray. Anxiously seeking reinforcements, Gibbon tried to contact other members of King's division. Fortunately enough, Abner Doubleday's brigade received the call, moving to bolster the Westerners, enabling them to maintain their stand before the larger number of Rebels. Until night fell, men fought and died, neither side willing to yield an inch, the rookies of Gibbon's brigade fighting like seasoned veterans before some of the most valiant men the South had to offer. Finally, after the battle ended at 2100, Gibbon withdrew from the face of larger numbers to safety near the turnpike. Thoroughly mauled by the fight, the Confederates were in no mood to pursue.

In what was to be known as the Battle of Groveton, or the Battle of Brawner's Farm, was severely costly for both sides with neither attaining any great yields from the spectacular bloodshed. In showing the unyielding fighting character that was to be its trademark, Gibbon's brigade lost almost a third of its number, holding off Jackson's division under Taliaferro and about half of Ewell's men. Jackson's officer corps also lost some indispensable leaders: Taliaferro had been wounded in the foot, neck and arm, leaving him incapacitated for some time. Leading an advance by his troops, Ewell suffered a shattered knee when a bullet hit him, entailing the amputation of his entire leg.

As night fell, Blackford recalled the field of battle following the fight,

> A fresh battlefield is an interesting sight, though a terrible one, and darkness by stimulating the imagination increases inexpressibly its gloomy grandeur. Human nature confronted with death and stripped of all disguise is here presented in the noble calmness of hero or the abject groveling of the coward. While regular details for duty were engaged in removing the wounded, many friends of the wounded and dead were wandering about the field looking for their friends, ministering to their wants, or taking last messages sent by those who were expecting to die.

As his men enjoyed a well deserved rest, Gibbon rode to join King to discuss further operations with his commander. Joined by his fellow brigadiers, the meeting was a somber one set before a large fire, with commanders and their division commander, who had taken ill, grimly looking on as they discussed their miserable options. Obviously the command had to retreat from Jackson and his superior numbers, but to where was the problem. Original orders from Pope were to move on Centreville where Jackson supposedly was. However, not only was Stonewall not where he was supposed to be, but he was also blocking King's path to his objective. Worse still, corps commander McDowell was nowhere to be found, having left earlier in the day to find Pope's headquarters in order to grant his superior the benefit of his knowledge of the area—but got miserably lost. It was Gibbon who suggested the course King's division would ultimately follow, to return to Manassas Junction, the last point of Federal concentration, where support was the most likely to be found. The Federals left at 0100 in the morning of 29 August. While appearing to be the most logical decision, this action had an unforeseen repercussion that was to have a serious impact on the upcoming battle. Isolated by the move, Ricketts' division was left without support at Thoroughfare Gap and was forced to retreat to join the rest of the army, leaving that pass open for the Confederate army under Longstreet to pass through and join Jackson.

Irvin McDowell.

CHAPTER III

SECOND MANASSAS
29 – 30 August, 1862

By 2200 on 28 August, Pope had learned of the Battle of Groveton and more importantly of the illusive Jackson's location. Believing King had blocked the attempted retreat of the Rebel force, he was prepared to finally smash his adversary with all the forces at his command. Being in the vicinity of Jackson's front at Henry House Hill, Sigel's corps and Reynolds' division were directed to lead the attack the next morning. The rest of the Army of Virginia spread out from Bristoe Station to Centreville would have to be concentrated in the enemy's front: Reno and Heintzelman were ordered to move their corps at Centreville south in the direction of Gainesville while Porter's V Corps at Bristoe Station was to head north joining with King's division at Manassas Junction. Remaining at Bristoe Station, Banks' Corps would happily miss out on the action.

Entrenched behind an old abandoned railway embankment located on the base of Stony Ridge, the Confederates were in an excellent position to withstand and repulse any Union attack. The left of their line was anchored on the Sudley Springs Church near the Catharpen Run, a tributary of the Bull Run extending to the southwest for two miles along the embankment. Before this position were rolling fields of dips and rises, cut by meandering streams. Occupying the Confederate left was Hill's division, operating with a possibly severe tactical handicap; the portion of the embankment his men would have to defend was covered with a dense wood affording the enemy some protection. Holding the center of the Confederate line was Ewell's division, now under the command of Brigadier-General Alexander Lawton, with Ear-

ly detached to the right and rear to block against a flanking movement and to watch out for Longstreet. Maintaining the right, taking the place of the wounded Taliaferro, was Starke commanding the depleted Stonewall Division.

The Federal attack began early the next day with the Teutonic divisions of Sigel's I Corps moving out around 0530 on 29 August. Commanding the First Division was Brigadier Robert C. Schenk following the Warrenton Turnpike

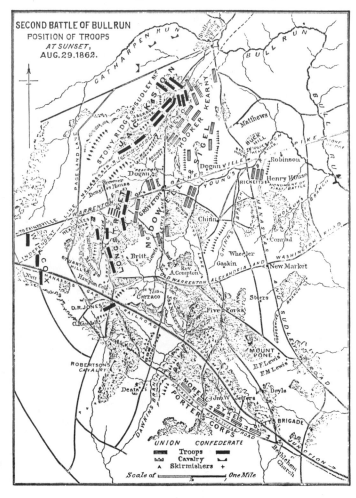

west with Brigadier-General Robert H. Milroy moving to hit the Confederate left. Heading north to confront Hill's men was Sigel's Third Division under Brigadier-General Carl Schurz. Schurz's men entered the woods, attempting to maintain formation in the thick underbrush as they moved against the embankment. Pushing up against Hill's line, they attempted unsuccessfully to break the right flank. Meanwhile, the unenthusiastic Schenk and Milroy refrained from an all out attack and instead offered an artillery duel with Confederate batteries while sending some troops to assist the embattled Schurz. During this early action, a Federal major was shot down leading his men into combat by Company A of the 15th Alabama. While a captain remonstrated these men for killing so brave an adversary, Jackson himself rode up to say, ''No, Captain, the men are quite right. Kill the brave ones; they lead the others.''

Reynolds came forth to bolster the courage of the Federal left moving forward then doubling back when enemy forces were spotted closing in on their flank.

Franz Sigel's I Corps led the Federal attack on Second Manassas.

At the helm of a division in Sigel's corps, Carl Schurz adeptly led his men into combat in the fight at Second Bull Run. Schurz would distinguish himself as a politician after the war.

At roughly 1030, a moving column appeared on the Confederate right rear emerging from the direction of Bull Run Mountain. Uncertain if they were friend or foe, Starke dispatched a courier to discover their allegiance. After a time, the courier rushed back with good news: it was Longstreet. Knowing that with the rest of the Army of Northern Virginia close by the day would be theirs, the men of the Rebel line sent up a roaring cheer. Longstreet's men filed into a line anchored to Jackson's right and extending out to the southeast. Lee desired Longstreet to make an attack as quickly as possible to relieve some of the pressure on Jackson. However, the subordinate demurred, desiring instead to launch a reconnaissance of the field before he advanced in force.

Before noon, an exultant Pope arrived on the field to take full control of the situation. Irritated by the absence of the commander of the III Corps, the General muttered, ''God damn McDowell, he's never where I need him.'' With Reno and Heintzelman coming in from the north, and Porter arriving from the south, the Union General Commanding hoped to combine all of these units in an all out assault against Jackson. Unfortunately, Pope was operating under confused perceptions of reality, refusing to consider even for a moment that the rest of the Confederate Army had already arrived on the

Jubal Anderson Early (1816-1894)

Virginian and West Point graduate, Jubal Anderson Early resigned his commission to take up law, although he participated in the Mexican American War as a major in the Virginia volunteers. After voting against the secession of his native state in the Virginia Convention, he joined the Confederate military when war broke out and commanded a regiment at First Bull Run. Attaining brigade command a short time later, Early, called "Old Jube" by his men, fell wounded in an impetuous assault at Williamsburg, Virginia, during the Peninsular Campaign. After returning to command in time to participate in the Battle of Malvern Hill, he provided a stoic defense at Cedar Mountain, even after the famed Stonewall Brigade cracked and had took flight, gaining time for Jackson to commit reinforcements to turn the tide. At Second Manassas, Antietam, and Fredericksburg, his services won him the rank of major general in

January of 1863. After becoming a lieutenant general in 1864, Early led an audacious assault against the Federal capital itself, winning the Battle of Monocacy, only turned away from the gates of Washington, D.C., by Major General Horatio Wright's Federals of the VI Corps. After razing the city of Chambersburg Pennsylvania, Early's troops embarked on a long duel with the command of Major General Philip Sheridan in the Shenandoah Valley, their continuing clashes culminating in the Battle of Cedar Creek. While winning some initial success there, the Confederates were totally wrecked after the Federals rallied. Following the conclusion of the war, Early fled to Canada, returning to Virginia in 1869. A general who could conduct a formidable defence, Early constantly proved himself a frightening adversary capable of launching a vicious blow.

Troops of Longstreet's command march unopposed through Thoroughfare Gap on the way to join Jackson near the old battlefield of First Bull Run.

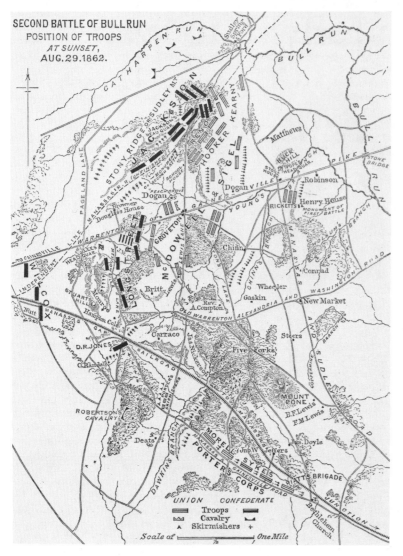

SECOND BATTLE OF BULL RUN
POSITION OF TROOPS
AT SUNSET,
AUG. 29. 1862.

Reorganizing his men, Schurz pressed forward once more in a futile attempt to take the embankment before the battle shifted to Reno's and Hooker's men.

Hooker's division entered the fray to launch powerful assaults against Hill's line, marching through fires ignited in the underbrush by shot and shell from both sides. Attempting to storm the embankment, the Yankees blindly rushed forward time and time again, climbing through the smoke and hail of bullets, only to fail for lack of strength to carry their objective. Falling back, the blue coats reorganized to come on again. Caldwell, of Gregg's brigade, wrote of the murderous onslaught:

> The woods swarmed with them (Yankees), they closed in upon us from the front and right and left pressing up with an energy never before witnessed by us, and certainly never surpassed since. . . . The firing was incessant. They seemed determined not to abandon the undertaking; we were resolved never to yield. All the sounds of Babel roared about us; the trees were raked by musket balls. Standing, kneeling, lying, we fought them, so close that men picked out their marks and on occasion saved their lives by anticipating the fire of someone on the other side.

In a desperate gambit to drive a wedge in Hill's line, Hooker called upon a sledge hammer blow to be led by Brigadier-General Cuvier Grover and his brigade. In planning his attack, Grover intended his men to move slowly forward at a walk, bravely receive a volley from the enemy, rush forward, fire a blast of their own, and then storm the embankment with bayonet. Grover's advance was under way at 1500, his men dutifully doing as they were told. After firing a destructive burst, they quickly rushed forward over the mutilated corpses of the dead men that had gone before them. Standing where the embankment was about ten feet high, the Rebels continued to fire their muskets into the advancing crowd. Expecting a blast in return, some defenders sought protection from the feared bullets. Instead of shooting, Grover's brigade

scene, and would tragically fail to compensate for that possibility.

From 1330 until evening fell, elements of the Army of Virginia and the Army of the Potomac were hurled time and time again against the fortified embankment in uncoordinated bloody attacks. Schurz's division took the lead by launching a successful drive against Hill when a gap was found in his line. With the left in serious danger, two Confederate regiments counterattacked the advancing Federal center shoving it bloodily out of the woods. However, Schurz was not without surprises of his own; the pursuing Confederates ran smack into a battery supported by a regiment of infantry. Volleys of molten lead and iron shot down a large number of Rebels with the survivors rushing back to safety in the woods.

A group of Federals pose before a monument to their comrades who fell at First Bull Run on 21 July 1861. A similar one was erected to honor the sacrifice of those who gave their lives during the battle of Second Bull Run.

The scene of two great battles: First and Second Manassas.

surged up the height, engaging in a cruel blood fest of hand-to-hand combat with its defenders. Caldwell remembered this vicious fighting:

> It is these hand to hand fights that makes war devils work; for it is they which excite all the blood thirsty passion and utterly silence every sentiment of humanity. One may fight at long range as a patriot and a Christian, but I believe that no man can engage in one of these close struggles, where he can look into the eyes of his adversary and see his blood, but he becomes for the time at least, a mere beast of prey.

For a few gruesome moments, bayonet pierced flesh as musket cracked skull spewing brains onto the bloodied ground. Finally, it seemed as though the Rebels could take no more, quickly fleeing from their position to the rear. Feeling that victory was in their grasp, the Yankees gave pursuit smashing through Hill's supporting line. With reinforcements, they might well have been victorious, but none were ordered forth. The Rebels soon rallied, hitting Grover's flank with a destructive fire forcing the Yankees back over the embankment. For roughly twenty minutes, Grover's brigade engaged the enemy and lost some 487 men.

Next to go into battle was Colonel James Nagle's brigade of Reno's corps. Men were ordered forth under the encouragement of officers shouting that Porter was on his way to join them. Comprised of men from Pennsylvania, New Hampshire, and Maryland, the brigade moved forward storming a cut in the embankment and successfully seizing it. Of the combat, a captain in the 48th Pennsylvania wrote:

> Off we moved, over a clear field into a dense wood, out of which we were to drive the rebels. The wood was skirted by a fence, which we had scarcely crossed, in fact, our regiment was just getting over it when bang! bang! whiz! whiz! and the battle commenced. There was no use in talking however. Our brigade went right in; walked steadily on, driving the rebels quickly before them, but losing men fast. A ditch or embankment, in which the rebels shielded themselves . . . our brigade assailed so fiercely, that it was soon cleared.

Their success was short lived as Nagle's Yankees came under a flanking fire from the left and rear. Believing they must be accidentally receiving friendly fire, regimental color bearers waved

Sudley Church, a Methodist Episcopal house of worship near the Catharpen Run, was the anchor of the Confederate right during the battle on 29 and 30 August 1862.

Second Manassas / 47

their flags but received even more intense volleys. Finding the position untenable, Nagle's men were also forced to retreat. After repelling the attack, John H. Worsham with the 21st Virginia witnessed a grotesque sight,

> . . . I heard a thud on my right, as if one had been struck by a heavy fist. Looking around , I saw a man at my side who was standing erect, with his head off and a stream of blood spurting a foot or more from his neck. He was Captain Nicholas Cabler of the 42nd Virginia, and his brains and blood bespattered the face and clothing of one of my company who was standing in my rear. As I turned farther around, I saw three others, all killed by cannon shot, lying on the ground.

As Nagle's men fell back, Hill did his best to brace the line for the next inevitable assault. Despite the intense pressure they had been under for most of the day, the morale of the Light Division was still high. In response to a query about his ability to hold his position, Gregg responded," . . . our ammunition is exhausted,

Members of fearless Phil Kearny's division that bravely stormed, but failed to take, Jackson's position on the railway embankment.

but rocks are very plentiful, and we can hold our position with them until we get ammunition." Soldiers were sent among the dead and wounded to seek out every cartridge that might be of use in combat. To encourage his men, Hill called out, "Good for you, boys! Give them rocks and bayonets, and hold your position, and I will have ammunition and reinforcements for you." No doubt many a Confederate soldier on the left looked to the reddened horizon to see the sun set, hopelessly urging it on, desperately waiting for darkness to bring an end to the fighting and give them a respite from their deadly work. Kyd Douglas of Jackson's staff remembered, "For the first time in my life I understand what was meant by 'Joshua's sun standing on Gideon,' for it would not go down. No one knows how long sixty seconds are, nor how much time can be crowded into an hour, nor what was meant by 'leaden wings' unless he has been under the fire of a desperate battle, holding on, minute after minute, waiting for a turning or praying that the great red sun, blazing and motionless overhead would go down." Even Powell Hill was increasingly becoming concerned with the tenuousness of his position, glumly telling Douglas he intended to hold on, but couldn't tell for sure if he would be successful. When this depressing news was related to

Jackson, he only said, "Tell him if they attack again he must beat them." When Hill appeared to report to Jackson personally, Stonewall plainly told him, "General, your men have done nobly; if you are attacked again you will beat the enemy back."

Just then, the right exploded once more with the din of battle. Hill started to ride back to his men shouting, "Here it comes," while his commander called after him, "I'll expect you to beat them." Despite the growing disgust and hatred growing between these men, they were professional enough not to allow such animosities to interfere with their business on the battlefield.

The next Union attack came at 1730 with Reno's and Kearny's troops slamming against the tired and depleted Confederate left. Kearny's division flung itself against the embankment with extreme vigor despite the storm of bullets and shells raining down on them from the enemy. For a moment it appeared that the Confederates finally could take no more punishment. Hill's extreme left slowly creaked back to a 90 degree angle with the rest of the line. In the middle of the unrelenting combat, Gregg stood amidst his men waving an unwieldy saber above his head shouting, "Let us die here! Let us die here!" Such an extreme sacrifice was not necessary, for just as disaster seemed imminent, the brigades of Forno and Early, relieved from the right by Longstreet, appeared to give

aide to their hard pressed comrades. With the Rebels slamming into the attackers with bayonets fixed, the stalling Federals could not maintain their momentum and fell back as quickly as possible.

While corps of Heintzelman's, Reno's, and Sigel's were desperately fighting before the embankment, Porter's V Corps and the III Corps under McDowell, who had since made a reappearance, were dawdling to the southwest at Dawkin's Branch. Out in the distance, ominous clouds of dust were being kicked into the air, a sure sign that Longstreet had arrived on the scene before them. This assumption was bolstered by a communication from cavalry man Brigadier-General John Buford, reporting the rest of the Rebel army was on its way to the battle field. Both corps commanders were acting upon a cryptic order from Pope, dispatched earlier in the day, giving them the latitude to use their own judgement in deciding possible moves.

While McDowell decided to head up the Sudley Springs Road in search of Pope, Porter decided to remain at his present position. With the sizable command of Longstreet ahead of him, Porter saw no reason to endanger his entire command in a foolish attack. No doubt, as a staunch McClellan supporter and enemy of Pope, he was not disposed to be especially helpful to the General Commanding or consequently therefore to the rest of the Union Army on the field. At 1630, not even considering that Longstreet was on the field, Pope sent a definite order for the V Corps to flank on the enemy right. However, by the time the order reached Porter at 1800, he was only able to get his troops under way when it was too late to do much of anything.

Lee was also having problems with a subordinate who refused to move. As reports of reinforcements on the Federal left came in, Longstreet politely opted against launching an attack, his troops quietly waiting while Jackson's men suffered severely. Finally, in the growing darkness of that August evening, "Old Pete" sent Hood out on a probing mission which took him into a short mild fight. So ended 29 August.

After a horrible day of bloody fighting, the wounded on both sides are gathered to receive care at field hospitals as night descends on 29 August.

Hood's Texas Brigade

One of the most notorious fighting units in the Confederate Army was a brigade of Texans initially under the command of Kentuckian John Bell Hood. Composed of the 1st, 2nd, 4th, and 5th Texas after the outbreak of hostilities, the soldiers from the Lone Star State absolutely refused to submit to the rigorous discipline of army training. Early in the war, the 1st Texas, without orders, crossed the Potomac to give the Federals in Washington, D.C., a good natured scare. Later joined by the 18th Georgia, the Hampton Legion and 3rd Arkansas, the brigade's first real engagement was at Eltham's Landing on the Peninsula where they routed Franklin's Yankees attempting to make a landing on Virginian soil. Originally, the commander of the Confederate forces, Joseph E. Johnston had intended Hood's brigade to lightly engage the enemy, he berated the Kentuckian, "General Hood, have you given an illustration of the Texas idea of feeling an enemy gently an then falling back? What would your Texans have done, Sir, if I ordered them to charge and drive back the enemy" to which his subordinate replied, "I suppose, General, they would have driven them into the river, and tried to swim out and capture the gunboats." Serving in the Seven Days and at Second Bull Run, the Texans won a fearsome reputation amongst the Yankees for their destructive charges. At Antietam, the brigade shattered Hooker's drive on the Confederate left, though losing two thirds of the command as casualties with 82 per cent of the 1st Texas falling either dead or wounded.

After seeing service in the bloody campaigns of Fredericksburg, Chancellorsville and Gettysburg, the Brigade headed west to join Bragg's Army of Tennessee only to find the Western ways of combat, which one soldier described as "stand-up and-fire or lie-down-and-shoot," ill suited them. At the great battle of the West, Chickamauga, the Brigade displayed its patented style of charging as it participated in the fatal breakthrough of the Army of the Cumberland's line. Returning to the Army of Northern Virginia, the depleted ranks of the Texans served with Lee until the final surrender at Appomattox. There, only some 600 of the 5,300 men that had served with the brigade remained with the colors.

That night, feelings around Federal Headquarters were a mixture of adulation and anger. Of the days events, Union commanders were confident the battle was all but won with Jackson suffering most horribly from their attacks. Surely the next day would bring ultimate victory. Despite his exultation, Pope still found time to vent his rage over Porter's inaction, arguing that if only the V Corps had made an attack, Jackson could have been driven unmercifully from the field. The General Commanding sent a terse order to Porter at 2050 commanding him to move to the battlefield immediately. Complying with this order, Porter got his troops under way at about 0300 on 30 August.

Turning to more important matters, Pope began to plan the next day's attack with Reno and Heintzelman renewing their attacks on the Rebel left to be joined by Porter's fresh corps. Despite Buford's dispatch stating that Longstreet was seen moving in the direction of the battlefield, Pope still refused to believe the rest of the Confederate Army could be anywhere near Jackson. Thus, his plans discounted the existence of almost half the enemy force, allowing himself to be set up for a military disaster of the highest magnitude.

Across the field, the Confederates were likewise exuberant also claiming the day had been theirs. Confidently, Lee himself was predicting

Federals on picket duty during Pope's campaign against Lee.

Pope would soon retreat across Bull Run and was planning a pursuit. In the meantime, the Confederate lines called for some readjustment. Hood had advanced beyond the rest of Longstreet's men while some of Hill's troops had pressed beyond the protection of the embankment, both having to be recalled to rejoin their compatriots. Despite these movements, the Johnnies sought an unpleasant rest while anticipating another day of heavy combat.

In between both armies lay large numbers of dead and wounded where they had so tenaciously fought several hours earlier. Yankee Private Warren Lee Gross described that night at Manassas:

> At the end of the first days battle, so soon as the fighting ceased many sought without orders to rescue their comrades lying wounded between the opposing lines. There seemed to be a mutual understanding between both armies that such parties were not to be disturbed in their mission of mercy. . . . When the firing had died away along the darkling woods, little groups of men from the Union lines went stealthily about, bringing the wounded from the exposed positions. Blankets attached to poles or muskets often served as stretchers to bear the wounded to the ambulances and the surgeons. There was a great lack here of organized effort to care for our wounded. Vehicles of various kinds were pressed into service. The removal went on during the entire night, and tired soldiers were roused from their slumbers by the plaintive cries of wounded comrades passing in comfortless vehicles.

As dawn arose on 30 August, the entire area maintained an ominous calm as Douglas described, "The stillness was unnatural—or was it the calm repose of the thousands of dead, the resigned silence of the thousand living." For Pope, the morning yielded a most illustrious discovery: the Confederates were not to be found in their lines of the day before—obviously they must be in a head long retreat. Reconnaissance patrols and the testimony of captives seemed to indicate this assumption to be true. Tremendously elated, the "five cent Pope" evoked his infamous capacity for windy bluster, writing Washington at 0500 that victory was almost certainly his. Unfortunately for the Federals, Pope managed to entirely misread the rearrangement of the Confederate lines during the previous evening as a total withdrawal. In fact, the Army of Northern Virginia remained on the field in strength patiently awaiting their enemy's attack. Orders were given for a general pursuit under the leadership of McDowell. As the Army of Virginia got under way, it was rudely awakened to the fact the their adversaries were still on the battlefield when Federal units encountered fierce enemy fire.

Awakened to the fact that the Rebels were still before him, Pope called for one more heavy assault to finally break Jackson's line. The freshest corps, Porter's, was ordered to make up the initial attack with Heintzelman on his right with Hatch's (commanding the division of the incapacitated King) and Ricketts' divisions in support. Sigel's and Reno's men would comprise the reserve to be used if needed. Holding the left was Reynolds's division set up to the just west of an eminence called the Bald Hill.

Of the utmost importance to success of Pope's army on 30 August were supplies and reinforcements from McClellan's Army of the Potomac. Unfortunately, Little Mac was not disposed to give his rival and the Army of Virginia a great deal of assistance (he even wrote Lincoln that the Westerner should be left to get of his "scrape" on his own). In response to Pope's call for food and forage on 28 August, McClellan replied that wagons would be dispatched with such stores, though only if Pope would see fit to send the cavalry to protect them en route. With all of the Army of Virginia's available troops needed for the days action and its troopers and mounts exhausted from many days on the move, one general on Pope's staff claimed that McClellan was essentially telling Pope, "that he and his army could go starve." Worse still was

McClellan's reticence in dispatching the necessary reinforcements to Pope. On 26 August, Halleck repeatedly pressed Little Mac to send the Army of the Potomac's VI Corps under Major-General William B. Franklin from Alexandria to the battle raging near Manassas. Finding McClellan had disobeyed his instructions and arguing that the corps was hardly in the proper condition to march or give battle, the General-in-Chief intended to impress upon Little Mac the gravity of the situation in issuing the following order at 1940 on 28 August:

> There must be no further delay in moving Franklin's corps toward Manassas. They must go tomorrow morning, ready or not ready. If we delay too long to get ready there will be no necessity to go at all, for Pope will either be defeated or be victorious without our aid.

At 2200 on 29 August, McClellan responded that Franklin would finally get under way at 0600 the next day. Indeed, the VI Corps got under way at the specified time only to halted at Annandale by the request of McClellan who still believed it was still unwise to move the unit forward to join Pope. An incensed Halleck wrote at 0940 on 30 August:

> I am by no means satisfied with General Franklin's march of yesterday. Considering the circumstances of the case, he was very wrong in stopping at Annandale. . . . He knew the importance of opening communication with General Pope's army and should have acted more promptly.

When Franklin finally did get underway, his command was far too late to assist Pope in avoiding the terrible calamity that was to befall him.

While McClellan stalls sending troops to aid Pope, these members of the VI Corps languish away at Alexandria as a major battle rages at Second Manassas.

The headquarters of Matthew Brady, one of the greatest pioneers in the art of photography, during the fighting at Second Bull Run.

As most of the day passed without any serious engagement, Confederate leaders were still under the assumption Pope might actually be on the retreat. Around 1500, Jackson was preparing a note to Lee, writing, "Notwithstanding the threatening movements of the enemy, I am of the expressed opinion that he does not intend to attack us. If he does. . . . " All of a sudden, the air was punctuated by a single shot. Immediately, Jackson looked up from his writing saying, "That's the signal for a general attack." Indeed, the man's instincts were remarkably correct, for just at that moment Porter's V Corps came into view, headed for the embankment, divided into three lines. The sight was an awesome one as Blackford described:

> The advance began in magnificent style, lines as straight as an arrow, all fringed with glittering bayonets and fluttering with flags. Between the lines officers in gay uniforms galloped back and forth with drawn swords waving on their men. But the march had scarcely begun when little puffs of smoke appeared, dotting the field in rapid succession just over the heads of the men, and as the lines moved on, where the little puff had been, lay a pile of bodies, and half a dozen or more staggering figures standing around leaning on their muskets and then slowly limping to the rear.

When the Federals reached the Rebel defenses, both sides clashed with a fury which, up to that point in time, was probably the fiercest fighting encountered in the year-old Civil War. As on the day before, the Yankees weathered tremendous fire as they tenaciously fought their way up the embankment. Blackford recounts the combat:

> . . . all along the crest of the cuts and fills of the railroad a dark, low line arose, of men showing less than half their bodies; there was an instant's pause as their bright musket barrels were leveled, and then through a bursting cloud of light blue smoke gleamed a deadly flash of flame. The first line of the attacking column looked as if it had been struck by a blast of a tempest, and had been blown away.

Still the Yankees came on, taking horrendous casualties, one officer in Pender's brigade observing, "We slaughtered them like hogs."

To protect Porter's flank, Hatch's division was sent in on his left while joining Heintzelman's corps on the right were Reno's corps and Ricketts' division. On the left, Colonel Timothy Sullivan's brigade of New Yorkers from Hatch's division was routed and fled smack into Brigadier-General Marsena R. Patrick's brigade catching them up in the retreat. As this mass of men headed towards the Iron Brigade, Gibbon drew his pistol shouting, "Stop these stragglers . . . shoot them if they don't." The combined effect of fixed bayonets and the impassioned pleas of officers was enough to stem the initial panic. The right did not fare much better with Reno and Heintzelman also failing to make any solid gains.

McClellan's most loyal lieutenant, Fitz-John Porter. His controversial actions at Second Manassas later led to his court martial in January 1863.

As the fighting on Jackson's front raged on for about two hours, the Confederates ran dangerously low on ammunition, many desperately pelting the ranks of Porter's men with rocks. As the situation reached a critical point, Jackson was forced to call to Lee for help from Longstreet's legion. At the time, Old Pete, watching the attack off in the distance found a rise from which some well placed batteries could unleash a destructive fire on the Union flank. When the call came to reinforce Jackson, Longstreet replied, "Certainly, but before the division can reach him, the attack will be broken by artillery." Putting his cannons on the eminence he had found earlier, the guns opened a terrific bombardment on the Yankees sending their lines into confusion. Continuous attempts to rally under the tremendous fire met with failure as masses of troops broke and ran for the rear. Crumbling under the pressure, Porter's lines were forced to fall back leaving hundreds of dead and wounded. In a move that was to seal the fate of the Army of Virginia, McDowell called upon Reynolds to join the fight raging off to the north, leaving Pope's entire left flank unprotected save for one lone battery later supported by the 5th and 10th New York regiments.

At 1600, all hell broke loose. Longstreet, losing all hesitation from the previous day, deemed the time propitious for attack and sent his five divisions forward in a trademark smashing blow. The 5th Texas and the Hampton Legion of Hood's division advanced against the embattled 5th and 10th New York, the regiments maintaining a fierce stand despite being heavily outnumbered. After delivering vollies at a distance of about 50 yards and in some places at bayonet point, the New Yorkers were forced to give up the contest to head for safety . . . the 5th New York, a Zouave regiment suffering the worst of it, having lost 297 out of 490 men. One Texan recalled that the red pantaloons of the dead Zouaves gave the ground upon which they lay, "the appearance of a Texas hillside when carpeted in the spring by many hues and tints." Longstreet's massive tide swept even further crashing into one of Reynolds brigades moving to join the Federal right. The stunned Yankees gave off a volley harmlessly into the air above the heads of their attackers. Taking far better aim, the Confederates mowed down those who stood against them, forcing the rest to flee. Standing with his battery, Captain Mark Kerns continued to load and fire his guns with canister even after most of his men fled. Mortally wounded by a Rebel bullet just as he prepared to pull a lanyard, Kerns said to the Confederates that rushed to his dying body, "I promised to drive you back, or die by my guns, and I kept my word." Continuing onward, Longstreet intended to cut Pope's only available line of retreat across the Bull Run, the Stone Bridge. If something wasn't done quickly, the Army of Virginia would be doomed.

With the left broken, Pope immediately tried to rectify the damage by sending reinforcements from Sigel's corps and Rickett's division to block Longstreet. As the Rebel right had moved to join the attack, the Union troops that had advanced earlier against his front, fell back to a defensive position on Henry House Hill, ironically where Jackson had made his famous stand just a year earlier. While covering Hatch's retreat, Gibbon ordered one of Sigel's battery's to

Fighting on the Federal right on the second day of fighting at Second Manassas.

Reinforcements from Sigel's corps and Rickett's division head towards the rapidly collapsing Union left to halt Longstreet's oncoming divisions.

Brigadier General Nathaniel C. McLean was one of the many Federal commanders that risked all to prevent Longstreet from getting into Pope's rear on 30 August.

cease fire in order to blast the oncoming Confederates at close quarters. Confused by the General's command, a German soldier called out, "Gott in Himmel! General, Vhy you no zay schoot by my battery! I vill be disgraced by New York!" Gibbon's intentions became all too clear when he finally allowed the guns to fire. Double shotted canister knocked out Rebels by the scores.

On the left, Colonel Nathaniel C. McClean's Ohio brigade advanced to Chinn Ridge, just east of where the 5th New York had made its stand, to obstruct Longstreet before he could threaten the new line going up around Henry House Hill. The troops from the Buckeye State opened up with muskets and cannon to deadly effect; soldiers were ripped apart by grapeshot, canister and minnie balls. For a moment at least, the Rebel advance was checked by the Ohio brigade. From the south through the dense fog of grey smoke from guns, McClean spotted what appeared to be Federal reinforcements. Only when the approaching troops reached his line did he discover his deadly error—it was a detachment of Confederates who lay down a heavy flanking fusillade against the Ohioan left. McClean desperately attempted to defend against the new attack by refusing his left while his cannons opened up with double shotted canister. After two of his regiments broke for the rear, it was no longer possible to hold off the

enemy in such great numbers.

However, reinforcements were on the way. Going in on the left of McClean were Colonel John A. Koltes' and Brigadier General George L. Hartstuff's brigades maintaining a brief stand before going to the rear. Taking the field on the Bald Hill to the east of McClean's previous position came the Second Brigade of Rickett's division under Brigadier General Zealous B. Tower. The historian of the 88th Pennsylvania, John D. Vauntier, remembered the scene that awaited them there, "The confusion among the troops on the hill was great; officers and men shouting, shells tearing through and exploding, the incessant rattle of muskets, the cries of the wounded,-all combined made up a scene that was anything but encouraging, yet every one appeared anxious to get in the proper place where they could do the most good." Both Longstreet's and Towers men slugged it out for what must have seemed to be an eternity. Tower's brigade, increasingly came under such an intense sweeping fire in his front from Longstreet's men, was to come under further pressure when a Confederate division came up on his left flank. Still, the Yankees made the Rebels pay for their advance, Vauntier stating:

> The Federal troops not withstanding their desperate resistance, were being slowly but surely forced back. The men in front rank would fire, then fall to the rear to force another cartridge down their heated and befouled rifles, but by the time they were loaded they would be in front again, the rear rank having performed the same movement. The enemy was returning this salute with interest, aided by superior numbers and a concentric fire, and the ground was thickly strewn with the dead and wounded, while the rear presented a woeful mass of wounded soldiers and the inevitable stragglers, who, taking advantage of the confusion, were making lively tracks to the rear.

Though the Federals were slowly forced back, they had valiantly bought the time needed to build the final defensive line on Henry House Hill.

Unnerved by the day's events, an anguished Kearny told the battle was all but lost. "I suppose you appreciate the condition of affairs?" he cried out, "It's another Bull Run, sir, it's another Bull Run!" "Oh," replied Gibbon, "I hope not quite as bad as all that, General." Musing over the situation, Kearny agreed, "Perhaps not. Reno is keeping up the fight. He is not stampeded, I am not stampeded, you are not stampeded. That is about all, Sir, my God that is about all!" Fortunately for the Yankees, Kearny's concern was a little over worked; the

On the Field after Second Manassas

One of the major difficulties facing the men of Lee's Army of Northern Virginia was the crippling lack of shoes among the common soldiery. Of the men in the force that fought at Second Manassas and later entered Virginia, a significant majority were forced to march long distances over rough terrain in their bare feet. For the lack of any better sources, many butternuts were forced to scour the field after a battle to search over the bodies of the dead to find pair of shoes.

One Rebel, a sergeant of the 16th Mississippi, was engaged in such a practice on the battlefield of Second Bull Run when he espied a group of horsemen approaching him. When one of the riders demanded to know what the soldier was doing away from his command, the Mississippian curtly responded, "That's none of your business, by God!" When one of his inquisitors charged him with being a straggler, he angrily defended himself, saying, "It's a damn lie, sir! I only left my regiment a few minutes ago to

hunt me a pair of shoes. I went through all the fight yesterday, and that's more than you can say; for where were you yesterday, when General Stuart wanted your damned cavalry to charge the Yankees after we put 'em to running? You were lying back in the pine thickets and couldn't be found; but today, when there's no danger, you come out and charge other men with straggling, damn you!" Initially stunned by the soldier's raging tirade, the mounted men looked at each other before they let out a roar of laughter. Before the horsemen continued on their way, the sergeant was asked if realized whom he just spoken to in such a harsh manner. The man replied it must have been "a cowardly Virginia cavalryman," but learned the stunning truth; the man had been none other than Robert E. Lee, himself.

Robert E. Lee.

Landmark for both battles at Manassas, the Henry House of Henry House Hill after its destruction in the first fight.

final Union line resisted the final attacks made against it with Reynolds' Pennsylvania Reserve Division launching a counter attack that finally blunted Longstreet. Holding until nightfall, Pope ordered a general retreat across the Stone Bridge towards Centreville at 2000. A mass of worn and beaten troops, wagons, artillery, and ambulances crowded across the Stone Bridge that night in search of safety. All in all, the Army of Virginia lost some 20 percent of its 70,000 men between 29-30 August with 1,750 killed, 8,480 wounded, and 4250 captured. The Army of Northern Virginia lost 17 percent of its numbers of 55,000 men with 1,550 killed, 7,750 wounded and 100 captured or missing. After Second Manassas, the entire campaign would turn to new ground as Lee would shift his operations north of the Potomac on Union soil in Maryland.

*Whipped once again, Federal soldiers retreat over
the Stone Bridge in search of safety at Centreville.*

CHAPTER IV

INTO MARYLAND

31 August - 10 September, 1862

While John Gibbon said Second Manassas could hardly be considered another Bull Run, it might as well have been. Dejected in their humiliating defeat, the Federal Army of Virginia suffered from plummeted morale as it left the field of battle in search of safety at Centreville. The roadway to the town was jammed with a tangled mass of dejected Yankees, supply wagons, artillery, ambulances, and cavalry. Through out the retreat, the Federals were plagued with the knowledge that they had fought with every fiber of their being, proving themselves to be the equal and in some cases even better than their adversaries. In the end they had lost, not as a result of the personal failings of the common soldiery, but due to the criminal ineptitude of their own commanders, primarily Pope and McDowell. Men were hardly at a loss to voice their disgust; as troops passed by these two leaders, shouts of "traitor" and "scoundrel" were heard. One even recalled the famous words of Horace Greeley, comically calling out to westerner Pope, "Go west, young man. Go west." Upon reaching the protection of the old Confederate entrenchments at Centreville on the evening of 30 August, the Army of Virginia was received by taunts and catcalls from the newly arrived corps from the Army of the Potomac, the troops of Franklin and later Sumner who had considered Pope and his men rivals.

Evidently indifferent to the angry condemnations from his own soldiers, Pope sent a dispatch to Halleck from Centreville at 2145, attempting to defuse his recent defeat:

> The troops are in good heart and marched off the field without the least hurry or confusion. Their conduct was very fine.

> The battle was most furious for hours without cessation, and the losses on both sides very heavy. The enemy is very badly crippled, and we shall do well enough. Be easy; every thing will go well.

The General in Chief sent a reassuring reply asking his subordinate to, if possible, return to the offensive against Lee, promising more reinforcements from Washington.

Safe haven for the beaten Army of Virginia, Centreville, Virginia. Here Pope's forces linked up with the II and VI Corps of the Army of the Potomac.

The Quaker guns that fooled the Federals in the old Confederate fortifications at Centreville.

Receiving news of the defeat at 0800 the next day, Lincoln met with Secretary Hay and calmly told him, "Well, John, we are whipped again, I am afraid. The enemy reinforced on Pope and drove back his left wing and he has retired to Centreville where he says he will be able to hold his men. I don't like that expression. I don't like to hear him admit that his men need holding." Unfortunately, the capital was not taking the situation in such a composed manner as the President, with its population collapsing almost into a state of panic as news arrived of Pope's defeat.

Meanwhile at Centreville on 31 September, Pope was attempting to maintain his optimism in his communications to Halleck while beginning to hint of possible disaster writing, "I should like to know whether you feel secure about Washington should the army be destroyed." In fact, Pope had good reason to be concerned as Lee had barely consented to let his foe off the hook just yet. Wishing to get one more blow in on his demoralized adversary, the Confederate General divided his army yet

A promising commander killed at Chantilly, Isaac I. Stevens.

again; placing the fatigued and battle-weary divisions of Jackson on the move, crossing the Bull Run at Sudly Ford on 31 August, moving north onto the Little River Turnpike and following the road to the southeast, threatening Pope's lines of communications with Washington. When Pope detected the move on the 31st, he proved unwilling to bring on a large engagement; the fighting General had been finally fought out. On 1 September, he put his army on the road to Fairfax Courthouse while Major General Isaac Stephens' division of Sumner's corps supported by Kearny's division were sent to field Jackson's move.

While approaching the crossroads of the Little River and Warrenton Turnpikes, the two forces collided just east of Ox Hill near the Chantilly Mansion. Though a thick cloud cover seemed to present the possibility of rain, soldiers on both sides went about their deadly tasks undaunted. Jackson's Confederates formed a line to the south of the Little River Turnpike in front of Ox Hill facing southeast. Stevens organized his men into three lines and came in on the attack. Advancing into a heavy fire, his front began to waver, threatening to collapse entirely. Seeing the colors of the 79th New York, a unit comprised of Scotch immigrants, Stevens himself ran past his own son lying wounded on the field to snatch up the flag crying out, "Follow me, my Highlanders!" Personally rallying the troops, he led his men forward only to fall dead when a bullet pierced his skull. Increasingly hard pressed, Jackson was forced to call on his reserves, but the Federals countered this move as Kearny's division entered the fight.

All of a sudden, the clouds finally burst with a torrential downpour, dampening all concerned in the conflict. Still, Stonewall was hardly about to give up the contest on account of rain. When one of his officers requested to be pulled out of line as his men's cartridges were wet, the General curtly sent the reply "tell him the enemy's ammunition is just as wet as his."

On the other side, Philip Kearny showed an equal determination to keep the fight going, a desire which unfortunately turned out to be fatal. As he rode among his men attempting to drive them on, he accidentally ran straight into the enemy line. Immediately, he wheeled his horse around only to be shot down and killed by Rebel troops. When A.P. Hill came to view the body, he said sadly, "Poor Kearny, he deserved better than this."

Rain and impending darkness put an end to battle and the Virginia phase of the Antietam

The most belligerent of the fighting generals in the Federal army, Brigadier-General Philip Kearny. His arm was amputated after he received a wound in the Mexican American War.

Campaign. All told, the Federals lost roughly 1000 men while the Rebels lost half as many in a battle which turned out to have no great strategic significance save letting Pope get back to Washington without being forced to fight another great battle.

While the Union lost two valiant officers at what came to be known as the Battle of Ox Hill or Chantilly, the rest of the Federal forces under Pope's control filed off towards Fairfax Courthouse, reaching the town on the evening of 1 September, the misery of the Yankees augmented as they were drenched by the sudden rainstorm. Pressing through the cold dampness, the defeated soldiers plodded along through the thick muddy slime of the road. Unable to keep up with the march due to the weather or sheer

After accidentally riding into the enemy line, Phil Kearny is shot down by Confederate soldiers as he attempts to escape.

exhaustion, thousands of stragglers left the marching columns to find rest in the roadside fields. That night, Fairfax seemed to be possessed of a disorganized mass of stragglers rather than a regular army as Alexis De Trobriand, a French officer serving in the Army of the Potomac, reported:

> . . . everything was in terrible confusion. By the light of the fires kindled all around in the streets, in the yards, in the fields, one could see the confused mass of wagons, ambulances, caissons around which thousands of men invaded houses, filled up barns, broke down the fences, dug up the gardens, cooked their suppers, smoked or slept in the rain. These men belonged to a different corps. They were neither sick or wounded; but, favored by the disorder inseparable from a defeat: they had left their regiments at Centreville, to mingle with the train escorts, or had come away, each by himself, hurried on by the fear of new combat: stragglers and marauders, a contemptible multitude, whose sole desire was to flee from danger.

By the next day, the army was ordered to take cover in the defenses of the Washington, D.C.. As the troops approached the capital, it was in evidence to everyone that the army needed some serious help to recover from ordeals of the previous weeks. The men were totally worn out, as one soldier in the 11nth Pennsylvania, noted; "The men had marched and counter-marched, fought and skirmished unceasingly for ten days. Their rations had been insufficient; their sleep broken and scanty. The cavalry men reported that the saddles had not been removed from the backs of their horses since the opening of the campaign, and the condition of the animals assigned to the artillery and wagons was no better. The Army might justly be described as used up." Obviously, the situation was criti-

Fairfax Courthouse, Virginia, a stop in Pope's retreat to Washington. After Second Bull Run the town was swamped with masses of dejected Union troops.

cal. Someone was needed to whip these fatigued Federal soldiers into shape and get them back out into the field to go against Lee.

It increasingly became clear that John Pope was not the man for the job. Rightly or wrongly, he received the blame for the current crisis and there was some doubt the Army of the Potomac would follow him to the best of their ability. Moreover, Pope had begun to lash out against his subordinates, most of them McClellan's officers of the Army of the Potomac, charging them with treasonous behavior that had ultimately sabotaged his campaign. Charges were brought against several generals, the most notable being Fitz-John Porter though these were soon dropped while the Westerner found himself transferred to the Mid-West to fight Indians in Minnesota. While Pope's complaints against

McClellanist officers could be dismissed as an attempt to escape blame for the catastrophe at Second Bull Run, Lincoln had since come to the conclusion that the personal jealousies of McClellan and his clique sabotaged John Pope.

Ironically, the only person Lincoln could count on to restore the Army of the Potomac to fighting condition was the man Lincoln blamed for the North's recent defeat: George Brinton McClellan. McClellan's blatant list of misdeeds against Pope included the withholding of vital supplies and even more vital reinforcements and, worse still, implying that the western Major General should be left to get out of his "scrape" on his own. While such actions could

*Regis De Trobriand, a Frenchman who command-
ed a brigade in the Army of the Potomac.*

into the Army of Virginia. On 30 August he
wrote to his wife ''I never felt worse in my life.''
Upon receiving the news he was reinstated to
control of the Army of the Potomac, McClellan
was ecstatic; once again writing his wife, telling
her,

> I was surprised this morning when at breakfast by
> a visit from the President and Halleck - in which
> the former expressed the opinion that the troubles
> now impending could be overcome better by me
> than by anyone else. Pope is ordered to fall back
> on Washington and as he reenters everything is to
> come under my command again! A terrible and
> thankless task - yet I will do my best with God's
> blessing to perform it. . . .

Hardly enthused with Lincoln's decision to
restore McClellan to command were Secretary
of War Stanton and Secretary of the Treasury
Salmon Chase. Both men, being enraged by his
supposedly treasonous activities during Pope's
campaign, were already engaged in the enterprise to purge the Young Napoleon from the
army. Fearing further military disasters and
possibly an attempted coup, they absolutely refused to see the general retained in a military
position of real power. Under the auspices of
Stanton and Chase, a petition was organized
against McClellan and signed by most of the
members of Lincoln's cabinet. Though a cata-
strophic showdown between Lincoln and his
subordinates appeared imminent over the Mc-
Clellan issue, the situation would prove anticli-
mactic; Lincoln delivered his decision to restore
the general firmly explaining his feelings to
Hay, '' . . . we must use what tools we have.

*One of Little Mac's many political enemies,
Lincoln's formidable secretary of war, Edwin M.
Stanton.*

be considered treasonous and at least serve as
enough evidence to cashier Little Mac, Lincoln
knew McClellan the was only individual capable of salvaging the Federal war effort in the
East. As Gideon Welles noted, only the Young
Napoleon commanded the respect and admiration of the army and would follow his direction,
''The soldiers whom McClellan has commanded
are doubtless attached to him. They have been
trained to it, and he has kindly cared for them
while under him. With partiality for him they
have imbibed his prejudices . . . '' Moreover,
perhaps only McClellan with his organizational
capabilities would be able to reorganize the defeated army entering Washington, and put it in
the field once more. Lincoln himself said, ''I
must have McClellan to reorganize the army
and bring it out of chaos.''

With his decision made, on 2 September, the
President went with Halleck to McClellan's
quarters in Alexandria to request him to take
command of the troops coming into Washington. Previously, the General had fallen into a fit
of depression at having his troops siphoned off

A good judge of character, President Abraham Lincoln was aware of McClellan's faults but also his usefulness as an organizer and an inspiration to fight.

The Young Napoleon and the lovely Ellen McClellan. McClellan confided more with his wife about military affairs than with any general or public official.

There is no man in the entire army who can man these fortifications and lick these troops of ours into shape half as well as he. . . . Unquestionably he has acted badly towards Pope! He wanted him to fail. That is unpardonable, but he is just too useful just now to sacrifice." Faced with the President's decree, the cantankerous secretaries backed down from a derisive confrontation.

After receiving command once more, McClellan's first action was to ride out to meet his incoming troops. Some distance out of Washington, he ran into a downcast Pope and McDowell leading the retreating army. As he informed both he was in charge once more, John Hatch eavesdropped in on the conversation. Upon hearing the news, Hatch saw the perfect opportunity to get back at Pope for relieving him of command back in July. While knowingly in earshot of his now former commander, he shouted to soldiers close by, "Boys, McClellan is in command of the army again! Three cheers!" The effect was instantaneous. All of a sudden, the Federals forgot their defeat, weariness, and hunger and exploded into triumphant hurrahs; multitudes of caps were thrown into the air. One soldier described the scene as shouts of "General McClellan is here" went up through the entire army during the evening.

> The enlisted men caught the sound and those who were awake aroused their sleeping neighbor. Eyes were rubbed and those tired fellows, as the news was passed down the column, jumped to their feet and sent up such a hurrah as the army of the Potomac had never heard before. Shout after shout went out into the stillness of the night and as it was taken up along the road and repeated by regiment, brigade, division and corps, we could hear the roar dying away in the night.

By 3 September, what had once been Pope's Army of Virginia, but was now McClellan's Army of the Potomac, took up position to defend the capital. Entrenched in fortifications on the Virginia side of the Potomac were Sigel's corps, now the XI Corps of the Army of the

Members of the II Corps parade in Washington, D.C..

Potomac, Heintzelman's III Corps, and Porter's V Corps. The defenses on the Maryland side of Washington included Banks' corps (now the XII Corps) and Sumner's II Corps at Tenallytown while Burnside's IX Corps was stationed in the suburbs of the capitol. The reserve consisted of McDowell's III Corps now called the I Corps of the Army of the Potomac. This was McClellan's legion. Along with the troops defending the city and new recruits, he commanded some 125,000 men, an awesome force of tremendous power, if only he could just use it. Among the command changes in the army the hapless McDowell was relieved and his corps was taken over by the dashing Fighting Joe Hooker. With Banks directed to command the defenses of Washington D.C., the XII Corps fell under the temporary direction of Alpheus Williams.

While the Army of the Potomac moved to take up position around Washington, Lee took his army to Leesburg, Virginia, 30 miles to the northwest of Washington, while pondering the possibilities his magnificent victory at Second Manassas opened up for him. The idea of staying on the defensive and awaiting another Federal attack was just not within Lee's character; he was above all a man of action who wished to keep his foe continuously off balance whenever the opportunity could be found. He had won the initiative back at Jackson's uncertain victory at Cedar Mountain and he was not about to surrender it or his campaign. He found the only viable course of action was to head north, to take on the Yankees on their own ground in what would amount to the first invasion of Union soil in the East.

Indeed, there were many reasons making this scheme so inviting. The North was still off balance from Second Manassas; its army both beaten, demoralized and disorganized. Though the Army of the Potomac had been reinforced in Washington, many of these new troops were complete rookies; their regiments mustered just a few days or weeks previously. Better still, Lee's good fortune was complemented by the victories of the Confederate armies under Brigadier General Braxton Bragg and Kirby Smith in the west. Lexington Kentucky was already in Confederate hands and there was boisterous talk of moving above the Ohio River against Cincinnati. With the Confederates running rampant on northern territory, the Unionists would be increasingly hard pressed.

An invasion would also help alleviate supply problems facing Lee's army and perhaps even

The Grand Ball at Urbana

While the rest of the Confederate Army encamped at Frederick from 6-10 September, the Confederate Cavalry set up its headquarters at the nearby town of Urbana. Impressed with the welcome he had received so far in Maryland, J.E.B. Stuart, very fond of dancing, decided he and his men should take a brief respite from the trials of warfare to hold a ball for his troopers and the local belles. Commandeering a large room in an abandoned ladies academy, he festooned walls with regimental flags while the services of the regimental band of the 18th Mississippi were acquired to play the music. On 8 September, invitations were sent out and by that evening, a large crowd of partiers had arrived to take part in the dance. Despite the gaiety of the occasion, cavalry officers left their swords nearby just in case of an emergency.

Master of ceremonies Major Heros Von Borcke (a German citizen serving with the Confederate cavalry) began the festivities with a polka. Turning to dance with his partner, he was introduced to the native customs as he recalled, " . . . my surprise was great indeed when my fair friend gracefully eluded my extended arms, and with some confusion explained that she did not join in round dances, thus making me acquainted for the first time with the fact that in America, especially in the South, young ladies rarely waltz except with brothers or first cousins and only in reels and contredanses with strangers."

As the evening passed on and the dashing cavalry troopers and their guests enjoyed dance after dance, all

Federal and Confederate cavalry in combat during the campaign in Maryland.

were reawakened to the war when a brusk fire of musketry and cannon opened up in the distance as Federal cavalry arrived to spoil the occasion. Immediately buckling on their sabers, the Confederates turned to their partners, bidding them to await their return before heading off into the darkness to do battle. When the soldiers finally returned, a woman screamed upon seeing the bloodied bodies of the wounded as they were brought into the building for care. Immediately, the ladies became "ministering angels," attending to the care of those unfortunate soldiers who had become casualties on the field of battle. One wounded Confederate smiled at the attention

he received, declaring he wouldn't mind getting hit any day with surgeons such as those attending him. Finally, with the grand ball ended, the soldiers escorted their partners home, keeping with them always the memories of one of the most pleasant experiences of the war.

the entire Confederacy. Shortly after the war began, the Rebels found themselves continuously suffering shortages of food, clothing, and other necessities for comfort and survival. The states supporting the Union had these objects in abundance, if the Confederates could only lay their needy hands upon them. Not only that, by living off Federal soil and occupying the atten-

tion of the enemy's armies, the Army of Northern Virginia would effectively spare Virginia's farmers the ravages of another enemy campaign and allow them to reap their fall harvests unhindered.

Political arguments for moving north also worked in Lee's mind. In invading the North, the general took it for granted that, when he crossed into Maryland, he would be welcomed as a liberator rather than shunned as a conqueror. Supposedly, the Free State was loyal to the Confederacy, with many of its citizens maintaining Southern sympathies as evinced by riots against Federal troops in the city of Baltimore in 1861. To bring Maryland under the heel of the Federal government, civil liberties had been suppressed, constitutional rights abrogated, and people unjustly arrested: all in the name of Union! Surely the results of loyalty to the South and Yankee despotism would lead to the Marylanders support for Lee's army, in the form of both badly needed men to fill the ranks and supplies. Lee also realized the psychological impact his crossing of the Potomac would have upon the North, especially after the defeats of the Seven Days and Second Bull Run. Perhaps the presence of Confederate troops on Yankee soil would convince the Northerners of the hopelessness of their desire to bring the Southern states back into the Union and influence them to pressure the Federal government to sue for peace or to vote for antiwar candidates in the upcoming congressional elections.

Perhaps the most important factor that influenced Lee was the possibility of foreign recognition after a victory across the Potomac. By running loose in the North, he might encourage European countries such as France and England to intervene; forcing both sides to mediate. This would effectively legitimize the Confederacy's existence and future autonomy. As word of Northern defeats was spread across the Atlantic, there were indications that Prime Minister John Templeton Palmerston and Foreign Secretary Lord John Russel were contemplating such a move.

Thus, a complete overview of the situation seemed to lead to one conclusion: ultimate victory could possibly lie on the other side of the Potomac, if Lee and his army could attain it. Could the Army of Northern Virginia prove equal to the task? For the previous few weeks it had attempted and accomplished herculean feats. The men were, dirty, tired, hungry, and lacked supplies and proper clothes; but still they would go on. In appraising the state of the Confederate Army after Chantilly one soldier wrote, "In all these weeks we had no change of clothing and were laterally devoured by vermin. . . . A prize fighter trains about two months to get himself in perfect condition, but we had been training in a more vigorous manner for nearly two years, and the men were skin, bone, and muscle." On 3 September, Lee notified the

After suppressing John Pope, Lee decided to go in search of bigger game north of the Potomac.

President of the Confederacy, Jefferson Davis, telling of possibilities and the obstacles his invasion would entail:

The present seems to be the most propitious time since the commencement of the war for the Confederate Army to enter Maryland. The two grand armies of the United States that have been operating in Virginia, though now united are, are much weakened and demoralized. Their new levies, of which I understand 60,000 men have already been posted in Washington, are not yet organized, and will take some time to for the field. If it is ever desired to give material aid to Maryland and afford her an opportunity of throwing off the oppression to which she is now, subject, this would seem the most favorable. . . . The army is not properly equipped for an invasion of an enemy's territory. It lacks much of the material of war, is feeble in transportation, the animals being much reduced, and the men are poorly provided with clothes, and

The president of the Confederacy, Jefferson Davis.

in thousands of instances destitute of shoes. Still, we cannot afford to be idle and though weaker than our opponents in men and military equipments, must endeavor to harass if we cannot destroy them. I am aware that the movement is attended with much risk, yet I do not consider success impossible, and shall endeavor to guard it from loss.

Moving north, Lee opted to move to the east of the Blue Ridge Mountains, going for the town of Frederick, Maryland, situated between the mountain range and Washington, D.C.

This move seemed to flaunt the Confederate advance before the enemy entrenched behind the Washington's extensive fortifications. No doubt the wily Confederates hoped to lure the Federals out of the safety of the capital into fight before they were ready with their supply lines stretched over a dangerously long distance. Furthermore, Frederick, one of Maryland's biggest cities, served as a perfect location to attract support from the state's citizens, collect supplies, and launch further operations. However, there were two possible obstacles to Lee's plans in the near vicinity: the Federal garrisons in Northern Virginia at Harper's Ferry (10,400 men) and

Martinsburg (2,500 men). Both threatened the planned lines of communication for the Army of Northern Virginia during operations in the North which ran south from Shepardstown through the Shenandoah Valley via Winchester and Harrisonburg before moving onto Richmond. However, it was hoped once the Rebels moved north of the Potomac, the Federals would show the good sense to remove these isolated commands from the danger of being captured by Lee and his lieutenants while unknowingly assisting them in their ventures. Unfortunately, the Yankees would not be so gracious and the commands remained where they were.

Reinforced by the divisions of Generals D.H. Hill, Lafayette McLaws and John G. Walker, Wade Hampton's cavalry brigade and William

A rather sinister depiction of the Confederate invasion into Maryland.

Johnny Rebs take off their shoes and roll up trouser legs to cross the icy waters of the Potomac River.

Nelson Pendleton's Reserve Artillery, Lee had some 50,000 men available for the invasion. From 4 to 7 September, the Rebel army began to cross the Potomac at White's Fords into Northern territory as a regimental band struck up the stirring and very appropriate tune "Maryland, My Maryland". So jubilant was the crossing that one of Kershaw's troops saw fit to apply a historical allusion to the movement, saying, "Never before had an occurrence so excited and enlivened the spirits of the troops as the crossing into . . . Maryland. It is said the Crusaders, after months of toil, marching, and fighting on their way through the plains of Asia Minor, wept when they saw the towering spires of Jerusalem, the Holy City, in the distance; and if ever Lee's troops could have wept for joy it was at the crossing of the Potomac." The river crossing was tough going for some troops, gingerly walking barefoot over the rocky ford. Some Texans complained that the water was so cold that all the ice houses in western Maryland must have been emptied in the river. Another blissfully recounted the relief of the cool river, saying, "The river was shallow and clear, and some of us dallied merrily in its bright waters, glad to be refreshed after the tedious, dusty marches of the past month."

However cheerful the crossing was, a few incidents occurred which seemed to bode ill for the coming campaign. Three of the leading Confederate commanders, Lee, Longstreet, and Jackson, all received injuries from various freak accidents. Shortly after Second Manassas, Lee, dressed in rain gear, tripped on his bulky rubber poncho when his mount Traveler started. Falling to the ground, he injured both hands which had to be bound in unwieldy and embarrassing splints. Longstreet's heel was chafed by his boot, causing painful blisters. The remedy for his discomfort ingloriously consigned him to the wearing of a pair of carpet slippers. Like Lee, Jackson also suffered from an unfortunate bout with a horse, presented to him by a group of Marylanders. When Jackson mounted the beast, it suddenly reared harshly throwing the general to the ground leaving him in some pain for quite awhile.

As if these incidents were not troublesome enough, a plague of arrests struck the officer corps of the Army of Northern Virginia. The antipathy between Stonewall Jackson and Powell Hill finally exploded. Smarting from earlier criticism from Jackson about moving his troops too slowly during the Second Manassas Campaign, Hill decided to press his troops unnecessarily hard as he moved them from Leesburg to the crossing of the Potomac on 4 September; blatantly ignoring his superiors' request to rest his men in order to stop straggling. When Stonewall called the Light Division to a halt himself, Hill rode up to his commander and presented his sword saying, "If you take command of my troops in my presence, take my sword also!" to which Jackson replied "Consider yourself under arrest for neglect of duty." John Bell Hood also found himself in trouble after getting into an argument about the possession of some captured Federal ambulances with his superior, General "Shanks" Evans. When Evans demanded the ambulances be turned over him, Hood refused and was put under arrest by Longstreet for insubordination. Fortunately, Lee realized it would be foolhardy to lose the talents of Hill and Hood in the coming campaign for such petty offenses; he kept them with their commands though under arrest, to be called upon when needed.

Frederick was to be very important for Lee's affairs in the state: there he wanted to proclaim his aims to the people of Maryland and claim his army did not come to conquer but to liberate; the actions of his men would confirm that statement. The Confederates were to be on their best behavior; troops weren't allowed in the town without a pass and the provost marshall's troopers patrolled the streets to ensure that the butternuts refrained from any infractions. Anything needed by the army would be purchased, albeit with Confederate script (worthless in the North save if the Confederacy could win the war). Wily soldiers managed to evade regulations against foraging, some killing livestock in "self defense" as the animals had unpatriotically attacked them. No doubt a lot of Rebels enjoyed a hearty meal by employing such a ruse.

The Confederates were excited to find an exuberant reception awaiting them in the town of Frederick. Von Borcke cheerfully wrote:

> Entering the old city of Frederick, I found it in a tremendous state of excitement. . . . Flags were floating from the houses, and garlands of flowers were hung across the streets. Everywhere a dense multitude was moving up and down, singing and shouting in a paroxysm of joy and patriotic emotion, in many cases superinduced by an abundant flow of strong liquors.

Confederate David E Johnston wrote, "In Frederick our hearts were made glad by unmistakable signs of friendship and sympathy. A bevy

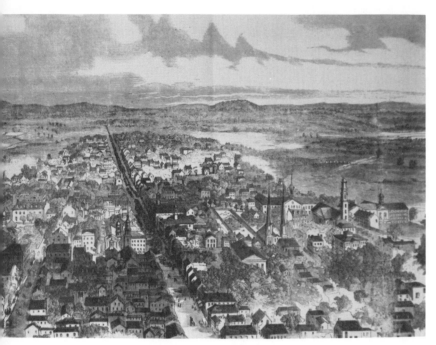

The city of Frederick during the Army of Northern Virginia's visit to the area in early September of 1862.

of pretty girls, singing 'Maryland, My Maryland' on seeing inscribed on our battle flag Seven Pines, proposed 'Three cheers for the battle flag of Seven Pines,' which were heartily and lustily given by us." Troops were fed with cakes, pies, bread, applebutter, milk and other treats, which for many of these men comprised the first good meal they had eaten in quite a while. Curiosity seekers flocked to see the mythic figures of whom they had heard so much, struggling to get a glimpse of the gallant Lee, Longstreet, Jackson, and Stuart. Officers and cavalry troopers were constantly accosted often times being mistaken for one of these great personages. While Lee and Jackson tended to refrain from much social contact, Longstreet and Stuart enjoyed the attention and were quite willing to enjoy the company of friendly and curious ladies.

On 8 September, Lee chose to deliver an address to state his aims to the people of Maryland:

> It is right that you should know the purpose that brought the army under my command to the limits of your State. . . . The people of the Confederate States have long watched with deepest sympathy the wrongs and outrages that have been inflicted upon the citizens of a commonwealth allied to the States of the South by the strongest social, political, and commercial ties. They have seen with profound indignation their sister State deprived of

every right and reduced to the condition of a conquered province. . . . our army has come among you, and is prepared to assist you with the power of its arms in regaining of the rights of which you have been despoiled. . . . No constraint on your free will is intended; no intimidation will be allowed within the limit of this army, at least. Marylanders shall once more enjoy their ancient freedom of thought and speech. . . . .It is for you to decide your destiny freely and without constraint. This army will respect your choice, whatever it may be; and while the Southern people will rejoice to welcome you to your natural position among them, they will only welcome you when you come of your own free will.

Lee gave the people of Maryland the choice of joining with him or staying with the Union. Unfortunately for the Confederates, most chose the latter course. The numbers of new recruits Lee expected to join his army never materialized. Maybe a couple hundred at best joined the Confederate standard, certainly crushing Lee's expectations; and many of these soon deserted the ranks after a few days in the Rebel army. Also disappointing was the general lack of food in the area. Most farmers had not yet harvested their crops and their barns were either empty or closed to the Confederates. There were many reasons for the notable lack of help from many

Citizens of the Free State during Lee's invasion of Maryland. Despite a warm reception in Frederick, Lee found a lack of enthusiasm for the Confederate cause in Western Maryland.

Maryland, My Maryland

Perhaps the most symbolic battle cry of the Southern soldiers during the Antietam Campaign was the anthem ''Maryland, My Maryland,'' written by a 22-year-old denizen of the Free State, James Ryder Randall. While teaching in Louisiana, he read an account of the riot by Confederate sympathizers against the 6th Massachusetts in Baltimore on 19 April 1861. Inspired by the incident and his hatred for the Yankees, he immediately put his words to

Author of My Maryland, James Ryder Randall.

verse, creating an epic work displaying his yearning to see his native state free from Federal dominance. It had what one writer called ''the fire and dash of Southern temperament through an impassioned crescendo.'' The song later fell out of favor with Confederate troops after their ill reception by the primarily pro-Union elements of western Maryland during their campaign there in September of 1862.

My Maryland
by James Ryder Randall
The despot's heel is on thy shore,
   Maryland!
His torch is at thy temple door.
   Maryland!
Avenge the patriotic gore
That flecked the streets of Baltimore,
And be the battle-queen of yore,
   Maryland, my Maryland!

Hark to an exiled son's appeal,
   Maryland!
My Mother State, to thee I kneel,
   Maryland!
For life and death, for woe and weal,
Thy peerless chivalry reveal,
And gird thy beauteous limbs with steel,
   Maryland, my Maryland!

Thou wilt not cower in the dust,
   Maryland!
Thy beaming sword shall never rust,
   Maryland!
Remember Carroll's sacred trust,
Remember Howard's warlike thrust,
All thy slumberers with the just,
   Maryland, my Maryland!

Come! 'tis the red dawn of day,
   Maryland!
Come with thy panoplied array,
   Maryland!

With Ringgold's spirit for the fray,
With Watson's blood at Monterey,
With fearless Lowe and dashing May,
   Maryland, my Maryland!

Come! for thy shield is bright and strong,
   Maryland!
Come! for thy dalliance does thee wrong,
   Maryland!
Come to thine own heroic throng,
Stalking with Liberty along,
And chant thy dauntless slogan-song,
   Maryland, my Maryland!

Dear Mother, burst thy tyrant's chain,
   Maryland!
Virginia should not call in vain,
   Maryland!

She meets her sisters on the plain,—
''Sic semper!'' 'tis the proud refrain
That baffles minions back amain,
   Maryland, my Maryland!

I see the blush upon thy cheek'
   Maryland!
For thou wast never bravely meek,
   Maryland!
But lo! there surges forth a shriek
From hill to hill, from creek to creek,-
Potomac calls to Chesapeake,
   Maryland, my Maryland!

Thou wilt not yield the Vandal toll,
   Maryland!
Thou wilt not crook to his control,
   Maryland!
Better the fire upon thee roll,
Better the blade, the shot, the ball,
Than crucifixion of my soul,
   Maryland, my Maryland!

I hear the distant thunder-hum
   Maryland!
The old Line's bugle, fife, and drum,
   Maryland!
She is not dead, nor deaf, nor dumb;
Huzzah! She spurns the Northern scum!
She breathes! She burns! She'll come! She'll come!
   Maryland, my Maryland!

Marylanders. The Southern sympathies that Lee had counted upon were upheld by citizens in the eastern part of the state around Baltimore. Out in western Maryland, most people stuck with the Union. Those who were either neutral or stood by the Southern cause might have been turned away by the ragged appearance of the Confederate troops. One citizen of

Frederick wrote of their strange appearance and manners, "They were the dirtiest, lousiest, filthiest, piratical-looking cut-throat men I ever saw. A most ragged, lean, and hungry set of wolves. . . . Many of them were from the far South and spoke a dialect I could scarcely understand. They were profane beyond belief and talked incessantly." Many Marylanders also believed, despite Lee's words, that the Army of Northern Virginia was only going to stay in their state for a short time. Once the Rebels left, those who had supported them would be at the mercy of vengeful Unionists. Not even pro-Southern Governor Enoch L. Lowe showed up to support the Rebels and their aims to liberate his own state. So far for Lee, his advance into Maryland had been a complete bust.

Worse still, the Army of Northern Virginia had actually lost troops due to a crippling plague of stragglers. Some soldiers just couldn't keep up with the rest of the army after the intense campaigning of the previous month and the current brakeneck pace. Others had simply remained on the Virginia side of the Potomac, refusing to cross the river, on the reasoning that they had enlisted to defend the South not to invade the North. Once across the river, the Army of Virginia's crippling lack of shoes began to tell as mens' feet, used to the soft dirt roads of Virginia, were painfully cut and scraped as they marched on the hard, rocky roads of Maryland. One soldier complained that while his heart was brave he was cursed with "unpatriotic feet." This combined with the rampant diarrhea, dysentery and hunger served to force many other men to fall from the ranks.

All told, Lee claimed to have lost from 8000 to 10,000 men from straggling. To avoid losing those who couldn't keep up to capture, the Pro-

A Confederate straggler leaves the ranks in search of food and rest.

vost Marshal was ordered to collect these masses of individuals and direct them to Winchester in the Shenandoah Valley to be reorganized and brought back into the rest of the army at a latter date.

Though the campaign had not yet lived up to Lee's expectations, he had yet to attempt to achieve the fruit of his military ambitions. To attain them, he would have to campaign against the garrisons of Harper's Ferry and Martinsburg. In this endeavor, he was to draw up a plan breathtaking in scope, taxing the very limits of his officers and soldiers, exposing them to more exhausting marches and tremendous risks. Still, his legion had done the impossible before and could surely so again.

CHAPTER V

"The Best Laid Plans . . ."
10 - 13 September, 1862

Cutting through the countryside of Western Maryland and heading up through the sleepy farmlands of Pennsylvania is an extension of the Blue Ridge, the imposing South Mountain. About six miles to the east is a low range called the Catoctins, to the southwest a prominence called Elk Ridge. But rising up 1300 feet, South Mountain dominates them all. In Western Maryland, the mighty height yields only a few crossings through its coarse features, the most prominent passes being Turner's Gap, almost 15 miles from Frederick, and Crampton's Gap, six miles to the south of Turner's. Ultimately,

South Mountain would prove instrumental for Lee's operations against Harper's Ferry and Martinsburg for in using the looming ridge as a massive blind, shielding his movements from the enemy, he could easily take both commands without the Yankees discovering him on the move until it was far too late.

While the size of the force at Martinsburg presented no real threat of opposition, Harper's

Harper's Ferry at the time of the Civil War. Armies from both sides took and retook the town several times so that by Antietam a good deal of it lay in ruins.

Ferry was an appealing target because it was almost indefensible. Overlooking the town from every angle rose massive wooded heights; the most important of these, Maryland Heights, the southern most extension of Elk Ridge, stood to the north across the Potomac. At 1450 feet, it commanded the other rises in the area. The 1250 foot Loudoun Heights was to the south and east of Harper's Ferry, and 650 foot Bolivar Heights to the west. With these positions taken, Harper's Ferry would be at the Confederates mercy, enabling their artillery to launch an uncontested devastating plunging fire on the town's defenders. As one Federal officer noted, "The place was no more defensible than a well bottom, being surrounded by commanding positions on every side, and was incapable of being held by any garrison that could be spared to undertake its hopeless and perilous defence."

Despite the vulnerability of Harper's Ferry, it maintained some strategic value to the Federals, serving as a base for operations in the Shenandoah Valley, a post protecting Maryland from enemy advances above the Potomac, and a defense from guerilla attacks for the B & O Railroad. Defending the town was hardly a fearsome lot; rookie soldiers, some mustered in only days before Lee had entered Maryland. Their commander was a career military officer on the skids, Colonel Dixon Miles, exiled to the post after being accused of drunkenness at First Bull Run.

Federal troops at Harper's Ferry seek amusements during their otherwise dull routine of garrison duty.

In developing a plan to take both towns, it was Lee's hope to have his armies surround and swallow both of the garrisons whole. To do so, he effectively decided to disassemble his army into different commands, sending them in separate directions to accomplish assigned tasks. Jackson was ordered to go from Frederick west with his own division under Brigadier General J.R. Jones, Ewell's division under Brigadier Alexander R. Lawton, and A.P. Hill's Light Division, all told 14,000 men, across the Potomac to move on Martinsburg, either destroying the garrison there or forcing it into the main trap at Harper's Ferry. Following this action, he would then take up a position to the west of Harper's Ferry on Bolivar Heights. Taking the northern approach to the town was Major General Lafayette McLaws commanding his own division along with Major Richard J. Anderson's division with the total force consisting of 8,000 men. Closing the siege would be Brigadier-General Richard G. Walker's division of 2000 men, recrossing the Potomac to take position on Loudoun Heights. The rest of the army along with the reserve, supply, and baggage trains would move on to Boonsboro under Lee and Longstreet, with D.H. Hill's division forming the rear guard. All commanders were to begin their movements on 10 September and take their positions two days later forcing the Federal garrison at Harper's Ferry to surrender. After accomplishing the set objectives, the army was to reunite at Hagerstown to prepare for a destructive rampage in Pennsylvania. As usual, Lee's more defensive minded subordinate Old Pete Longstreet had strenuous objections to this incredibly audacious plan. Arguing the risks involved were far too great, the General firmly stated the army was in no condition to make the planned long marches in enemy territory necessary to carry out the objectives set. Furthermore, there was the threatening possibility McClellan might manage to get his army into fighting condition quickly, coming out to engage the vulnerable Army of Northern Virginia before it could be reunited. Instead, Longstreet urged caution and advised his commander to recoup the army's strength, recruit troops, and take in supplies.

Lee was not convinced by his subordinate's words of caution. He confidently believed his men able to achieve the monumental tasks set for them. Furthermore, Lee practically refused to believe McClellan possessed the initiative to advance from Washington with any great speed as he told General Walker after detailing his plans, "[McClellan] is a very able general but a very cautious one. His enemies among his own people think him too much so. His army is in a very demoralized and chaotic condition, and will not be prepared for offensive operations— or he will not think it so—for three or four weeks. Before that time I hope to be on the Susquehanna."

Unlike Longstreet, Stonewall Jackson was eager for the Harper's Ferry operation. As with the flanking maneuver around Pope, it was his kind of campaign. Besides, as he jokingly told Lee, he had "impolitely" neglected his "friends" in the Shenandoah Valley for far too long. On 9 September, Special Orders Number 191 detailing the commands for the Harper's Ferry operation were dispatched to the appropriate commanders: Longstreet, Jackson, McLaws, R.H. Anderson, Walker, Harvey Hill, and Stuart. Though D.H. Hill had been detached from Jackson's command, Stonewall scribbled down a copy of the order, sending it on to his subordinate. While Hill received this copy, somehow, the one sent from headquarters never arrived. The next day, the Confederates were on the move, disappearing behind the protective cover of South Mountain with Stuart's troopers defending the approaches to the gaps and depriving their arch-foes, the Yankee cavalry, of any useful reconnaissance.

Meanwhile, McClellan was busy restoring his fighting machine, the Army of the Potomac, to good working order with a speed belying his

Baltimore and Ohio railroad bridge destroyed to hamper Union lines of communication.

timidity and immense caution on the field. Stragglers were rounded up to be returned to their commands which were being reorganized and reinforced. As news arrived of Lee's moves across the Potomac, the army took position on the Maryland suburbs of Washington, preparing for an eventual rematch with the army that had bested them in the swamps before Richmond and on the fields near Manassas.

When McClellan was finally ready to take to the field, he brought five corps with him: the I, II, VI, IX and XII (falling under the command of

Sketch of Stuart's cavalry burning a bridge and the house of pro-Union farmer. Actually the Confederates upheld Lee's instructions not to disturb the citizens of Southern states.

Barbara Frietchie

One of the greatest points of contention Confederates found with the Maryland Campaign was not Lee's dividing the army before a numerically superior enemy nor the loss of the Special Orders 191 to the Federals, but instead what a little old lady did, or might have done, with the national flag.

As the Federals entered the city of Frederick, an elderly woman of 96 years, by the name of Barbara Frietchie could be seen gently waving an American flag to welcome the approaching troops. Touched by the scene, soldiers lifted their caps and cheered loudly, calling out, "God bless you, old lady!" "May you live long, you dear old soul!" The story of Frietchie's patriotism spread through the ranks, eventually reaching General Jesse Reno himself, who took the time to pay her a visit before he rode off to meet his death at South Mountain. Another citizen of Frederick, May Quantrall was also charged with waving an American flag before Stonewall Jackson, however, Confederate witnesses claim the general never saw her.

Evidently Frietchie's sudden status as a celebrity refused to remain in the ranks of the Army of the Potomac. The story of her waving the flag spread throughout the area, like all good yarns picking up a little something more at every retelling. Eventually it reached a Washington novelist, Mrs. E.D.E.N. Southworth, who related the events to poet J.G. Whittier. In putting the incident to lyrics, the account of an elderly woman waving a flag to welcome Union troops was transformed into Frietchie defiantly waving a flag before Jackson himself and his Rebel troops.

During and after the war, Confederate proponents were so disturbed by the poem that they heatedly disputed the validity of the work, with Kyd Douglas writing, "As for Barbara Frietchie, we did not pass her house. . . . She never saw Stonewall Jackson and he never saw her. I was with him every minute while he was in town, and nothing like the patriotic incident so graphically described by Mr. Whittier in his poem ever occurred. The venerable poet held on to the fiction with such tenacity for years after, that he

seemed to resent the truth about it." Unlike most his comrades, Moxley Sorrel admitted that if Whittier's work did not contain much in the form of historical accuracy, it could still be appreciated for the fine lyrics of the author, " . . . the poet Whittier has told of Barbara Fritchie and Stonewall Jackson—a stirring poem in winning lines, but quite without fact at bottom. But that matters not in the least. The lines are good and we can well afford to throw in with all the hard words and abuse of those days, the poet's ideas about our Stonewall."

Despite Confederate objections to the basis of Whittier's poem, the poet absolutely refused to acknowledge that the story he was told was false as he wrote in 1886, "The poem *Barbara Frietchie* was written in good faith. The story was no invention of mine. It came from sources which I regarded as completely reliable; it had been published in newspapers, and had gained public credence in Washington and Maryland before the poem was written. I had no reason to doubt its accuracy then, and I am still constrained to believe that it had foundation in fact. If

I thought otherwise, I should not hesitate to express it." True or otherwise, *Barbara Frietchie* provides a glimpse of the romanticism of the Civil War era.

Barbara Frietchie
by John Greenleaf Whittier

Up from the meadows rich with corn,
Clear in the cool September morn,

The clustered spires Frederick stand
Green-walled by the hills of Maryland.

Round about them orchards sweep,
Apple and peach trees fruited deep,

Fair as the garden of the Lord
To the eyes of the famished rebel
Horde,

On that pleasant morn of early that fall
When Lee marched over the mountain-wall;

Over the mountains winding down,
Horse and foot, into Frederick town.

Forty flags with their silver stars,
Forty flags with their crimson bars,

Flapped in the morning wind: the sun
Of noon looked down, and saw not
one.

Up rose old Barbara Frietchie then,
Bowed with her fourscore years and ten;

In her attic window the staff she set,
To show that one heart was loyal yet.

Up the street came the rebel tread,
Stonewall Jackson riding ahead.

Under his slouched hat left and right
He glanced; the old flag met his sight.

"Halt!"—the dust brown ranks stood fast.
"Fire!"—out blazed the rifle blast.

It shivered the window, pane and sash;
It rent the banner with seam and gash.

Quick, as it fell, from the broken staff
Dame Barbara snatched the silken scarf.

She leaned out the window-sill
And shook it forth with a royal will.

"Shoot if you must, this old gray head,
But spare your country's flag," she said.

A shade of sadness, a blush of shame,
Over the face of the leader came;

The nobler nature within him stirred
To life at that woman's deed and word:

"Who touches a hair of yon gray head
Dies like a dog! March on!" he said.

All day long through Frederick street
Sounded the tread of marching feet:

All day long that flag tree tost
Over the heads of the rebel host.

Ever its torn folds rose and fell
On the loyal winds that loved it well;

And through the hill-gaps sunset light
Shone over it with a warm good-night.

Barbara Frietchie's work is o'er,
And the Rebel rides on his raids no more.

Honor to her! and let a tear
Fall, for her sake, on Stonewall's bier.

Over Barbara Frietchie's grave,
Flag of Freedom and Union, wave!

Peace and order and beauty draw
Round thy symbol of light and law;

And ever the stars look down
On thy stars below Frederick town!

Major-General Joseph Mansfield on 16 September), and later the V, as well as a cavalry division under Brigadier General Alfred Pleasonton, all combined totaling some 85,000 not including the Federal's large pool of reinforcements in Washington D.C..

In setting out to make contact with the enemy, the Army of the Potomac was divided into three wings with the I and IX under Burnside taking the left, the II and XII under Sumner comprising the center, and the VI and Major General Darius Couch's unattached division taking the right under Franklin. The Army of the Potomac swept across the Maryland countryside, searching for Lee's Army, in a wide arc extending from the Potomac and back towards Baltimore. The basic idea behind this

Union troopers of Pleasant cavalry combing the Maryland countryside for signs of Lee's army.

formation was to ease Halleck's fears of an attack on Washington by blocking any attempt on the part of the Rebels to slip around either flank of the army and attack either the capital or Baltimore. On 9 September the army was on the move into Western Maryland. Pleasonton took the lead, skirmishing with Stuart's cavalry, slowly driving the enemy back, though failing to get any helpful reconnaissance. Holding the extreme left flank, Couch following the Potomac and watching the river fords, moved through Poolesville and Barnesville, reaching Lickville by the 13 September. Franklin headed up through Dawsonsville and Barnesville to Buckeyestown, arriving on the same day. Sumner's wing followed the Old National Road to Frederick where he arrived on the 13th and was joined by Burnside's men traveling via the Brookville Seneca road. The movement had been a slow one, the army making the 40 mile march to Frederick in four days, typifying McClellan's caution primarily due to his overwhelming uncertainty over the number of the enemy troops he was facing. Originally reports had estimated the enemy strength to be about 60,000 troops, but that was doubled by spies, cavalry, and intelligence from local citizens. Worse still, the enemy was operating behind the cloak of South Mountain, hiding their true plans and intentions from McClellan. The only way the Army of the Potomac could achieve a proper reconnaissance was to burst through one of the gaps of South Mountain in force, a move the enemy might anticipate and attempt to ambush. With this in mind, along his concerns over his foe's overpowering advantage in manpower, McClellan was not about to move with all due haste. In

Federal artillery bombard Lee's rear guard outside the town of Frederick.

Federal and Confederate cavalryman engaged in a bloody skirmish. In actuality, Pleasanton's men were no match for Stuart's skillful riders.

heading west, troops from the Army of the Potomac toiled along the Maryland roads, kicking up the familiar choking dust clouds; a symbol of an army on the move. The march caused some to reflect on the dramatic differences between their appearance now and a year earlier when the romance of war still prevailed. De Trobriand noted:

What a contrast between the departure and the return! We had started out in the spring gay, smart, well provided with everything. The drums beat, the bugles sounded; the flag, with its folds of immaculate silk, glistened in the sunshine. And we were returning before autumn, sad, weary, covered with mud, with uniforms in rags. Now the drummers carried their cracked drums on their backs, the buglers were bent over and silent; the flag, riddled by the balls, torn by shrapnel, discolored by the rain, hung sadly upon the staff without cover.

Still, many a Yankee was happy to be campaigning on friendly ground for a change, as one soldier wrote home, "I shall always remember the march through Maryland as among the most pleasant of my experiences as a soldier. The roads were splendid and the country as beautiful a country as I ever saw. It has but little of the desolate appearances of the devastated Old Dominion, but everywhere landscapes of exquisite beauty meet the eye. Pretty villages

are frequent, and pretty girls more so, and instead of gazing at passing soldiers with scorn and contempt, they were always ready with a pleasant word and a glass of water."

Combined with their reception in Maryland was the return of the army's determination from having their old favorite back in command again. As De Trobriand noted, "The confidence in McClellan had been restored, and the late reverses had much less beaten down the courage of the soldiers than excited his resolution to have his revenge."

As the Army of the Potomac arrived in Frederick, the city had seemingly changed its allegiances with the Federal arrival. The Yankees were received in the same resplendent fashion as the Rebels had been, as David L. Thompson of the 9th New York wrote, "The city was abloom with flags, houses were open everywhere, trays of food were set on window sills of nearly all the better class of houses, and the streets were filled with women dressed in their best, walking bareheaded, singing, and testifying in every way the general joy." John Gibbon recalled:

I did not much believe before coming here that there was so much Union feeling in the state as has been shown towards us. As the troops passed through Frederick, the houses were covered in

U.S. flags and the whole population seemed to turn out to Welcome us. When General McClellan came through he was overwhelmed by the ladies, they kissed his clothes, through their arms around his horses's neck and committed all sorts of extravagances. Those who saw it say there never could have been such a scene witnessed in this country since Washington's time. . . . The people come out and speak to us as we pass and show their delight at the idea of the rebels being driven out of the state. There is no question of the loyalty of this part of Maryland.

Despite their reception, the Yankees often took advantage of the Marylanders, foraging throughout the area, stealing food and other items when it suited them, defaming their reputation when compared with the better behaved Southerners. Some officers attempted to curb such crimes. In one instance a soldier stole two bundles of hay from a barn in the vicinity of Frederick only to run into the disapproving George Gordon Meade who ordered him to return the stolen booty immediately. The soldier audaciously grumbled, "General, I suppose I will have to obey your order, but if you were not wearing shoulder straps, I'll be damned if I would." To this, Meade immediately dismounted from his horse, threw down his coat and gruffly commanded, "Now, young man, the

Yankee fighting men find the citizens of Frederick kind and generous. The Confederates who passed through the town just days before enjoyed a similar reception.

straps are out of the way, you take that straw back.'' Taken aback, the soldier grabbed the bundles and returned them immediately.

Two soldiers of the XII Corps' 27th Indiana were up to more honest pursuits as their command went into bivouac in a camp abandoned by the Confederates just three days earlier. Corporal Barton W. Mitchell and Sergeant John M. Bloss were lounging around when the former discovered a stuffed envelope lying in the grass. Opening it up, he found a most pleasant discovery, three cigars wrapped in a piece of paper. Though no doubt excited by their find, the two soldiers took the time to examine the cigars' wrapper only to marvel at what was to become the biggest discovery of the war. The sheet of paper was in fact Special Orders 191 signed by Lee's Adjutant General Colonel R.H. Chilton and contained the movements of the entire Rebel army. The astute soldiers took the paper to their company captain, Peter Kop, who sent it on to the 27th's skipper Silas Cosgrove. Cosgrove then gave it to Alpheus Williams and his

aide Colonel Samuel E. Pittman. Fortunately for the Federals, Pittman, an acquaintance of Chilton, recognized the handwriting and verified the document as an original. Thus, the orders made their way into the hands of George Brinton McClellan just as he was receiving a group of prominent local citizens. It was the greatest fortune that any general could desperately hope for in wartime: the complete plans of the adversary. Even better than this stupendous discovery was the knowledge that his enemy was incautiously divided practically inviting the Federal Commander to beat him in detail. As Confederate Staff Officer Moxley Sorrel noted, ''Had Lee whispered into the Federal General's ear his inmost plans, the latter could have asked for nothing more than the information brought to him on that fatal paper.'' If McClellan could only take advantage of his find, the Army of

George McClellan enjoys a jubilant reception as his Army of the Potomac triumphantly enters Frederick, Maryland.

Northern Virginia could be totally crushed and the war a lot closer to a conclusion.

After getting word of the lost orders the General Commanding jubilantly informed Lincoln of his magnificent find at 2400 13 September:

> I have the whole rebel force in front of me, but am confident, and no time shall be lost. I have a difficult task , but with God's blessing will accomplish it. I think Lee has made a gross mistake, and will be punished for it. The army is in motion as rapidly as possible. I hope for great success if the plans of the rebels remain unchanged. . . . I have all the plans of the rebels, and will catch them in their own trap if my men are equal to the emergency.

John Gibbon happened to stop in on Little Mac as he was beginning to plot Lee's demise.

Though not showing him the order in its entirety, McClellan displayed Chilton's signature before his subordinate and confidently stated, "Here is a paper with which if I cannot whip 'Bobbie Lee,' I shall be willing to go home. . . . Tomorrow we will pitch into his centre and if you people will do two good hard days marching I will put Lee in a position he will find hard to get out of."

So McClellan had Lee's orders along with the unparalleled opportunity to crush the Army of Northern Virginia. Still, the Yankees would have to move quickly: the orders were four days old and it was already one day past the moment when Jackson's forces were to be arrayed around Harper's Ferry. In drawing up his plans, McClellan opted to send Franklin's men through Crampton's Gap to come up in the rear of McLaws in order to save the Garrison at

Little Mac in the field.

The Lost Order

One of the greatest mysteries of Antietam and the Civil War was the lost copy of Special Orders 191 that fell into McClellan's hands and informed the Federal general of all the subsequent movements of Lee's army, placing the Confederates in extreme danger. On 9 October, Lee dispatched his orders to the proper commanders, informing them of his intentions to divide the army to capture Harper's Ferry. Copies were drawn up by Lee's Assistant Adjutant General R.H. Chilton with one each going to Jackson (commanding the Harper's Ferry Operation), Longstreet, D.H. Hill, J.E.B. Stuart, Lafayette McLaws, R.H. Anderson, John Walker, and Major Taylor in charge of dispatching casualties to Winchester, Virginia. Of these, only the existence of three are certain; Jackson maintained his, Longstreet destroyed the order by ripping it apart and chewing on the pieces, and Walk-

er pinned his copy to a pocket for safekeeping. The fates of those delivered to McLaws, Taylor, and Stuart are not readily known and Anderson denied receiving a copy. One mysterious issue found its way into the hands of Confederate staff officer Moxley Sorrel who upon seeing the succinctness of the orders professed some anxiety over the possibility of what to do with the paper should he be captured with it on his person.

Of all these, the one to fall into Federal hands was the copy sent from Confederate headquarters to D.H. Hill, its disappearance unnoticed as Jackson had sent his subordinate a duplicate of the orders penciled by himself. Unfortunately, there is conflicting testimony as to whether Hill received a copy of Special Orders 191 from Lee's headquarters. No receipt for the order was ever returned to Chilton, although Lee's assistant adjutant general maintained he would have recalled if a courier returned without proper documentation proving Hill had received the order due to the severity of the resulting situation.

For many years after the war, Hill was blamed for the actual loss of the order, some people claiming the cigars the order were wrapped in served as ample evidence of the general's guilt as he was a notorious smoker. Disputing such claims, Hill steadfastly maintained his innocence, arguing he had never received any copy of Special Orders 191 save those sent from Jackson. He wrote "I went into Maryland under Jackson's command. I was under his command when Lee's order was issued. It was proper that order come through Jackson and not Lee. . . . My adjutant-general made an affidavit, twenty years ago, that no order was

received at our office from General Lee. But an order from Lee's office, directed to me, was lost and fell into McClellan's hands. Did the courier lose it? I don't know. Did Lee's staff officers lose it? I don't know.'' At any rate, he went as far as to argue that the lost order was actually a boon to the Confederate cause. Since the captured order placed Longstreet at Boonsboro, the Federals were inclined to believe his full force was on the mountain rather than merely Hill's weak command.

This mystery will probably never be explained with some of the most important facts remaining missing from the watchful eye of the historian. Did Chilton receive a receipt? Did a courier give the dispatch to Hill or somebody on his staff? Unless more evidence is forthcoming, the lost order will probably remain one of the greatest unanswered questions of the Civil War.

Harper's Ferry if that was still possible. The rest of the army with the IX Corps leading the advance, was to pitch forward through Turner's Gap interposing it between Lee's divided army in order to gobble up the scattered detachments as they presented themselves. In a communique to Halleck, McClellan plainly stated the army would move out early the next day making forced marches to save the beleaguered garrison at Harper's Ferry. But despite his enthusiasm, the general did not move as fast as would be expected under the circumstances, if he had faith in his men as he wrote in his dispatches, he would have had them on the road the night

A portion of Lee's army under Longstreet in Hagerstown, Maryland.

of the 13th rather than waiting till morning of the next day. Had the Federals marched that night they would have found the gaps unguarded and Lee's army invitingly open to destruction. Waiting until the morning of the 14th to get under way, they allowed the Rebels to take proper measures to safeguard themselves from an attack.

In fact, Little Mac was actually luckier than he had reason to believe. On 10 September, Lee divided his forces once more in response to rumors of a menacing Federal force coming down from Pennsylvania. Longstreet was dispatched with Lee to Hagerstown while Harvey Hill remained in Boonsboro, the sole defense of the Southern army should McClellan come suddenly bursting through South Mountain—but then Lee had no reason to expect him so soon. In fact, Lee had left the vital passes unguarded as a lure to bring the Army of the Potomac away from the security of Washington while extending its vulnerable supply line. In doing so, he hoped to bring the enemy to a pitched battle on terms favoring the Confederates.

Worse still for the Southerners, the Harper's Ferry operation was running increasingly late. Stonewall Jackson's 14,000 men had the toughest route, carving a circuitous trek through 51 miles of the Maryland and Virginia countryside. They were following the Old National Road up through Middletown and Boonsboro before turning off to the west, heading for a river cross-

ing at Williamsport, Maryland. The march was not a very cheerful one as the Rebels found themselves in unfriendly, pro-Union territory. Reaching Middleton, soldiers found the town inhospitable to say the least, with stores locked tight, their owners gone, and houses likewise closed. Those citizens who did come out were not at a loss to show their pro-Union sympathies. As Stonewall Jackson rode through the town, two young girls with red, white and blue ribbons in their hair rushed before him, audaciously waving the Stars and Stripes in his face. Instead of yielding to some sort of harsh reaction, Jackson chivalrously bowed, lifted his cap, and said, "We evidently have no friends in this town." Seeing a group of ladies wearing red, white, and blue cockades pinned to their blouses, a Confederate officer rode up to them, politely touched his cap in salute, and said, "If you will take the advice of a fool, you will return into the house and take off the colors; some damned fool may come along and insult you."

Crossing the Potomac on 11 September near Williamsport to the tune of "Carry Me Back to Ole Viginny," Jackson's men were relieved to find themselves in friendly territory once more. As they advanced on the Federal garrison at

Martinsburg, the post's commander, Brigadier Julius White, decided to abandon the town rather than risk a confrontation against such superior numbers of Confederates (the Yankees fleeing into the trap which awaited them at Harper's Ferry). In a stark contrast from their experiences in Middletown, the Confederates found themselves welcomed by an adoring populace. J.F.J. Caldwell recounted the reception after the liberation of the town:

> We were enthusiastically received. In addition to the sutler's goods and government provisions, which were found in abundance, the citizens of the place brought us baskets of food, and invited large numbers of us to go home and dine with them. I doubt not I saw a ton of bread devoured that day. The thanks and words of encouragement we received from fair lips, and the more moving attentions of fair eyes, perhaps deserve first place in the list of our enjoyments, but a soldier may be pardoned for dwelling on the more substantial comfort of bread and meat.

Meanwhile Walker and McLaws enjoyed a march confined to less social and more military affairs. Walker with his division of 2,000 men stopped at the Monocacy Aqueduct of the C & O Canal on the 10th to destroy the structure and disrupt the water way. His efforts were to no avail, the structure was so magnificently constructed, the Confederates could barely do any damage to it. Crossing the Potomac the next day, Walker was convinced by a heavy rain to rest his troops before progressing to Hillsboro

Reno's IX Corps on the advance after McClellan received Lee's lost orders.

Stonewall Jackson receives cheers from his troops during his daring 1862 campaign against Harper's Ferry.

Just before First Bull Run, Jackson's first command was at Harper's Ferry. His jubilant return in September 1862 was at the expense of Colonel Dixon Miles and his Yankees.

on the 12th. Though McLaws had the shortest route to march, about 20 miles, it took two days to move into the Pleasant Valley, between South Mountain and Elk Ridge. To gain Maryland Heights, his men had to assail wooded Elk Ridge and follow its treacherous crest south until they reached the cliffs overlooking Harper's Ferry. Though an old road was found leading from a pass called Solomon's Gap along the ridge's summit, the going over the small path was exceedingly difficult with the troops fighting their way through a tortuous and tangled wood land. One rebel recalled the great difficulty with which McLaws' men moved across the ridge, "the men had to pull themselves up the precipitous inclines by the twigs and undergrowth that lined the mountainside, or hold themselves in position by the trees in front." As they proceeded, Brigadier Joseph Kershaw's brigade of South Carolinians ran into a smattering of Federal picket fire. While sweeping this irritancy before them, another obstacle was found: a Yankee line of battle behind breastworks of logs and rock with an abatis of fallen timber and brushwood 400 yards in front of it. Faced with this sturdy defense, McLaws opted to attack the next day on 13 September, one day after Lee had expected to have taken Harper's Ferry and the day McClellan found the orders to the Confederate army.

What the Federals at Harper's Ferry desperately needed was a hero, a stalwart individual who could hold the garrison until help arrived. Unfortunately, Dixon Miles might have been just that man in his younger years during his respectable service in the Mexican American war. Now, 15 years later, he was a bitter old soldier, lacking the fervor to lead and enkindle the spirits of the troops under his command. As September dawned, he found himself face to face with a crisis of the greatest magnitude. On the third day of that month Miles was definitely aware of a Rebel advance across the Potomac. Three days later, telegraphic communications were cut off from the east while an ominous message was received by an operator, "How are you General Pope? General Jackson's Army."

Despite the growing threat the Rebel army posed to the Garrison at Harper's Ferry, Halleck sent only a reassuring dispatch telling Miles to hold, writing on 7 September, "Our army is in motion. It is important that Harper's Ferry be held to the latest moment. The Government has the utmost confidence in you, and is ready to give you full credit for the defence it expects you to make." Still, despite the harrowing situation, Miles did little to prepare himself for the worst, only having a defensive set of breastworks built on Maryland Heights. McClellan would request Miles men to reinforce his own army writing Halleck on the 10th, "Colonel Miles is at or near Harper's Ferry, I understand, with 9,000 troops He can do nothing where he is, and could be of great service if ordered to join me." Initially, on the 11th, Halleck refused, but the next day put Miles within the command of the Army of the Potomac, telling him, "You will obey orders General McClellan may give you. You will endeavor to open communication with him and unite your forces to his at the earliest possible moment." Of course with Jackson moving to surround the town, there was little chance that Dixon would ever have the chance to establish communications with the Army of the Potomac.

On the twelfth, Harper's Ferry received horrible news. From Martinsburg came Brigadier General Julius White with the news that Stonewall Jackson was close behind. Furthermore, there were reports of a Confederate advance on Maryland Heights. Despite the fact White outranked Miles, he deferred to the Colonel in command due to his knowledge of the town's defenses as well as his long experience in the military.

Impressed with an increasingly darkening predicament, Miles turned his attention to his defenses. Loudoun Heights was ignored, as it was believed to be indefensible and could only be taken if the Federals lost Maryland Heights. With Maryland Heights serving as such a keen position, 2000 men were instructed to hold there with two batteries defending a naval battery of seven heavy guns including two nine-inch Columbiads, overlooking Bolivar Heights, supporting positions there from attack. To guard the town itself from attack, 7000 men were set up on Bolivar Heights to block any move made by Jackson. These troops were supported by a brigade, with batteries of 20—pound Parrotts and 24—pound howitzers. After preparing their defenses, all the Federals of Harper's Ferry could do was wait and hope some reinforcements were on their way.

As dawn broke on the critical day 13 September, the commander of Maryland Heights, Colonel Thomas Ford of the 32nd Ohio, prepared to meet the attack of seasoned Confederate troops with the 1st Maryland, 39th New York, 32nd Ohio and the rookie 126 New York, in the army for only six days. All were entrenched behind breastworks and a log abatis. At 0630, the confrontation began with Brigadier General Joseph B. Kershaw's South Carolina brigade hitting the Yankee front and left, while Brigadier General William Barksdale attempted to turn the Federal right. The Rebels found the battle tough going, clinging to bushes on the incline of the mountain while they loaded and fired.

As Captain A.T. Harllee saw a standard fall, he rushed up to grab the flag, urging his comrades on, only to collapse himself with wounds in both thighs. Though in extreme pain, the officer called out to the skipper of the 8th South Carolina, Colonel John W. Henagan, to take the flag. The Colonel rushed forward, the banner waving, only to fall wounded as well. While being taken from the field he saw his men beginning to waver. Immediately, he called out desperation, "About face! Charge and take those works."

Upon hearing these words, the Palmetto state troopers renewed the contest with vigor. After valiantly holding off the Southerners for four hours, the 126th New York broke in panic when its commander Colonel Eliakim Sherril was severely wounded by a minie ball which struck him in the mouth. With the rest of the Federals joining the wild retreat, all seemed lost.

Seeing his troops routed, Miles and his staff

rode up to the fleeing soldiers, imploring them to return to the fight. To impress upon his troops with the gravity of his commands, Miles ordered a nearby regiment was told to bayonet anyone trying to run away. The effort was successful as a new line was formed a mile away from the abandoned breastworks.

Miles returned then to Harper's Ferry despite Ford's insistence that his position could not be held. To this, Miles responded "You can and you must." Then occurred one of the many strange events during this strange campaign: an unnamed lieutenant rode up to the troops as they waited for the Confederate attack and gave orders for a general retreat. The Yankees were flabbergasted at the command, Captain Philo D. Philips of the 126th New York refused to obey saying later, "The Rebels could be seen over the abatis and the breastworks in force; but as we were holding them in check at all points, it was a mystery why we should be ordered to fall back." However, other regiments followed the orders given, spiking the battery of naval guns and leaving Maryland Heights at 1530, effectively handing the key to Harper's Ferry to McLaws. Down in the town, Miles looked up to see his men filing off the mountain. His curse was a loud one, "My God, Colonel Ford is evacuating his position; we must stop it." But it was already too late.

As the Federals retreated from Maryland Heights, the rest of Jackson's men were busy surrounding the garrison; Walker had arrived at Loudoun Heights and Jackson was already in

The key to the defense of Harper's Ferry, Maryland Heights.

sight of Bolivar Heights. Now came the task of getting artillery together to bombard the town. Meanwhile in the town, Miles, impressed with the growing hopelessness of the situation he was facing, called in Captain Charles H. Russel of the 1st Maryland Cavalry and ordered him to attempt to break through enemy lines and to reach "somebody who had ever heard of the United States Army, or knew anything about the United States Army, and report the condition of Harpers's Ferry."

Despite Jackson's success, Lee was increasingly finding his great campaign slowly collapsing into what appeared to be a major disaster on the evening of 13 September. Though the Harper's Ferry operation was already running a day late, he was still confident the garrison would be taken soon, allowing the Army of Northern Virginia to move on to bigger and better things. Then came news that McClellan was on the move much sooner than Lee had anticipated. With Federal Cavalry troopers supported by infantry forcing back Stuart's cavalry screen, Hill dispatched Colonel A.H. Colquitt to Turner's Gap who then reported seeing campfires of a large force through the darkness at Middletown. Deciding it would be best to hold Turner's Gap as Harper's Ferry had not yet been taken and the enemy was advancing when his own army was still vulnerable, Lee directed Hill to take the pass. Hill dispatched Brigadier Samuel Garland's brigade to join Colquitt while leaving the rest of his division at Boonsboro. Finally at 2400, the worst news of all arrived. A Southern informer had been among the group of private citizens when the lost order was before McClellan. Seeing the Federal general's enthusiasm and, later, preparations for an assault under way, the informer had passed through Confederate lines to inform Lee of the danger. The threat facing the Army of Northern Virginia was now a certainty. But what to do about it? Unenthusiastic about the idea of dividing the army in the first place, Longstreet suggested falling back to the town of Sharpsburg to join Hill and flank any force going to the aid of Harper's Ferry. However, Lee ignored this advice, planning to go to the aid of Hill at South Mountain, further disregarding Longstreet's protests that the march from Hagerstown to Turner's Gap would so tire his men that they would be of no help during a pitched battle. With both armies converging on Turner's Gap, the scene was set for the Battle of South Mountain.

CHAPTER VI

TO THE ANTIETAM

14 - 16 September, 1862

The terrain of South Mountain looked like an awkward place to hold a battle. For the most part, the heights consisted of heavily wooded clefts, ravines, and hollows, making complicated military maneuvers a nightmare. Remarkably, some farmers managed to carve out a living on the tangled mountainside, leaving cultivated fields, both wood and stone fences and lanes interspaced upon the rise.

Causing considerable anxiety to Hill was the large amount of ground he was going to have to cover in the face of a Yankee advance. The most important feature of his position was the pass at Turner's Gap. Carving its way through the gap was the Old National Road running from Frederick over the Catoctin Mountains through Middletown and South Mountain before going on to Boonsboro and Western Maryland. A mile to the south, the Old Sharpsburg Road climbed through another pass called Fox's Gap. Just before this small gorge, a farm road went off in a circuitous route before heading up an eminence just above Fox's Gap and continuing across the summit to link up with the Old National Road at Turner's Gap. To the north, the Old Hagerstown Road veered off from the National Road at the small town of Bolivar, swinging off to the north before rejoining it at Turner's Gap.

Early on Sunday 14 September, Daniel Harvey Hill rode to South Mountain to make his first real examination of the ground he was to defend. Upon arrival, he had a few nasty shocks. Stuart, who Hill believed was to assist in the defense of the pass had disappeared. Thinking the real threat to be against McLaws' rear at Crampton's Gap, the cavalry commander had gone south with most of his force, leaving only a token 200 men and an artillery battery

Terrain of Turner's Gap around which the Battle of South Mountain was fought.

under Colonel Thomas L. Rosser. Worse still, the shouts of Federal commanders and the movements of Union troops could be heard from the enemy now pressing up the mountain. Realizing his danger, Hill readied his line for a possible attack while calling up G.B Anderson and a regiment of Ripley's brigade, the 4th Georgia under Colonel George Doles from Boonsboro.

89

In setting up his defenses Hill had given the task of protecting Turner's Gap to Colquitt, placing his 1,100 man brigade before the National Road where some men found a good defensive position behind a farmer's stone wall. Garland's brigade of 1000 was ordered to the right to hold the road running from Fox's Gap towards the Old National Road.

In the early morning hours around 0600, Pleasonton's cavalry advanced towards South Mountain supported by Colonel Eliakim Scammon's brigade of the Kanawha Division of the IX Corps. Riding amongst these troops was divisional commander Brigadier General Jacob D. Cox. Arriving outside the town of Bolivar, he found Colonel Augustus Moor, captured by Rebel cavalry during a skirmish in Frederick, walking back to Federal lines after being paroled. Learning of Cox's intentions to cross South Mountain, Moor exclaimed "My God! Be careful" Realizing the enemy was probably in force on the heights ahead of him, Cox called up Moor's old brigade under Colonel George

Member's of Cox's division assail South Mountain to engage Hill's Confederates.

Daniel Harvey Hill (1821-1889)

South Carolinian Daniel Harvey Hill embarked on a short military career after graduating from West Point in 1842, only to take up an unglorified post as teacher in a military school in North Carolina. Returning to the military to fight for the Confederacy, Hill led the 1st North Carolina Regiment in one of the South's first major victories at Big Bethel. Promoted to the rank of major general, Hill served under Joseph E. Johnston and later Robert E. Lee in the Peninsular Campaign when his troops met a bloody repulse in an attempt to storm Federal positions at Malvern Hill.

During the Antietam Campaign, Hill held out against incredible odds battling the Union I and XII Corps to a standstill at South Mountain with his lone division, thus buying precious time for Lee's army to reunite and make a stand near Sharpsburg.

In the summer of 1863, Hill headed west with Longstreet's command to fight under Braxton Bragg in the Battle of Chickamauga. There his criticism of Bragg won him not only the lasting enmity of that general, but of his good

The man who led the initial Federal assault on Turner's Gap, Jacob D. Cox.

friend Jefferson Davis as well. After being removed from command as a result of charges brought against him by Bragg, Hill managed to return to command to see some service at Petersburg and in North Carolina with Joseph E. Johnston.

The conclusion of the war allowed

Defender of Turner's Gap, Daniel Harvey Hill.

Hill to return to more academic pursuits, some writing on the great conflict as well as becoming president of the University of Arkansas and later of the Middle Georgia Military and Agricultural School. Hill was brother-in-law to his illustrious comrade, Stonewall Jackson.

Crook to follow Scammon as he proceeded up the Old Sharpsburg Road towards Fox's Gap. All in all, Cox was taking some 3000 men on the advance. After sending a dispatch to his corps commander Jesse Reno, he turned his affairs to the battle at hand. Up near South Mountain, Pleasonton's troopers were already skirmishing with the enemy, waiting for a flanking force to arrive. Cox sent Scammon up the Sharpsburg Road around 0730 with Crook following a half an hour behind to eventually take a position on the left of the former's brigade. After coming under some fire, Cox felt around the Rebel line, following the farm lane from the Old Sharpsburg Road, searching for the enemy's flank while driving off the skirmishers that opposed him. The going was quite rough as troops advanced with bayonets fixed, single file in some places, through the tangled wood of laurel trees. The terrain caused some commands to break apart and soldiers ended up fighting individually at times, but each, as one Ohioan put it, "struck were he saw his blows were most

needed." Eventually around 0900 Scammon's men came before a pasture with Garland's Rebel line behind a stone wall. A growing fight ensued between Cox's Ohioans and Garland's Tarheels. When the Federals finally got all their men up, a charge was made through a harrowing storm of grape and canister from well placed Confederate batteries. During the growing conflagration, Garland was struck down, with a wound which proved to be fatal.

As the Scammon and Crook drove most of their troops in a headlong charge against the Butternuts behind their stone wall, the 11th Ohio and 23rd Ohio were sent to flank the Rebel left from higher ground, enabling them to get a plunging fire on the enemy. When the Federals reached the wall, a bloody struggle of fierce hand-to-hand combat ensued, with the Rebels taking the worst of it. In face of the sheer terror of combat, the rookies in the Confederate ranks could not endure; the green 12th North Carolina almost entirely collapsed in a panicky flight.

The combined effect of Garland's death and

Scammon's and Crook's brigades attempt to crush the frail Southern Line guarding Turner's Gap on South Mountain.

the Federal charge led to the complete disintegration of the center of the brigade, with the flanks crumbling soon after. Those who could fled down the western mountainside leaving some 200 of their fellow soldiers prisoners in Yankee hands. Faced with the advancing Federals, Rosser's cavalry and his battery were also forced to fall back to a new position where his field pieces could still blast the enemy advancing up the lane. For a moment, it seemed as though all Cox needed to do to eject Hill from his position was to sweep north along South Mountain and roll up the Rebel flank. With the Federals advancing on Colquitt as far as the fields of one Daniel Wise at Fox's Gap sometime after 1000, Hill sent two guns to block the oncoming enemy which unleashed a tremendously destructive fire on the Ohioans. To deter any attempt to rush the guns, Hill set up a line of staff officers, couriers, teamsters, and cooks to present the appearance of a strong infantry line standing in support. Fortunately for the Confederates, the Yankees by this time had enough,

being low on ammunition as well as exhausted from the climb and heavy fighting. Believing he faced a force far stronger than that actually present, Cox decided to fall back. If anything more was to be done, reinforcements would be needed. By 1100, the fighting had lulled to an artillery duel as both sides awaited supports and the chance to renew combat.

Realizing the seriousness of his plight, Hill called for the rest of his division to join him from Boonsboro. As he waited, the general felt an increasing anxiety over the possibility that the rest of his troops might not arrive before the Yankees returned to the offensive. Recalling the situation, he later wrote, "I do not remember ever to have experienced a feeling of greater loneliness. It seemed as though we were deserted by 'all the world and the rest of mankind.'"

Still the fates and Federal commanders conspired to aid the lonesome Hill. While Reno had promised Cox the support of the rest of the corps after receiving word about the situation at South Mountain at 0800, real help would be a long time coming. Though dispatched from Middletown at 1030, Brigadier Orlando Wilcox's division managed to get lost on the way to the battle, arriving tardily between 1300 and 1400. They went into position on Cox's right, while

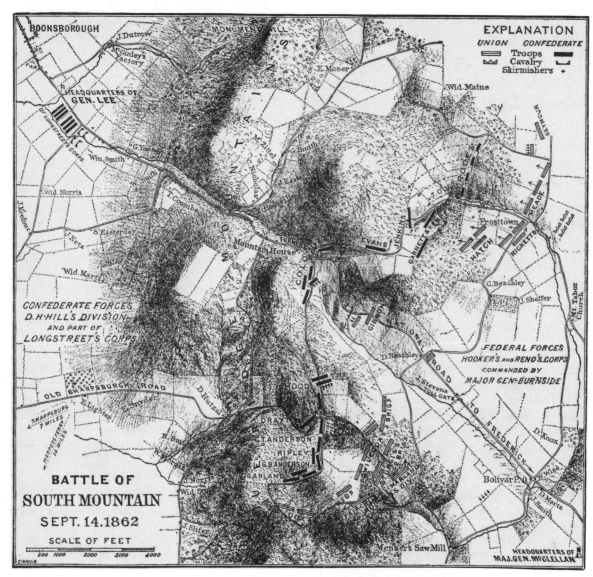

Brigade commander at South Mountain, Samuel Garland.

dispatching two regiments to bolster the left. Wilcox was followed by the two other divisions of the IX Corps under Brigadiers Samuel P. Sturgis and Isaac Rodman; both moved into supporting position behind the rest behind the Federal line at Fox's Gap. Even when these units were on the field, an advance was delayed. Once wing commander Burnside arrived to take control of the situation, he refused to consider attacking until Hooker's corps came up. Finally arriving sometime before 1600, the I Corps moved to the north, following the Old Hagerstown Road, to prepare operations

The Wise fields, scene of part of the fighting on South Mountain.

against Hill's left. To many soldiers, the sight of the Federal army on the move was incredibly awe inspiring. One soldier of the 125th Pennsylvania recalled, "... through the shimmering heat waves we could see lines of infantry—which looked like ribbons of blue—being rushed to the front; the rays of the sun glinted from musket barrel and bayonet and polished brass cannon; batteries.... It was a panoramic moving picture." Even Harvey Hill was impressed by the spectacle as he watched this mighty host draw closer, calling it both "grand and sublime," invoking the phrase of a Hebrew poet, "Terrible as an army with banners."

Despite its picturesque qualities, another advance by the Federal army would be a long time coming, at least until late afternoon, giving Hill all the time he needed to prepare a proper reception. The first of his brigades to arrive was under Brigadier General George B. Anderson; it moved into the position vacated by Garland's disintegrated command before 1400. In attempting to drive Cox back, his bold thrusts were easily repulsed. Between 1400 and 1500, Ripley's brigade came up in support of Anderson. Passing Ripley on the way up the mountainside, Brigadier General Robert E. Rodes was directed to a knoll to the north of the National Road where the Old Hagerstown Road rose up South Mountain. As the Federals stalled, Longstreet's tired men appeared on the scene after marching 17 miles in nine hours, leaving a trail of stragglers in its wake. Hill directed the arriving brigades of Colonel George T. Anderson and Brigadier General Thomas F. Drayton to the right to fend off Reno's newly arrived Corps.

Attempting to lead an assault, Ripley had directed his own, Anderson's and Drayton's brigades to move against Cox's men. Unfortunately, Ripley's brigade somehow managed to get lost leaving a gap in the rest of the line for the Federals to exploit and put the Confederates under a vengeful fusillade which forced them back.

While Lee watched the rest of Longstreet's troops go into battle, Hood's Texans filed by, some shouting, "If there's any fighting to be done by the Texas brigade, Hood must command it." To this, Lee raised his hat and called out "You shall have him, Gentlemen." As the gallant Texan thus took to the field once more to lead his troops into battle, a wild shout went up from the Texans, as one Confederate described, "the cheers deepened into a roar that drowned out the volley of a hundred cannons that were then vengefully thundering at the gap." While Brigadier Generals James L. Kemper, Thomas F. Drayton and Richard B. Garnett were sent to help maintain the left, these commands only managed to get lost in the rough terrain of South Mountain. When they finally found their designated positions, their troops were much too exhausted to do much of anything.

While Reno conferred with Burnside on a strategic prominence before the field of battle, McClellan appeared on the scene to get an appraisal of the situation. The commanders decided to renew the attack, with Reno's men moving across the ridge to the north, while Hooker, following the Old Hagerstown Road, struck on the Rebel left, forcing the entire enemy legion on the mountain to splinter under the pressure. In order to turn up the heat at the most dramatic moment, Gibbon's Western brigade would lead an attack against the Confederate center at Turner's Gap.

By the late afternoon, the Federal attack was finally renewed, with the IX Corps plunging through the woods and farms of South Mountain into the blaze of musketry, canister, and shell awaiting them. During a lull in the battle, Reno rode forward to take a personal look at the situation. Arriving near the 51st Pennsylvania, he directed the regiment into a field for a brief respite. All of a sudden the Confederates from Hood's division appeared in the woods in the Federal front to let loose a volley, felling several soldiers including General Reno. Reno was carried to the rear with a wound he knew to be mortal. Seeing General Sturgis while being taken to the rear, he called out cheerfully, "Haloo, Sam, I'm dead." His tone was so natural, Stur-

The Union's Best: The Iron Brigade

Probably the toughest Federal brigade in the Civil War was a unit comprised solely of Westerners and called the Iron Brigade or the Blackhat Brigade. On 15 October, 1861, four regiments from western states, the 2nd, 6th, 7th Wisconsin, and the 19th Indiana were organized into a brigade under brigadier general Rufus King. This unit was the only such unit comprised solely of men from the west that fought in the East. It wasn't until an officer from the Regular Army, North Carolinian John Gibbon, assumed control of the command that it won the distinctive characteristics that would make the brigade famous. While Gibbon put his raw troops through rigorous drill and ruled with iron discipline to turn them into real soldiers, he had the men wear a uniform different from that of the ordinary Federal fighting man. A long blue frock coat with a turned up light blue collar, light blue trousers and dressy white gaiters set them apart. Unlike the rest of the troops in the Union Army, these westerners wore black hardee hats instead of the kepi, thus giving the unit one of its nicknames. By 1863, the Iron Brigade Uniform had abandoned the frock coats, unnecessary leggings and even the black hats.

Only the 7th Wisconsin had seen service at Bull Run when the brigade faced its first real fight at Groveton on 28 August 1862. Going into battle against the elite of the Confederacy, Jackson's Brigade, the Westerners performed their duties valiantly, losing 731 men; a 33 per cent casualty loss. Another test of combat quickly followed in the Battle of Second Manas-

sas with Gibbon's men maintaining order in the midst of the chaos along the Federal line.

While serving in Hooker's corps in Maryland, the brigade advanced unsupported against the Rebel center at South Mountain on 14 September, giving a good account of themselves though losing 318 men. Watching the fight, McClellan reportedly asked Hooker what brigade was fighting on the heights before them. When told it was Gibbon's Brigade of Western men, the general commanding mused, "They must be made of iron." To this, Hooker claimed, "By the Eternal, they are iron! If you had seen them at Bull Run as I did, you would know them to be iron." Though this story may be somewhat too fanciful to be true, the unit's tenacity in combat won the Western unit the title of the Iron Brigade sometime after South Mountain or its next big fight, Antietam. Involved in Hooker's drive on Jackson's left on 17 September, the Blackhats managed to press back the Confederates only to be forced to retreat by the countercharge of Hood's brigade. Despite this setback, the Westerners held together on the field, eventually repulsing the attack and holding the line after Sedgwick's division collapsed in the West Woods, threatening to take the rest of the Federal right in their retreat. To replenish the ranks of the Iron Brigade after the costly fights from Groveton to Antietam, Gibbon requested and got another Western regiment, the 24th Michigan.

While not fiercely engaged at Fredericksburg and Chancellorsville, the Iron Brigade would face its penulti-

mate conflict in the greatest battle of the war, Gettysburg. On going into action at McPherson's Ridge on the first day of the contest on 1 July 1863, some of the opposing Confederates were heard to exclaim, "Here are those damned black hatted fellers again." The Westerners managed to completely crush Brigadier General J.J. Archer's brigade and captured Archer himself along with 75 men. When the reinforced Confederates began to drive back the Federal right, the reserves of the Iron Brigade under Colonel Rufus Dawes were committed to the fray. In assisting in the destruction of Brigadier General Joseph R. Davis' brigade, a whole regiment, the 11th Mississippi was captured. When finally forced to give ground, the Blackhats did so grudgingly, ensuring that the enemy paid for every step it took. Though not significantly engaged in the next two days of fighting, the Westerners lost 1,900 of their number, a 65 per cent casualty loss, the highest toll of all brigades engaged in the battle.

Though serving in the rest of the war until its conclusion at Appomattox, the Iron Brigade lost its distinctive character after Gettysburg. Easterners, substitutes and conscripts were added to its rolls, men poorly received by the proud veterans who had seen and done so much together. Some of the old regiments were also either detached or consolidated, leaving the unit a mere shadow of the brigade's former glory. Still, the Iron Brigade had forged a legacy that would live forever after both Federals and Confederates had laid aside their arms in peace.

gis thought he was making some sort of morbid joke and replied, "Oh, no, General, not so bad as that I hope." "Yes, yes," lamented Reno, "I'm dead, good by." Cox then took command of the corps, launching another furious offensive against the Rebel line, driving within a half a mile of Turner's Gap. Oliver C. Bosbyshell of the 48th Pennsylvania recalled of the furious musketry, "Shot was answered by shot, sixty

rounds of ammunition per man was expended, and some of the boys were so excited they forgot to withdraw their ramrods. . . . " However, the momentum was not enough; the Federals slowly ground to a halt even though they were so close to their goal, and the battle puttered out into the growing darkness of the night.

Meanwhile, further up to the north, Hooker's men had joined the attack just as dusk was settling in with the divisions of Meade and Hatch in the advance. As the men of the 21st New York approached the enemy line, an old woman vainly attempted to warn the troops away. "Don't go up there," she cried waving her arms, "There are hundreds of them up there." It took some time to get men into proper formations with one brigade getting entirely lost in the thick woodland of the area. Once on the move, all that lay in their path was the 1000 man brigade of Rodes' Alabamians.

To flank Rodes' force, Brigadier General Truman Seymore of Meade's division was directed to move his brigade around the enemy left only to be checked by the 6th Alabama under John B. Gordon. Though the Federals pressed Rodes with impossible odds, the Confederates managed to hold on desperately. To protect their cannons, Rebel gunners fired their pieces, pulling them back to reload in safety before sending them back up to the front to fire once more. In this mighty contest, the colorbearer of the 76th New York rushed ahead of his regiment, shoving his flagpole into the ground and challenging his compatriots, "There, boys, come up to that;" only to receive an enemy bullet in the skull. Finally, Hatch's division, now under Brigadier General Abner Doubleday after Hatch fell wounded, managed to turn the Confederate right at a corn field near the summit. All of a sudden, Rodes' command was flanked. Colonel B.B. Gayle of the 12th Alabama was caught up

Jesse Reno. While commanding the IX Corps on South Mountain, he was struck down by a mortal wound.

A powerful battery of 20-pound Parrotts bombards Confederate positions on South Mountain.

Federal artillery going into position under a heavy shelling.

in the Federal advance on his regiment, but refused to surrender, crying out, "We are flanked boys, but let us die in our tracks." Firing into the advancing line, the Colonel himself was finally shot down, his body riddled with bullets. Hooker had finally managed to crush the Rebel left, only to fall short of his goal as darkness fell forcing the fight to an uncertain conclusion. During the night as the firing slowed, the Rebels managed to unleash one last terrific volley, scattering some Federals. In trying to calm their unnerved men, officers called out, "Why, boys, what are you running for? We've beaten the enemy. Three cheers for victory!"

There was one more Federal attack launched that day by Gibbon's Western men against Colquitt's line located behind a strong defensive position in the gorge through which the National Road passed as it traveled over South Mountain. Some of the Confederates were fortunate enough to find protection behind a stone wall running to the south from the road. After getting the orders to move out, Gibbon placed two of his regiments in front, the 19th Indiana and the 7th Wisconsin, in double columns with the rest of the brigade coming up in support. Brushing aside the annoying picket fire, the unit was torn by death yielding shots of shell and canister as they continued their march: seven unfortunate men were cruelly taken out by one blast. Running into an advance of the enemy behind a stone wall, the Black Hats fired away defiantly as the 7th Wisconsin attempted to flank the enemy, only to get an enfilading fire itself from a detachment of Southerners concealed in some woods. After throwing in the rest of his men, Gibbon advanced his line forward once more, driving the Confederates from the wall back to their main line. As the Federals pressed against

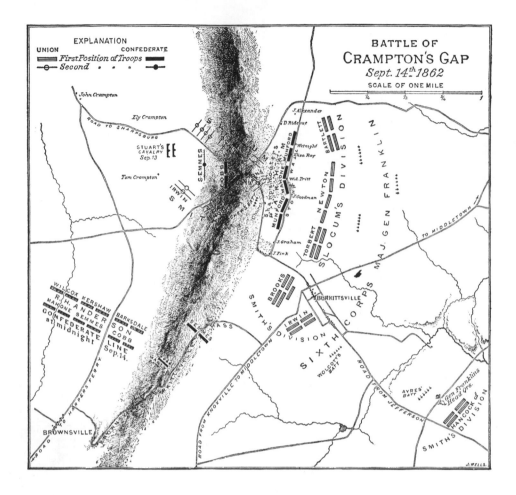

Colquitt's command at Turner's Gap, the Rebels could be heard taunting their foe, crying out, "O, you damned Yanks, we gave you hell again at Bull Run!" Responding in kind, the Black Hats cried out, "Never mind Johnny, its not McDowell after you now. Little Mac and Johnny Gibbon are after you now." Throughout the waning hours of the day, the two forces slugged away into the coming night; when they couldn't see their targets anymore through the darkness, men aimed at the flash of firing guns.

Thus ended the battle of South Mountain with the Confederates suffering harshly, losing around 2300 men, while the Federals lost some 1800. Informing Halleck of the situation, McClellan wrote, "After a very serious engagement, the corps of Hooker and Reno have carried the heights commanding the Hagerstown Road. The troops behaved magnificently. . . . It has been a glorious victory." In actuality, McClellan did not have much reason for such optimism. Hill's masterful defense upon South Mountain against huge numbers of Federals had managed to impede plans to crush Lee's

army while it was still divided. In effect, Harvey Hill had bought his commander a present he desperately needed, time to capture Harper's Ferry and reunite.

As Burnside's wing drove up South Mountain, William B. Franklin took on what appeared to be a far easier contest at Crampton's Gap in the attempt to relieve Miles' garrison. Earlier, McLaws had sent Mahone and Semmes to the area with their brigades to protect his rear at the Brownsville Gap. Discovering Crampton's Gap had gone unnoticed by Confederate commanders and realizing the possible threat this position posed to McLaws' rear if unguarded, Semmes wisely determined to dispatch a battery and some of Mahone's men there. On the morning of the 14th, Stuart arrived, informing the commander of Maryland Heights of an approaching enemy force and advising him that more troops would be needed to hold the pass. Instead of learning the size of the enemy force on the way, Stuart continued on to Harper's Ferry, believing the Federals might be making a move against Jackson's forces there. He dispatched Colonel Thomas Munford there with only 300 cavalry troopers leaving yet another of his comrades in the lurch. Responding to the threat, McLaws dispatched Brigadier General Howell Cobb and his brigade to the gap. Fortunately for the Confederates the Federals of the VI Corps were moving with a slowness that belied the importance of reaching Harper's Ferry before it could fall into enemy hands. Though Franklin had taken to the road around 0600, he had stopped at the town of Jefferson to wait for Darius Couch's division which had mysteriously disappeared from the vicinity. After wasting enough time, Franklin took to the road once more reaching the town of Burkitsville before Crampton's Gap around 1200, finding 1000 Confederate troops entrenched defiantly behind a stone wall at the base of the mountain.

It took some three hours to get the attack going and even then the Yankees made things more difficult than they needed to be. While Franklin could be a tough fighter at times he was certainly not the most imaginative officer in the Union Army. The Confederate detachment before him so occupied his attention, he ignored the possibility of using his overpowering numbers, 12,300 men, to easily outflank his enemy by moving through the Brownsville Gap to the south. Union commanders merely planned for a full frontal assault. With Major General Henry W. Slocum's division on the right and Major General William F. Smith's division on the left,

the Federals advanced against the comparatively tiny line of Munford and Mahone who were awaiting reinforcements from Cobb's brigade. Slocum's division bore the brunt of the attack; forming up in line and firing away at the enemy 300 yards away from behind a rail fence. Eventually, the Yankees, tired of the fight, decided to break it up with an all out attack. All of a sudden the Bluecoats silenced their rifles and the shout of "Charge" went up. The Confederate position at the wall was easily overwhelmed and crushed; those who weren't captured made a hasty retreat for the summit. Though the Federals swept up the ridge, their ascent was slowed as the Rebels peppered the advancing line with well placed shots from behind trees and boulders. Of the carnage and debris from the battle lying before their advance, one Federal recalled:

> Their dead strewed our path, and great care was required, as we passed along the road, to avoid treading upon the lifeless remains which lay thickly upon the ground. On every side the evidences of the fearful conflict multiplied. Trees were literally cut to pieces by shells and bullets; a continual procession of rebel wounded and prisoners lined the roadsides, while knapsacks, guns, canteens and haversacks were scattered in great confusion.

Finally, joined by reinforcements from Semmes and Cobb at the top of the gap, the Confederates attempted to make a stand but could take no more from the enormous numbers of Yankees and fled into Pleasant Valley. As McLaws approached the scene with more reinforcements from Kershaw's and Barksdale's brigades, he found his commanders and troops in a state of utter panic.

Undaunted by the desperate situation,

Franklin's VI Corps advance against Confederate positions at Crampton's Pass.

Federals advancing on Confederates.

McLaws gathered up what troops he could, throwing up a thin defensive line before the Yankees in the Pleasant Valley, determined to meet the overpowering numbers of the enemy with rifles and cold steel. The sight of these troops were enough for Franklin, who evidently believed he was confronted by a larger force than that actually present and fearing the possibility of the rest of the Rebel army falling down upon his rear from the north, he decided to halt for the night. The VI Corps lost 545 men that day inflicting about an equal number on their foes while taking 400 prisoners.

Essentially the inability of the Northerners to break through the Confederate lines at Turner's and Crampton's Gaps meant the garrison at Harper's Ferry would have to fend off Jackson and his men on their own. As battles raged miles away, McLaws and Walker were busily hauling cannons up the heights around the town, the former having to cut a path through the thick woodland of Maryland Heights to make room for the 200 men needed to drag a single piece up to the summit. Around 1000 on the 14th, Walker had three 10—pound Parrots and three other rifled guns stationed on Loudoun Heights. Two hours later, McLaws had two of his cannons in position ready to fire and would have the two others up by 1400. Originally, Jackson intended to have all his guns open fire simultaneously, but was forced to delay the bombardment due to difficulties in communicating with his subordinates through the use of

signal flags. After learning of the Federal presence threatening McLaws, rather than wait for Jackson's command to open the cannonade, General Walker on Loudoun Heights took it upon himself to open fire. Once Walker's guns had fired, the rest of the Confederate guns churned in, sounding the death knell of Harper's Ferry. Finding themselves in a rain of plunging fire, the desperate Bluecoats scram-

The man who took Maryland Heights and defied Franklin's corps, Lafayette McLaws.

Overpowered by the overwhelming superiority of the Yankees, the Confederate defenders at Crampton's Pass flee to safety.

bled for whatever cover they could find. Lieutenant Henry Binney, Miles' aide-de-camp, wrote of the bombardment, "The cannonade is now terrific; the enemy's shell and shot fall in every direction; houses are demolished and detonation among the hills terrible." An officer in the 126th New York wrote, "From the Maryland Heights came shells which exploded before they reached us, showing a fleecy white cloud with a spiteful white flash at its center, giving our boys their first experience of 'bombs bursting in air.'" Meanwhile, Federal cannons attempted to respond in an angry retort, but out of range of the enemy's guns there was very little they could do. To turn up the pressure, Jackson had Powell Hill move against the left flank of the Yankee position on Bolivar Heights. The commander of the Light Division headed his troops toward a hill commanding the Union flank, taking it while encountering only a feeble resistance. With the Confederates in possession of an ideal position to enfilade the Federal stations on Bolivar Heights at a distance of only a 1000 yards, cannons were ordered to take position on the prominence. As darkness fell upon the town and its surrounding heights, so fell the hopes of Miles' troops, for they knew that the next day

Maryland Heights, key to the seizure of Harper's Ferry.

View of the Harper's Ferry area as seen from Walker's position on Loudoun Heights.

would probably bring the most ultimate humiliating disaster, abject surrender. Lamenting over the situation he knew to be lost, Miles turned to his aide Lieutenant Binney, saying, "My last order from headquarters was to hold at all hazards and I shall hold until my last shell is expended. O where is McClellan and his army?" Indeed, McClellan had gotten word of the plight of Harper's Ferry when Captain Russel managed to sneak through the Confederate siege early on the 14th; but the general commanding had done all that could immediately be done to save the garrison at Turner's and Crampton's Gaps. In the attempt to inspire hope amongst Miles and his men, couriers were sent out to break through Jackson's lines around Harper's Ferry to deliver news that help was close by. None of these messengers would reach their destination. In the Confederate camp, Jackson, confident that the fate of Harper's Ferry was most surely sealed, wrote Lee at 2015 on the night of the 14th, "Through God's blessing, the advance, which commenced this evening has been successful, and I look to

Him for complete success to-marrow. The advance has been directed to be resumed at dawn tomorrow morning."

Before Lee received these jubilant tidings from Jackson, he was coming to the disheartening conclusion that his great campaign would have to be terminated, as the fighting on South Mountain began to slacken in the darkness of the September night. By the next day, McClellan would most likely burst through the feeble Confederate defenses in the Pleasant Valley and Turner's Gap, threatening to gobble up most of the Army of Northern Virginia. Solemnly and with much regret, Lee considered having his army retreat to Sharpsburg to cross the Boteler's Ford into Virginia, drawing McLaws with him and effectively lifting the siege of Harper's Ferry. Upon receiving Jackson's 2015 dispatch, all feelings of defeatism passed from the General's mind; he was not going to run; on the contrary he was going to stand and fight, preferably on good defendable ground near Sharpsburg. On the night of 14 September, the Confederates abandoned their position on South Mountain and fell back to the peaceful town near the banks of the Antietam Creek.

As the dawn arose on the fateful day of 15 September, an ominous mist covered the town of Harper's Ferry, mercifully shielding it from the watchful eyes of the cannoneers upon the heights surrounding the town. Miles' Federals found the respite a short one as the fog was slowly burned away by the rising sun. Once again taking aim, the Rebel guns, at least 50 of them now brought to bear on the town, opened fire almost at once. One Confederate artillery-man noted of the commencement of the bombardment, "Simultaneously the great circle of artillery opened, all firing to a common center, while clouds of smoke, rolling up from the tops of the various mountains, and the thunder of the guns reverberating among them gave the idea of so many volcanoes." Once again, the embattled Yankees scrambled to reach whatever cover they could find in the face of the falling exploding shells. The unfortunate troops on Bolivar Heights found themselves raked by a barrage from Hill's guns set up on their left during the night. The day's prospects for Miles did not bode well.

Still there was some hope for the garrison, as Franklin was still close by with enough numbers to brush off McLaws and break the siege if he so chose. Tragically, the Federal commander deluded himself into the belief he was outnumbered two to one and would not budge, leaving Miles and his men on their own. At just about 0800, the fire from the Union guns began to slacken as the last supply of long range ammunition was expended. Rather than risk a needless effusion of blood, Miles prepared to surrender. To the great satisfaction of the Confederates and the horror of the Federals the white flag was sent up. Despite the odds against them, some Yankees wanted to fight it out; Captain Philo D. Phillips of the 126th New York, believing help was on the way, rushed out to Miles pleading, "For God's sake, Colonel, don't surrender us. . . . Our forces are near us. Let us cut our way out and join them." Miles merely replied such action was impossible. "They will blow us out of this in half an hour." After Jackson's guns silenced in honor of the white flag, Miles and Binney approached Confederate lines

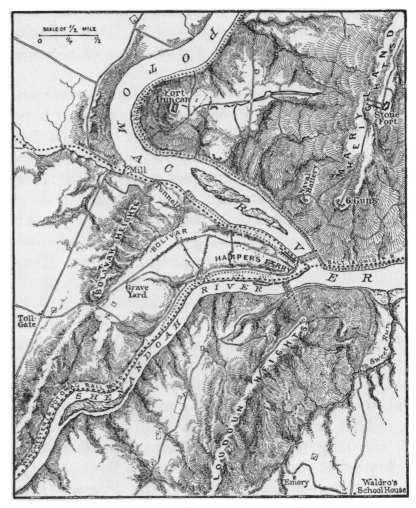

to seek terms. The Colonel said passively, "Well, Mr. Binney we have done our duty, but where can McClellan be? The Rebels have opened up on us again; what do they mean." Indeed, some battery commander had not paid attention to the truce and had continued to fire. By pure chance, a shell exploded right before Miles with a piece of shrapnel tearing away part of his leg. Seeing their commander fall, Captain Phillips grumbled, "Good," writing later, "The rest felt it if the did not say it." The wound would prove mortal; as the Colonel passed away, he was confident that he had done his duty, and as an old soldier was willing to die.

Taking Miles' place, General White rode up to give the surrender attired splendidly in a fine dress uniform with a gleaming sword sheathed in its scabbard. Concomitantly, Jackson appeared in garb weathered from many months of

A pastoral morning scene from Maryland Heights.

campaigning, as a reporter from the *New York Times* noted, "He was dressed in the coarsest kind of homespun, seedy and dirty at that; wore an old hat which any Northern beggar would consider an insult to have offered him, and in his general appearance was in no respect to be distinguished from the mongrel, bare footed crew who follow his fortunes." After receiving White, Jackson had Hill work out the surrender while he prepared to put his army on the road to join with Lee. The magnanimous Confederates offered generous terms to the defeated Federals; all personal property and side arms of the officers were to be retained by their owners while all troops were to be paroled, agreeing not to fight until exchanged. Hearing news of the surrender, Mclaws' men in Pleasant valley let out a mighty roar, prompting a Federal picket to jump up on a rock to inquire what all the racket was about, shouting, "What in hell are you fellows cheering for?" To which he got the reply,

"Because Harper's Ferry has gone up, damn you!" "I thought so," grumbled the Yank. Exultant over the surrender, Stuart told Von Borcke, "My dear Von, is not this glorious? You must immediately gallop over with me to congratulate Stonewall on his splendid success." When he met with Jackson, the General could only say, "Ah this is all very well, Major, but we have much hard work before us."

A bountiful stash of supplies was gathered to equip the Southern army, including 13,000 small arms, 200 wagons, 73 cannons, as well as plenty of ammunition and food. Starved Confederate soldiers rushed to get what they could of the available supplies of food and clothing, greedily grabbing meat, hardtack, sugar, coffee, shoes, undergarments and blankets. One biblically minded South Carolinian drew an allusion to the sight saying, "It really looked like Pha-

John George Walker (1822-1893)

Unlike most of his comrades, Missourian John Walker received his education outside West Point in the Jesuit College in St. Louis, and entered the army after he received a commission in 1846. A captain when the Civil War broke out, Walker threw in his lot with the Confederate States, becoming a lieutenant colonel in the 8th Texas Cavalry. By the summer of 1862, he was commissioned a brigadier and took command of a division in Lee's army. Serving with Jackson during the campaign in Maryland, Walker was charged with taking Loudoun Heights in the plan to capture Harper's Ferry. Promoted to the rank of major general, he was shipped out west to join the Trans-Mississippi Department and led the Texas Infantry Division. Helping Kirby Smith to thwart the designs of the hapless Nathaniel Banks, Walker commanded the District of West Louisiana and the District of Texas, New Mexico, and Arizona before the end of the war. Though briefly fleeing to Mexico, he returned to serve the Federal Government in the area of Pan-American affairs in the post of Consul-General to Colombia and commissioner in the Pan-American Convention.

raoh's lean kine devouring the fat.''

Looking on in dismay, the Yankees could only curse their humiliating plight. One New Yorker openly wept, crying out, "Boys, we have no country now." Another captive, a veteran of the fight on Maryland Heights, bitterly remarked, "Rather than let this happen, I gladly would have left my bones on the field." As Jackson rode through the town, Northern soldiers, crowded the roadways to get a look at the man who had bagged them. Throughout the mass of soldiers admiring shouts of "Boys, he's not much to look at, but if we had him we wouldn't have been caught in this trap" and "Ah! If we had him we should whip you in short order" were heard from troops who had been his enemies. As soldiers from both sides mingled together, Yankees and Rebels marveled at the appearance of the other, the Federals well groomed and washed in clean almost pristine uniforms, the Confederates dirty, ragged, and foul smelling. The observer from the *New York Times* wrote, "I've heard much of the decayed appearance of rebel soldiers, but such a looking crowd! Ireland in her worst straits could present no parallel and yet they glory in their shame." Of the Federals, Blackford recalled they looked as though they had just stepped out of a "bandbox" with their clean uniforms, white shirts, and polished boots. Both factions found the time to trade jokes as one Reb called out noting the pale complexion of his Northern adversaries, "I say Yank, what kind of soap do you fellows use? It has washed the color out of your faces." A cocky Yankee quickly retorted, "You don't look like you ever used soap of any sort," winning a hearty laugh from all around.

All told the Federals had lost a total of 12,500 men as prisoners to the Confederacy, 44 had been killed and 173 wounded during the entire affair with most of the casualties suffered during the fight on Maryland Heights. Jackson suffered sparingly, losing only 286 men in killed and wounded; most of these also suffered on Maryland Heights.

Almost immediately after taking the town, Jackson put his divisions on the road to Sharpsburg, leaving A.P. Hill's division to gather sup-

plies and parole the prisoners.

Sharpsburg had always been a quiet town, its inhabitants knowing only the peace of rural life as they farmed the fertile ground around the Antietam Creek. On the morning of the 15th all this was about to change as the air was filled with the noise of tramping feet, the cries of officers shouting orders, and the creaking of wagon and cannon wheels. The illustrious Army of Northern Virginia was bearing down on the town, coming in from the east along the Boonsboro Turnpike, its leaders determined to use the ground at Sharpsburg to make a decisive stand against the Army of the Potomac.

The area around the town yielded a fine defensive position for the Confederate Army which precluded the need for building trenches and extensive breastworks. Running due south from Hagerstown ran a turnpike, following a low ridge line as it approached Sharpsburg. Along the rise was a large patch of woods bordering the western side of the Hagerstown turnpike: the West Wood. Standing before the Southern portion of the woods stood a small white structure which might be mistaken for a one room school house. In fact, this austere building belonged to a pacifistic German Christian sect called the Dunkers. Across from the unpretentious house of worship was an inter-

Harper's Ferry once again in Confederate hands after Miles' garrison ignominiously surrendered.

section in the Hagerstown Turnpike where the Smoketown Road turned off to run northeast through a plot of trees: the East Woods. Overlooking this ground to the northwest was a prominence called Nicodemus Hill. Interspersed throughout the area were a series of a pleasant farms and cultivated fields belonging to families German stock that had settled in the area. To the East, the Antietam Creek meandered south cutting through the Maryland countryside as it approached the waters of the Potomac. There were three immediate crossings over the stream available: the Upper Bridge with a road leading to the town of Keedeysville, the Middle Bridge maintaining the Boonsboro Road, and the Rohrbach Bridge with the road running from Sharpsburg to Rohersville, called the Rohrbach Bridge.

Set up on the slight ridge and the gently rolling ground of the area, finding protection behind rises, trees, limestone outcroppings, and farmers fences, Lee's men would have plenty of cover from which to field the blows of their enemy's attacks. However, the ground also came with a price that could prove to be disastrous. Just a few miles behind Sharpsburg snaked the waters of the noble national river, the Potomac, a mighty obstacle to any withdrawal. With the only crossing nearby being Boteler's Ford near Shepardstown, Lee readily and knowingly risked ultimate disaster in choosing to make a stand at Sharpsburg. If he should at any time be forced to retreat, a quick and orderly passage across the Potomac would be close to impossible.

The idyllic village of Sharpsburg, Maryland.

In setting up his army's position, Lee had part of his force head to the north of the town, just east of the Hagerstown Road; Hood took the left flank just above of the Dunker Church, followed by Hill's division, and Evan's Independent Brigade, with D.R. Jones' division extending south of Sharpsburg. Since the Antietam was neither wide nor deep enough to provide a natural defensible barrier, Lee only chose to contest a Federal crossing of the stream at the Rohrbach Bridge. In deciding to make his stand, Lee only had some 15,000 of the 35,000 troops he would later wield against McClellan's 78,000 available men including the V Corps which had recently joined the rest of the army. The VI Corps was also ordered up from Pleasant Valley to participate in the coming conflict. Correctly reading his enemy, the Confederate General believed McClellan would stall just long enough

for Jackson to arrive with the rest of the army. Even then, the odds would be at least two to one against him, but the men of the Army of Northern Virginia had faced an overwhelmingly superior force before only to humiliatingly best their foe.

As the sun rose on South Mountain on the 15th, Federals were exposed to sights of frightful carnage from the contest of the day previous. However, most men were heartened by their first substantial victory in quite a while as one soldier noted in viewing the debris left behind in the wake of the Confederate retreat, "The summit and westerly side of the moun-

Pile of Confederate dead near Wise's field after the Battle of South Mountain.

The Great Escape of Grime Davis

While the situation for the Federals at Harper's Ferry was growing exceedingly dim on 14 September 1862, a few officers were not about to meekly submit to their fate. One such officer was the commander of the 8th New York Cavalry, Lieutenant Colonel Benjamin "Grimes" Davis, a Mississippian loyal to the Union. With Stonewall Jackson's Confederates bombarding the garrison from the heights surrounding the town and resistance seemingly futile, Davis and his fellow troopers decided to attempt a breakout rather than be trapped in an ignominious surrender. Informing the garrison's commander, Colonel Dixon Miles, of his decision, Davis argued over the merits of the action. Miles was forced to give his approval once Davis made it clear he was determined to go with or without his commander's assent.

At 2000 that night, the Federal cavalry of Harper's Ferry, consisting of 1500 men of the 1st Maryland, 1st Rhode Island, 12th Illinois, 8th New York, and a detachment of the Maryland Home Brigade, set out across a pontoon bridge over the Potomac into the night's inky blackness under the eyes of McLaws' and Richard Anderson's troops atop Maryland Heights. With the moon missing from the sky that evening, the Federal movements were concealed from Confederate detection. Taking a winding road from the base of Maryland Heights towards Sharpsburg, the cavalry proceeded in a column almost 12 miles in length across the Maryland countryside, the only source of illumination being the sparks of horseshoes striking the pavement of the road. Leading the way was an area native knowledgeable about local roads, enabling the Federals to sneak their way through Confederate lines without being detected. Still, there was plenty of room for error with one company threatening the success of the entire mission when it made a wrong turn and ran into a Rebel picket. The men managed to get back on the right track, however, before the enemy was any wiser.

The long trek through the night was as exhausting as it was tense, with men slumping in the saddle to get a few minutes of sleep before forcing themselves awake again to stay on guard for enemy pickets. Entering Sharpsburg, the Federals stumbled on a few Confederates, but managed to escape unharmed. Fortunately, a friendly local citizen informed Davis and his men of the position of a large enemy detachment near Hagerstown.

Turning off to the west to avoid this force, the troopers continued on into the approaching morning until they reached the Hagerstown Williamsport Road and a far off creak and rumble of wagon wheels could be heard. Finding a file of enemy wagons with a cavalry escort coming down the road, Davis cleverly applied an ingenious ruse to take possession of the supply train. His blue uniform disguised by the fading night, the Mississippian employed the accent of his native South to fool the cavalry, who believed him to be a friendly officer, into halting, while the wagons were directed off onto a road which led into Pennsylvania. As the train was escorted away, the Federals surprised their unsuspecting Confederate counterparts and drove them off through the countryside. Meanwhile, as daylight illuminated the surroundings, Confederate teamsters were shocked to find themselves surrounded by Yankee cavalry. Crossing into safety in Pennsylvania on the morning of the 15th, Davis counted in his possession some 91 wagons belonging to General Longstreet's reserve ammunition train. Thus, the Mississippian brought the one bright chapter to the Federal stand at Harper's Ferry in September of 1862.

tain, down which the Confederates fled, gave proof of the extreme panic which seized them at the close of the battle; guns, blankets, and equipments were scattered about the ground in great profusion. It was encouraging to our soldiers to witness these indications of the retreat of their valiant old enemy of the Peninsula, who, less than two months before had put them in the same awkward plight, and caused them untold hardships."

Learning of the Battle of South Mountain, Lincoln sent a dispatch to his general to provide encouragement, "God bless you, and all with you. Destroy the rebel army if possible." Ultimate victory appeared at hand, Lee was on the run, his army had not yet united and there was still time to bag him if the Federals could just move fast enough.

Despite the necessity of moving quickly to catch the fleeing enemy while still without Jackson, McClellan did not attempt to drive his troops with all due haste. It wasn't until 1500 that the first Union troops of Sumner's corps arrived on the field near Sharpsburg. As McClellan joined his men there, he and Fitz-John Porter looked over the enemy defenses, taking some shots from Confederate artillery across the stream. Those vast numbers of troops supposedly possessed by the Confederate army loomed in Little Mac's mind, Lee had 120,000 men at his command, but just how many were across from him now he was not so sure. As usual, rather than gambling to bring the enemy army before him to battle while it was still weak, Little Mac stubbornly decided to plan safely, waiting until the rest of his troops came up before deciding on any aggressive action. An attack could always wait until the next day. By the end of the 15th, most of the Federal army had gone into camp at Keedysville to the northeast of Sharpsburg.

As dawn broke on the 16th, the monotonous deep thud of cannon fire opened up across the countryside as gun commanders from both sides duelled with each other, seeking out targets to play with. Frederick L. Hitchcock of the 132nd Pennsylvania watched the artillery contest, writing later:

The ball opened soon after daylight by a rebel battery, about three quarters of a mile away, attempting to shell our lines. Our division was massed under the shelter of a hill. One of our batteries of 12-pounder brass guns promptly replied, and a beautiful artillery duel ensued, the first I had ever witnessed at close quarters. Many of us had crept up to the brow of the hill to see the

"fun," though we were warned that we were courting danger in so doing. We could see columns of rebel infantry marching in ranks of four, just as we marched "en route," and as shell after shell of our guns would explode among them and scatter and kill we would cheer. We were enjoying ourselves hugely until presently some additional puffs of smoke appeared from their side, followed immediately by a series of very ugly hissing, and

whizzing sounds, and the dropping of shell amongst our troops which changed the whole aspect of things. Our merriment and cheering were replaced by a scurrying to cover, with blanched faces on some and an ominous, thoughtful quiet overall.

As a Confederate battery fired away, a young newly commissioned lieutenant, excited by the fire rode up amongst the gunners shouting,

"Let 'em have it." Irritated by this youthful show of exuberance, the cannoneers gave the officer icy stares, silently telling him they would "let him have it" if he didn't get out of their way.

McClellan with staff. His hesitation in confronting Lee cost him total victory at Sharpsburg as well as ultimate glory.

As the cannons thundered, McClellan thought over his options as he continued to survey the lines of the enemy. By 1400, he had finally devised the plan for defeating his enemy: a fierce blow would be launched against the Confederate left under Hooker supported by II and XII Corps while Burnside would take on the Rebel right in the vicinity of the Rohrbach Bridge. Holding the middle would be Porter waiting to hit the center at the appropriate moment as well as exploiting any opportunities that presented themselves. To bolster his strength on the field, Franklin was ordered up from the Pleasant Valley to arrive the next day. The plan essentially entrusted Fighting Joe Hooker with the major task of driving the line, giving him the ability to command a superior Bull Sumner while removing the I Corps from Burnside's wing, a move that was to provide some discomfort for the commander of McClellan's right wing. Overall, McClellan's planning was sound, but like all great designs, near perfect implementation is an important factor leading to success.

Back at Second Manassas, Jackson had anxiously waited for Longstreet and Lee to arrive to save the day; now eighteen days later, the question was would Old Stonewall arrive in time. At 1200, good news had come, Jackson was arriving in camp at the head of his and Walker's divisions. At the time, two soldiers had been arguing over whether Jackson was actually on the field. One maintained he had while the other plainly stated he was, "over in Virginny, somewhere, up to something lively I'll bound." To settle the dispute, Kyd Douglas of Jackson's staff approached the gentlemen pointing to Jackson as the General was talking to Longstreet, "That's he talking to your general, old Pete.—The man with the big boots on." "Is it?" replied one, "Well bless my eyes! Thakee, captain." He then turned to his friends saying, "Boys, it's all right."

Jackson's men filed in to the north above Hood's command raising Lee's effective strength to 26,500 men. The Confederate line now extended a full four miles running from the Nicodemus Hill all the way past the Rohrbach Bridge to the south with all 200 Rebel guns placed in strategic locations to hit the enemy the hardest when he finally did plan to attack. Still there was reason for much concern: McLaws, Anderson's, and A.P. Hill's divisions, almost a fourth of the army still weren't on the field and wouldn't arrive until the next day. Would they arrive in time?

CHAPTER VII

ATTACK OF THE I AND XII CORPS

16 - 17 September, 1862

At 1600 on 16 September, Hooker put his 8600 troops in motion across the Antietam Creek by the upper bridge and two nearby fords in search of an advantageous position on the farms and fields of Sharpsburg from which to launch an attack. Driving west towards the Hagerstown Pike and then south towards the East Woods, the I Corps slowly bore down on the Confederate left with Meade's Pennsylvania Reserve Division in front. Meeting this initial advance was Hood's division which engaged the Federals in a sharp firefight in the East Woods and the Cornfield on the David R. Miller farm only to have the conflict peter out as evening descended. Effectively blinded in the growing pitch darkness, the Federals withdrew, with soldiers clutching the bayonet scabbards and clothes of the persons nearby to stay with the command. As the I Corps went into bivouac to the north of the Confederate position on the Samuel Poffenberger farm near the North Woods, Hooker prophetically informed his men, "We are through for tonight, gentlemen, but tomorrow we fight the battle that will decide the fate of the Republic." This initial skirmish did nothing save to alert Lee to the direction of McClellan's initial thrust, allowing the Confederate General to respond accordingly, strengthening the left to meet the expected assault on the morrow and making Hooker's assault all the more difficult. After his men finished skirmishing with the Federals, Hood approached Lee, asking to have his men withdrawn as they had been without anything resembling a good hot meal in several days. Though necessity demanded all troops

available to be on the front line to meet the attack of the next day, Lee would only agree if Jackson gave his assent. With the usually stringent, but now sympathetic Stonewall agreeing, the gallant Kentuckian's division was pulled back to be replaced by Lawton's men. Meanwhile Hooker received his support in the form of Mansfield's command, his troops treading across the Antietam around 2200 to take position just to the northeast of the I Corps. With 7,200 men in the XII Corps, a combined attack from Hooker and Mansfield would outnumber Jackson by over two to one: however it never dawned on McClellan to ensure such a crippling coordinated attack took place.

As evening enshrouded the surrounding countryside in an ominous Stygian darkness, soldiers on both sides sought an uneasy rest, sleeping on their rifles, prepared to go to battle at a moment's notice. At first the men had to contend with the booming artillery, as cannoneers attempted to get their last shots of the day in on their foe. Vauntier described the effect of the night's cannonade, "Every time a piece was discharged the flash of the gun illuminated the surroundings, producing an effect similar to sheet lightning; and when the other fellows sent their howling compliments back, the flash of their exploding shell fitfully lit up the ranks, and the broken particle went buzzing around in search of victims." As if to compound the discomfort of the anxious troops on the field, a chilling sprinkling rain swept across the countryside during the night. A member of the Iron Brigade, Captain William Harries, recalled the freezing effect from the dampness, "I slept very little. The night was chilly, there seemed to be a cold sensation creeping up and down my spinal column. I could not have felt more cold in that region if a chunk of ice had been drawn up and down my back." The almost palpable tension between the opposing forces constantly burst out during the night as picket fire opened up the front lines. The apprehension also led to a great deal of confusion; in Burnside's command, two whole regiments fell into disorder after an unfortunate trooper from the 103rd New York stumbled onto the regimental dog and then into a stack of muskets, setting off an alarm of a possible attack.

Slowly dawn broke on that Wednesday of 17, September, 1862, as soldiers awaited the signal to begin their grim work. Initially, the pall of an early morning mist from the rain of the previous evening hung on the field, obscuring the forces of both sides. To many of those there, this was perceived as a good omen, they thanked God, exclaiming, "We have not got to fight beneath a blistering sun." Unfortunately, the weather was to prove them wrong. The sun would come out and the temperature would climb as the sights and sounds of battle arose during what would turn out to be the bloodiest of all days.

Off in the distance, before the I Corps, lay the rolling countryside of Maryland, which dipped into the farm of D.R Miller. Just south of the farm, between the East Woods and the post and rail fence bordering the Hagerstown Turnpike, stood flowing rows of corn stalks in a large rectangular field. In laying out his plan of attack, Hooker picked a course that was painfully simple, throwing his force of 8,600 men to the south along the Hagerstown Turnpike in order to take the high ground dominating the Rebel line at the Dunker Church, a mile away, thereby making the rest of the enemy's position untenable. Advancing down the right of the Hagerstown Turnpike would be Hatch's old division under Doubleday with Ricketts' division on the left moving through the Cornfield and East Woods.

Hooker's corps splashes through the Antietam on their way to engage Lee's army.

Lee with his son, G.W.C. Lee, and his aide, Colonel Walter Taylor.

The only problem with Hooker's plan was in the fact that he was facing the uncompromising Stonewall Jackson who could reduce even the easiest plans of his enemies to tremendously embarrassing failures, as Pope had found out at Second Bull Run. Composing the immediate Confederate left was Jackson's old division, under Jones, in the northern edge of the West Woods with his right extending towards the Hagerstown Turnpike. Winder's old command, the Stonewall Brigade, now under the helm of Colonel A.J. Grigsby, and Jones' brigade led by Colonel Bradley T. Johnson held the front with Taliaferro's brigade, controlled by Colonel E.T.H. Warren, and Starke's brigade in support. Lawton, with Ewell's old division, was posted on Jones' right angling to the south towards the Smoketown Road with Lawton's old brigade under Colonel Marcellus Douglass extending east from the turnpike through the southern edge of the Cornfield. Brigadier Henry T. Hays' brigade, and Trimble's brigade led by Colonel James A. Walker set up before the East Woods on the Mumma Farm with General Ripley's brigade from Harvey Hill's division in supporting distance. Jubal Early had been detached to the far left with his brigade to protect the flank while supporting Stuart's Horse Artillery under Major John Pelham on Nicodemus Hill. Most of the Confederate artillery strength was massed on the high ground before the Dunker Church

Confederate cannoneer, Major John Pelham. His guns stationed on Nicodemus Hill plagued the Yankees all day on the 17th.

An assortment of 20-pound Parrotts. Though firing from heights across the Antietam, these guns put the Confederates through "artillery hell."

Joseph Hooker (1814-1879)

Born in Hadley Massachusetts, the son of a captain in the Revolutionary War, Joseph Hooker attended the Hopkins Academy before going on to receive instruction in the art of warfare at the United States Military Academy and graduating in 1837. Getting an early education in violence in the Second Seminole War, Hooker made a name for himself in the campaigns of Generals Zachary Taylor and Winfield Scott in the Mexican American War, impressively winning all brevets from first lieutenant to lieutenant colonel. Hooker abandoned his military career for a few years, Hooker resigned his commission and took up farming.

The Civil War caused him to return to active service and take command of a division in Heintzelman's III Corps. During the Peninsular Campaign, Hooker won his sobriquet "Fighting Joe" from a misinterpreted press dispatch which read "Fighting—Joe Hooker." During the Battles of Second Manassas, Antietam, and Fredericksburg, the belligerent general lived up to his name leading vigorous blows against his Confederate opposition after taking control of the I Corps in early September of 1862. When Burnside was relieved from the command of the Army of the Potomac, Lincoln entrusted Hooker with the command of the legion on 26 January despite the general's penchant for political opportunism in evidence when he claimed to a reporter that a dictator should assume power in Washington to wind the war. In regards to this statement, Lincoln plainly told Hooker, "Only those generals who gain successes can set up dictators. What I ask of you now is military success, and I will risk the dictatorship."

Whatever his aims might have been, Hooker's aspirations were shattered when he lost his nerve at the Battle of Chancellorsville, suffering a tremendous defeat at the hands of Lee. Though relieved of command, his military career was rejuvenated when he was ordered to lead the XI and XII Corps in the West and won a great victory at Lookout Mountain. Though participating in the Atlanta Campaign,

the spiteful Hooker, believing himself to be deprived of the proper praise and commendations for his efforts, asked to be relieved and went on to serve in various departmental positions before the end of the war.

Civil War Historian Francis W. Palfrey probably best assessed Hooker when he wrote, "As an inferior, he planned badly and fought well; as chief, he planned well and fought badly." Unfortunately, Fighting Joe's main claim to fame was having his name used forevermore to define the females of ill repute that frequented his headquarters.

Sharpsburg, Maryland, where one of the greatest battles of the Civil War was fought.

where it could draw a good bead on the approaching Federals. All in all, the Confederate left, presented a barrier of 7,700 men three-fourths of a mile in length, a mighty obstacle to any Federal advance.

As soon as the mist had cleared and enemy positions could be seen, the artillery on both sides opened up fiercely; Confederate guns rattled the Federals they could spot while Hooker's guns and the 20-pound Parrotts of McClellan's reserve artillery, located on heights across the creek, opened up in reply. In loading their guns, the Federals expertly timed the fuses of their shells with killing accuracy to explode at just the right moment for deadly effect. Some Confederates rightfully remembered Antietam as the day they were subjected to "artillery hell." One shell struck a member of the 4th Georgia in his cover in the West Woods sending a piece of his skull hurling into the ranks behind him. Another shell fell in the ranks of the 3rd North Carolina killing and wounding 16 men all at once. Watching Pelham's Southern gunners tirelessly unload barrage after barrage from Nicodemus Hill, a cannoneer of the 1st Rhode Island Artillery wrote their fire gave the hill an appearance of " . . . an active volcano belching forth flame." During the almost incessant shelling, a Pennsylvania battery had a good scare when a shell exploded near the muzzle of a gun felling three men and lighting off the fuse just being loaded into a cannon. The Yankee holding the deadly missile acted quickly to save himself and those around him by painfully extinguishing the fuse with his own bare hands.

In setting up the advance of his division, Doubleday directed Gibbon's Iron Brigade to take the lead, supported by Colonel Walter Phelps' and Brigadier Marsena R. Patrick's brigades, leaving the Second Brigade under Lieutenant Colonel J. William Hoffman's to support his batteries engaged in duelling Stuart's guns. In Rickett's advance, the First Brigade under Brigadier General Abram Duryea took the right, Brigadier General George L. Hartstuff's Third Brigade comprised the center and Colonel William A. Christian's Second Brigade was on the left.

By 0600, the I Corps of Joseph "Fighting Joe" Hooker was in motion against Jackson's line, thus inaugurating what was to become the bloodiest day in all of American History. Ricketts' division took the offensive in the East Woods and the Cornfield. Leading the advance, Duryea went into line to the north, in front of the rows of corn on the Miller farm pushing towards the field through a heavy bombardment from Stuart's guns. Noticing the sun glinting

Rebel eating what was sometimes standard fare for the Confederate army, green corn.

from the bayonets of some of Lawton's skirmishers in the Cornfield, Hooker, in his official
report, prepared an appropriate attack upon the
Confederates there, ''Instructions were immediately given for the assemblage of all my spare
batteries, near at hand, of which I think there
were five or six, to spring into battery to the
right of this field, and to open up with canister
at once. In the time I am writing every stalk in
the northern and greater part of the field was
cut as closely as could have been done with a
knife, and the slain lay in rows precisely as they
had stood in their ranks a few moments before.
It was never my fortune to witness a more
bloody, dismal battle-field. Those that escaped
fled . . . as there was no resisting this torrent of
death-dealing missives.'' Following the torrential volleys of canister from Hooker's batteries,
Duryea's men entered the sea of carnage bearing towards their goal of the Dunker Church.
Awaiting the approaching line, lying prostrate
in the pasture to the south of the Cornfield,
were Marcellus Douglass and his men. Seeing
Federal bayonets poking up from the corn,
Douglass advised his troops to pick out a row of
stalks, aim closely at it and fire when the order
was finally given. When the blue line emerged
from their cover, the Confederates let loose a
mighty fusillade. All of a sudden there was a
crackle, flash, and the acrid grey smoke from
ignited black powder covered the field. Now
came the painful screams and moans of scores
of Yankee wounded. Mauled but undaunted,

*Confederates cook a meager meal between
marches and battles.*

*Hooker's Yankees on a desperate charge through
the Cornfield.*

the Federals redressed their lines and came on again, advancing over the bodies of fallen comrades to within 250 yards of the enemy. For a while, both lines stood and blasted away at close range, each volley taking deadly effect. One soldier described the musketry as a "tremendous murdering fire." With men falling fast, those fortunate enough not to get hit got the good sense to forget romantic notions of bravado, and immediately scattered for cover. In an attempt to assist Douglass's line, Walker advanced on the Northerner's flank only to get hit in turn by enfilading fire from Federals within the East Wood. Since part of the 21st Georgia had failed to advance, Walker approached these men to urge them on, only to find most either dead or wounded. Unfortunately for Duryea, he discovered his command also suffering tremendously; roughly one-third of his men had fallen, and those still standing were becoming increasingly exhausted and quickly running low on ammunition. Faced with no other choice, he ordered his men to fall back in retreat through the Cornfield. Seeing their battle flag lying on the field under a pile of dead, J.C. Delancy of the 107th Pennsylvania called to two of his comrades, Captain H.J. Sheafer and Private James Kennedy, to retrieve the colors in the face of an advancing Confederate line. All ran back to recover the flags as quickly as possible and with their hearts in their mouths fled to the rear. Though the enemy troops behind the Yankees called for Pennsylvanians to surrender, they did not fire. Later in the battle, Duryea came upon some of General Hartsuff's men and asked if they had seen his command explaining, it was "all cut up."

After Duryea's men abandoned the field, his supports, Hartstuff and Christian, finally arrived to take up the attack. Both brigades were suffering from the loss of commanders, hampering their effectiveness in combat. Hartstuff's brigade advanced to find itself the target of Rebel cannoneers, but the first shots flew harmlessly over the heads of the advancing Federals. However, the aim of the guns quickly improved: explosions landed closer and closer to the brigade line. While taking stock of the ground before his command, Hartstuff fell badly wounded from enemy shrapnel, and brigade command fell on Colonel Richard Coulter. Eventually obtaining control of his brigade,

Federal and Confederate lines of battle slug away in what was to be the bloodiest day of the war and in all American history.

A Federal line of battle pauses before advancing against the enemy's position.

Coulter followed Duryea's path through the Cornfield, receiving the same terrible medicine as his predecessor. One Yankee recalled seeing the enemy line, "Never did I see more rebels to fire at than that moment. . . . It was magnificent and it was war." A member of the 13th Massachusetts remembered, "The rebels fired first but we being so near, many of the balls went over our heads, but still many took effect. We halted and commenced firing immediately. Men now commenced to drop on all sides; I remember now, as I stood loading my gun, of looking up the line and seeing a man of Company D who I was quite intimate with throw up his hands and fall to the ground; one last struggle and that was all." To drive the Yankees from his front, Lawton took to the offensive, throwing in Hays' crack brigade, the Louisiana Tigers. Joined by some of Douglass' Georgians, the Confederates pressed the new Union line back through the

Cornfield. There a huge conflagration transpired with both lines firing away at close range. In the 12th Massachusetts, as soldiers fell, the rest of those standing continued to close in on the colors until the size of the unit was just that of a mere company. Both Northern and Southern batteries were brought up to fire case shot, tearing huge holes in the ranks, mangling flesh and splattering the ground with fresh blood. The Confederates suffered horribly, with the Tigers taking 60 percent casualties. Still the Federals fared not much better. Taking heavy casualties, Coulter opted to retreat. During the fight, the 12th Massachusetts could only count 32 of the 345 men brought into action. Later in the day as the rest of the command filtered in, the regiment found it had lost 220 of its numbers.

As Christian's brigade was going in, the men were no doubt disgruntled from being forced to go to battle without having time to fill canteens with desperately needed water to wet parched throats, cook breakfast to fill empty stomachs, or even to shake the dirt off their uniforms. They moved forth in columns of division, officers barking out orders for the brigade to move first to the right and then to the left. As Vauntier recalled, " . . . we thought they were making a show of us for the benefit of the rebel artillery," yet the movements were executed, "as quietly as on parade." A flustered Colonel Coulter rode up to Christian, imploring him, "For God's sake come help us out." The troops were put in motion once more; all the while the ever present Confederate shells came screaming down upon the Federals, kicking dirt high up into the air. The historian of the 88th Pennsylvania noted of the bombardment,

> The hideous noise made by these projectiles as they screamed through the air was indescribable; it appeared to the blue masses in that advancing host as if all the devils infernal had been incarnated and assembled on this horrible field, with the power to make the most terrible noises that were ever heard. At any rate, the appalling sound was enough to terrify the heart of the bravest and cause the blood to chill in one's veins.

Evidently Colonel Christian found it so; the cannon fire completely terrorized the officer. Openly displaying the "white feather," he fled his command leaving his men to face open combat on their own. Though the artillery fire was feared, when a shell struck the line, men simply closed ranks to take the place of their comrades who had fallen from the blast. Entering the East Woods, bullets and shells clipped the trees while zipping through the forest. Advancing to the edge of the wood, Colonel Peter Lyle of the 90th Pennsylvania, assuming Christian's position, had his men engage the Confederates. Once in combat the mood of the Federals had changed from fear to ferocity. Again, Vauntier,

> Five minutes before more than one man would have been two hundred miles away from this unhealthy place, if wishing could have accomplished it; but now excited by the acts and presence of comrades, all sense of personal fear fled, the surroundings making every man as brave as a Trojan, forgetful of all personal danger, and intent only upon inflicting all possible damage on the enemy.

While on the right of Lyle's line, the flank of the 88th Pennsylvania found itself exposed to deadly shots from Confederates in the Cornfield, felling men "like autumn leaves."

Meanwhile, on the Federal right, the Iron Brigade was going into action. Gibbon advanced his troops in column of division until he deployed them in line of battle before the North Woods, with the 6th Wisconsin regiment taking the lead. Under heavy fire from Confederate artillery, the brigade pushed south along the Hagerstown Turnpike and reached the Miller farm. The Rebel guns severely punished the Iron Brigade as Rufus Dawes of the 6th Wisconsin recalled, "We had marched ten rods when whizz! bang! burst a shell over our heads; then another; then a percussion shell struck and exploded in the very center of the moving mass of men. It killed two and wounded 11. It tore off Captain David K. Noyes's foot and cut off both arms of a man in his company."

Seeing what appeared to be an enemy force bearing down on its right, the 6th Wisconsin opened fire quickly dispatching the supposed threat. In fact, the "enemy" located on the flank of the regiment were two companies from the same unit deployed there to protect the flank, which now remained invitingly open. The Westerners would cruelly discover this error when Grigsby's men, lying down before the West Woods for concealment and protection, rose up to throw a staggering volley into their line. While shouting orders to his troops during the awful combat, Captain William E. Brown was killed after receiving a musket ball in the mouth. Dawes recalled of the attack, "Men, I cannot say fell; they were knocked out of the ranks by the dozens." To meet this attack, Gibbon dispatched the 7th Wisconsin and the 19th Indiana to take the right of the 6th Wisconsin on the west side of the turnpike with Patrick's brigade going in as support. Together, these reinforcements returned a taste of hot searing musketry in revenge for their fallen comrades,

Brigadier General William Starke. He fell mortally wounded after being hit three times by bullets while leading Jackson's division.

Federal signal station situated atop Elk Ridge which afforded these Yankees a good view of the battlefield.

forcing Grigsby's Virginians to slowly fall back into the West Woods. Of the advance Dawes recalled, "There was on the part of the men, great hysterical excitement, eagerness to go forward, and a reckless disregard for life, of everything but victory." Joined by their compatriots from the 2nd Wisconsin on the left and support from Phelps' brigade, Gibbon's offensive down the turnpike was renewed, only to run headlong into a massive destructive fire in the Cornfield from Lawton's Georgians that had met Duryea and Coulter before them. Dawes had this to say as some of Phelps' New Yorkers joined the fray, "Men and officers of New York and Wisconsin are fused into a common mass, in the frantic struggle to shoot fast. Everybody tears cartridges, loads, passes guns, or shoots. Men are falling in their places or running back into the corn." To reinforce the ailing Confederate line, Starke brought up his and Taliaferro's brigades, falling into line near the turnpike fence, laying down an unmerciful fire upon the Blackhats. Unable to take the punishment, the Westerners fell back into the Cornfield, only to regroup and push on again. Despite some initial success, Starke was to find himself in a desperate situation. Sweeping down through the West Woods came the 7th Wisconsin and 19th Indiana joined by Patrick's brigade to hit Starke's Confederates in the left and rear while the rest

Some of those who lost their lives in the massive effusion of blood near the turnpike fence.

of the Iron Brigade played havoc with their front. Unable to take anymore, the rebel brigades fell back, Starke himself falling mortally wounded when struck three times by enemy bullets. As the Black Hats drew south toward the objective of the Dunker Church, the situation grew all the more serious for Jackson's line. If something was not done quickly, the entire Army of Northern Virginia would be in great peril. Dawes recalled, "The men are firing and loading in demoniacal fury and shouting and laughing hysterically, and the whole field before us is lying with Rebels fleeing for life, into the woods. Great numbers of them are shot while climbing over the high post and rail fences along the turnpike. We push over the open fields halfway to the little church."

Fortunately, Jackson had a superb reserve at his command to throw at the oncoming Federals; one of the toughest units in the whole Army of Northern Virginia: Hood's division. The desperate call for help went out just as the men were settling down to their first hot meal in days, cooking fistfuls of moistened flour on their ramrods to make a crude sort of bread. Stuffing down what ever could be eaten, Hood's men grabbed their rifles and ran into position. At 0700, from the woods in front of the advancing Federals came the ghastly haunting cry of the Rebel Yell. All of a sudden, 2300 howling mad Southerners of Colonel William T. Wofford's and Colonel Evander M. Law's brigades exploded from the West Woods, firing a withering volley that, in the words of Rufus Dawes, cut like a "scythe" through the Federal line. The Union soldiers not only stopped, but fled to the rear as quickly as possible over the mounting carnage of the day's fight, the enemy close on their heels. The Federal batteries did their best to check the oncoming horde firing case shot at increasingly short ranges.

Now Hooker found his own command in desperate peril. Immediately, he committed his reserve, Meade's division of Anderson's and Magilton's brigades while sending for assistance from Mansfield's XII Corps. Meanwhile Wofford pressed against the Federal right under Gibbon, Phelps, and Patrick driving them back through the Cornfield to the west. One soldier in the 24 New York called out to his men, shouting, "Hold on boys, I have a load in my musket that I want to fire before I go." As he turned to empty his gun, a load of grapeshot tore off his leg. The 4th Texas, 18th Georgia and the Hampton Legion wheeled to the left in the corn, ad-

RALLYING BEHIND THE TURNPIKE FENCE.

Jackson's Confederates attempt to make a stand along the turnpike fence.

Standing with the Colors

Perhaps the object of greatest importance to a Civil War regiment was the battle flag flown in combat. Serving as a means of identification, direction, and a rallying point for a unit, the flag maintained a great deal of symbolic value as well. Usually bearing the list of battles the regiment had fought in, the banner was a emblem of honor, to be flown at all times throughout any engagement; to lose it was the utmost disgrace. As a result, it was a distinction to serve as a colorbearer and soldiers displayed great bravery while wielding their flags despite imminent danger or wounds. At Antietam, a corporal of the 8th Pennsylvania Regiment continued to wave his regiment's colors despite a broken leg and an advance of the enemy. While calling out to his comrades not to desert the flag he was shot through the head by a Confederate soldier.

Troops were also known to risk their lives to capture enemy standards. During Hooker's attack, Lieutenant Lewis C. Parmelee of the 2nd U.S. Sharpshooters was killed near the Hagerstown Road by six or seven bullets from Rebel rifles as he attempted to capture a fallen Confederate flag as a trophy.

When the Federal garrison surrendered at Harper's Ferry, a few regiments escaped further dishonor by preventing the loss of their flags as trophies for the Confederates through various cunning maneuvers. One regiment tore their banner to bits, each soldier keeping a piece. Corporal Omar S. Lee managed to save the flag of the 32nd Ohio by wrapping it around himself under his clothes.

Though perhaps members of an honorable profession, there was always a high rate of mortality amongst color bearers. Due to their importance to the fighting effectiveness of the regiment and distinctiveness as a target, the flags made good targets for enemy soldiers. At Antietam, the 1st Texas lost eight colorbearers during the battle; the 9th New York also lost eight men carrying the flag into battle; the Hampton Legion lost four in succession while attacking Gibbon's men. Thus there is no wonder that enthusiasm among soldiers to serve as color bearer waned amongst soldiers on both sides.

vancing on Gibbon's men rallying around Battery B at the northern edge of the Cornfield. Seeing the Colors of the Hampton Legion fall, after a third bearer was struck down, Major D.H. Dingle grabbed the colors, shouting, "Legion, follow your colors!" Lieutenant Colonel M.W. Gary of the Hampton Legion described what happened next in his official report, "The words had an inspiring effect, and the men rallied bravely under their flag, fighting desperately at every step. He bore the colors to the edge of the corn near the turnpike road, on our left, and, while bravely upholding them within 50 yards of the enemy and three Federal flags, was shot dead." As the rest of the Confederate line approached, Battery B fired canister at a feverish pace and with deadly effect. In their haste, one battery sergeant failed to get out of the way of his piece as it recoiled after firing only to be crushed under the wheel. Each blast struck the Rebels like a huge shotgun, tearing gaping holes in the formation. With every shot, torn caps, broken rifles, and ripped haversacks filled the air. In one instance, an arm was torn off its owner, thrown into the air some thirty feet. Noting one of the cannon elevated too high, Gibbon rushed to the gun and turned the elevating screw down, yelling out, "Give 'em hell boys." As the Confederates drew closer, the gunners fired double shots of canister, which knocked out the Confederates by the scores, forcing them to fall back.

Meanwhile, on the northern edge of the Cornfield, the 1st Texas had advanced beyond any support and was rushing headlong into disaster. Awaiting the regiment, lying down before the fence bordering the cultivated ground, was Lieutenant Colonel Robert Anderson commanding the Third Brigade of Meade's division. As the unknowing Texans approached to close quarters, the Pennsylvanians fired a blaze of musketry, decimating the entire force opposing them. Under continuing blasts, which were beginning to catch the 1st Texas in flank, those who survived the killing volleys fled for cover, leaving 186 out of 226 of their comrades behind; a total of 82 percent casualties. In running out to grab the fallen regimental flag of the 1st Texas, a Yankee found the standard surrounded by 13 corpses, all lying within touch of it.

Taking on the Federal left in the East Woods and Cornfield were Law's 4th Alabama, 21st Georgia and 5th Texas which were followed by a few brigades from D.H. Hill's division from the Confederate center including Colquitt's, Garland's under Colonel D.K. McRae, and Ri-

Joseph Mansfield. Mansfield took command of the XII Corps on 15 September only to die two days later at Antietam.

pley's. While on the advance, Law's troops saw a foolhardy Union officer offering himself as a target for enemy guns as he urged his troops on from a white horse. All of a sudden, the unanimous call went up, the men shouting "shoot the fool!" Despite the many shots aimed at the Federal, he remained unscathed. Driving into the woods against Christian's brigade, the Confederates received a "lively cannonade and shelling." In the tremendous fire, a lieutenant in the 4th Alabama had his head taken off by a shell, splattering all those around him with brains, blood and gore. Still, the Confederates pressed on with the firing and yelling so loud that officers were forced to communicate by hand gestures, since their voices had no chance of being heard over the din. Under tremendous pressure, Lyle fell back, with the 90th Pennsylvania protecting his rear. The regiment retreated slowly, with the color bearer walking backwards to ensure he would not receive an ignominious death from Rebel bullets in the back. To stem the tide, Magilton's brigade of Meade's division arrived attempting to block the advance, only to melt away in the face of the furious assault of the Confederates. With the retreat of Christian's brigade, Ricketts' remnant of a division left the field after losing a third of the men that had gone into action.

Even Gibbon was forced to retire as he faced a new threat in his rear: Early had joined the fray after being ordered up by Jackson and was moving from his position near Nicodemus Hill to the rear of the Blackhats. Now, the Iron Brigade, along with Patrick's and Phelps' brigades, found themselves in severe danger of being flanked. Though hard pressed, the Yankees made a hasty retreat to the Miller farm to set up a new defensive position there. Within the mighty conflagration, the Iron Brigade, still depleted after the previous fights of Brawner's farm, Second Manassas, and South Mountain had lost 348 men, a 42 percent casualty loss.

As the battle entered a new phase, with the entrance of Mansfield, both sides had suffered horribly in only an hour and a half of continuous fighting. Already the I Corps had lost almost a third of its numbers, some 2500 men. Hood could have spoken for the entire Confederate left when he replied to a questioner asking where his command was, saying, "dead on the field." Jones' division had 33 percent of his soldiers in butternut killed or wounded; the strength of Lawton's division was cut in half with his old brigade losing 554 men out of 1150 of those going into combat. The mortality of officers in Lawton's brigade was astounding; only one of his regimental commanders escaped unscathed while all of the staff officers had fal-

Commander of a division in Hooker's corps, George G. Meade. In July of 1863, Meade led the entire Army of the Potomac at Gettysburg.

len from wounds. Hood's repulse cost the 4th and 5th Texas, and the 18th Georgia roughly half their men while the Hampton Legion and the aforementioned 1st Texas were completely decimated. While the fight was effectively over for Hooker's troops, Jackson's men had two more Federal corps to contend with.

The XII Corps goes into action at Antietam after Hooker's command had spent itself on the field.

In the face of disaster, Major General J.K.F. Mansfield answered Hooker's call for help, arriving with the 7200 men of the XII Corps at 0730. Though a veteran officer, this was his first time commanding a unit of this size. Most of his men were rookies as well; while a good many had fought with Banks at Cedar Mountain, at least half had never been in combat before. This being the case, Mansfield had his men approach the field in tight compact lines. Though this maneuver ran the risk of incurring increased casualties from exploding shells, Mansfield believed it was essential to keep all the troops, especially the newer soldiers, under the watchful eyes of the officers to insure the weak of heart wouldn't break to the rear once in combat. To encourage the troops, the general shouted words of encouragement: "Ah! boys. We shall do a fine thing today. We have got them where we want them. They cannot escape by the skin of their teeth." As the commander of the XII Corps approached the field, a flustered Hooker rode up to him requesting immediate assistance as the Rebels were breaking through his lines. Approaching the battle down the Smoketown Road, the new Federal corps entered the East Wood from the northeast. The depleted Rebels of Law's and Hill's detached brigades wisely fell back in the face of this new threat; one Confederate later said the soldiers' fighting instinct told them it was time to "git up and git." Many of Law's men were so low on ammunition; men with only two cartridges in their belts gave one to a comrade without any at all. Despite being low on ammunition and men, the Rebels gave the Yankees a tough time of it. As Mansfield's Federals drove through the wood they encountered irritating sniper fire from Rebels dodging from tree to tree or from behind rocks, fallen branches and wood piles.

Mansfield tried his best to get his troops into position in the East Woods, despite the blanket of smoke covering the area and the fire from the woods and corn. Seeing the 10th Maine firing into the Cornfield, Mansfield supposed they were accidentally shooting at some of Hooker's men attempting to retreat to safety. Interposing himself between what he believed to be friendly forces, Mansfield rode before the Maine regiment calling out, "You are firing into your own men." The men argued the contrary leading the General to scrutinize the opposing force. Realizing his mistake he exclaimed, "Yes, Yes, you are right," only to fall from his mount, which collapsed after receiving a bullet from the enemy's guns. Another shot found Mansfield in the

After Mansfield fell, the command of the XII Corps devolved upon Alpheus S. Williams.

chest giving him a wound that was to prove mortal.

Following Mansfield's fall, command devolved upon Alpheus Williams, who approached Hooker to get an appraisal on the situation which awaited him. While talking with the General, a shell struck Fighting Joe in the foot, forcing him to be carried from the field as well. As Williams tried to get the command sorted out of the confusion caused by Mansfield's loss, his Yankees came under a shattering fire from Hill's brigades in the Cornfield, which had followed Hood into combat.

Of course, there were many moments in which the new troops were introduced to the horrors of war. Lying down during a lull in the battle, one soldier of the rookie 125th Pennsylvania turned to his comrade next to him in order to discover why he was being so quiet. In doing so, he found his compatriot's skull pierced by a bullet with his brains oozing out. Eventually, Williams had his forces divided to reinforce the depleted commands of Meade and Gibbon with Crawford's brigade being sent to join the forces near the Miller farm and Gordon's taking position to the north of the Cornfield. Upon seeing reinforcements from Crawford's brigade, the remnants of the decimated 5th Pennsylvania gave them a few mighty cheers, calling out, "God bless you boys!" In attempting their

THE COMING STORM

Storm clouds gather over the site of America's single most bloodiest day, the Antietam National Battlefield.

Federal troops go into battle around the Dunker Church.

A row of slaughtered men killed at Antietam before receiving a hasty burial.

FEDERALS ON THE ADVANCE

Bank's corps makes a desperate charge against the Confederate ranks led by Stonewall Jackson at Cedar Mountain. The Federal defeat here would halt the advance of Pope's Army of Virginia and set the stage for Second Manassas.

McClellan's Army of the Potomac engages Joseph Johnston's Confederate legion in the inconsequential battle of Williamsburg. The confrontation was one of a series of many bloody clashes during McClellan's failed Peninsular Campaign.

A depressed and defeated Army of Virginia crosses the Bull Run after receiving a sound beating at Second Manassas.

John Pope

SECOND MANASSAS

Robert E. Lee.

Federal artillery battery attempts to stem Confederate advance on Henry House Hill on 30 August 1862.

BURNSIDE'S BRIDGE

A rather fanciful depiction of the bloody and tragic struggle for Burnside's Bridge.

Burnside's Bridge as it stands today. Some 550 Federals died attempting to take the structure on 17 September (photo by author).

ANTIETAM: AMERICA'S BLOODIEST DAY

Carnage of the Sunken Road also known as
Bloody Lane.

The Best Shots of the War as Seen by James Longstreet

While on the field at Antietam, Longstreet viewed the second best shot he ever was to see in the entire Civil War. While surveying the course of the battle with Harvey Hill and Robert E. Lee on a ridge under cannon fire, Hill imprudently remained mounted on his horse while his comrades dismounted, causing "Old Pete" to warn him, "If you insist on riding up there and drawing the fire, give us a little interval so that we may not be in the line of fire when they open on you." Sure enough, Captain Stephen H. Weed serving with the 5th New York Artillery spotted the mounted officer and aimed one of his cannons at the easy target, firing off a shot. Noticing the flash and smoke emanating from the Yankee gun as it unloaded its deadly missile, Longstreet turned to Hill to say, "There is a shot for you." The shell was so accurately fired that, after

hanging in the air for two or three seconds, it landed right in front of Hill's horse, cutting off both of the animal's forelegs. His mount falling upon its bloody stumps, Hill found himself ignominiously stuck in the saddle, desperately struggling to free himself. Amused by the spectacle, the generals and staff officers chuckled as Longstreet tried to aid Hill, saying, "Throw your legs over the pommel and try to get off that way."

The single best shot Longstreet was ever to see took place at Yorktown, when a Rebel gun dropped a shot right on the table of a Federal engineer as he was drawing up a map.

movement to get into position before the Cornfield, Gordon's brigade was subjected to a galling fire from the enemy; in the process, the 27th Indiana lost some of its celebrities; Corporal Bloss and Sergeant Mitchell, the finders of the lost order were both wounded. Still, the Confederates were having increasing difficulties in dealing with the new threat posed by the XII Corps. When Hill's detached brigades launched a counterattack against Gordon's men, the Yankees defiantly held. They were helped in part when Garland's brigade, still not yet recovered from almost being swept up by a flank attack at South Mountain, fled from the field, when shouts of a enemy force on their right went up.

Bearing down on the Rebels in the Cornfield was the division of General George S. Greene, son of the famous hero of the Revolutionary War, Nathaniel Greene. Lieutenant Colonel Hector Tyndale's brigade took Hill's troops in flank, driving them from the field into the West Wood, cutting apart the 6th Georgia, which lost 226 out of 250 men. A few members of the Peach State Regiment were attempting to make a stand before the oncoming blue lines, when one

called out, "Let's get out of here!" Seeing a number of Georgians remaining on the ground, a comrade replied, "We have a line, let them come." The soldier in favor of fleeing informed his misinformed friend that the men around him were all dead or wounded and proved his statement by shooting a nearby corpse after which he said, "The sooner we get out of here the better." During the advance, the men of the 8th Ohio found the fight an excruciating enterprise as most of the men had gone into the fight without water to spare them from the heat, exhaustion of battle, and thirst caused by biting off the paper cartridges filled with dry black powder. One Ohioan, despite the needs of himself and his fellow troops, came upon a Confederate who had his face partially blown away but was still alive. Halting amidst the fighting, he paused to give his unfortunate enemy a drink before he moved on. Pressing forward through the Cornfield, Greene's division moved to the south to take position on a plateau right before the Dunker Church, the objective of Hooker all along. A member of the 111th Pennsylvania remembered the heavy fighting there:

Without nervousness or haste the men monotonously loaded and discharged their pieces, and the officers walked back and forth shouting orders. . . . Every moment men went down, some with wounds so slight that they were unheeded, some disabled for life, and some to rise no more. Throats were parched from thirst. Faces were

This austere temple of worship of a pacifistic Christian sect, the Dunker Church, ironically became a symbol for the bloodiest day of fighting in American history.

blackened with smoke, lips smeared and cracked wit powder from bitten cartridges. The guns were so hot that their brass bands were discolored. Belts sagged loosely over empty stomachs. Hands were swollen with the incessant use of the ramrod. Shoulders were lamed by the recoil of pieces.

Hit in the stomach, Jacob E Miller of the 111th Pennsylvania died desperately trying to shove his exposed intestines back into his abdomen cut open by a hideous wound. Somehow, the 125th Pennsylvania from Crawford's division managed to get up into the West Woods right above the Dunker Church Now the Federals could seize the day, if they could just take advantage of their good fortune. By 0900, the plucky soldiers from the Keystone State were seemingly assured of possible success when reinforcements were approaching the field.

In engaging the worn out remnants of Jackson's command, the Federals of Mansfield's corps had lost 1,800 men, including its commander Joseph Mansfield while winning a significant foothold in the enemy's line. Still, thousands of men had been wasted upon the fields at Sharpsburg by none other than George Brinton McClellan, the man who professed to care for his troops so much. Remaining aloof from the battle at his headquarters across the Antietam at the Pry House, Little Mac allowed his corps to be thrown into battle piecemeal, one at a time, destroying the absolute power their combined numbers could wield. In the end, Hooker and Mansfield essentially wound up fighting separate battles while getting chewed up in the process. As McClellan failed to press attacks against the Confederate line in other areas, Lee could shunt reinforcements to blunt his enemy's assaults before they could seriously threaten his position. As Sumner's corps entered the battle, this type of move on Lee's part would work with deadly effect upon his enemy.

CHAPTER VIII

ADVANCE OF II CORPS

17 September, 1862

Responding to the 0720 call to reinforce the stalled Federal left, Major General Edwin Vose Sumner started his Second and Third Divisions, under Major General John Sedgwick and Brigadier General William H. French respectively, across the Antietam to take up the fight. The First Division, under Major General Israel B. Richardson, was held in position across the Antietam until 0900 due to a command mishap. Altogether, Sumner was initially taking 11,100 of his 15,400 troops into battle with him. Crossing the Antietam to the south of the Northern Bridge, the II Corps came onto the battlefield below Hooker's and Mansfield's positions.

As they approached the battle, musketry could be heard far off, sounding to one Yankee like a "rapid pouring of shot on a tin pan." Arriving where the two armies had fought and struggled for the better part of the morning, Sumner peered through the drifting smoke of battle only to find the remnants of a mighty bloodfest cast about the field: muskets, soldiers' belongings, torn cartridge papers, and the slaughtered bodies of the dead and wounded of both sides. Though the Major General had been told the I and XII Corps were holding their own against the Rebels, it appeared as though both sides had been driven off the field or completely annihilated, leaving the II Corps completely alone to face an unseen enemy.

Believing he must be above both the Union and Confederate positions, Sumner decided to push off to the west, hoping to get on the Rebel flank and then wheel around to the south to roll up the rest of the enemy's line, thus crushing the Army of Northern Virginia once and for all. In setting up the advance, Sedgwick was directed to take the lead with his brigades formed into three compact parallel lines about 60 to 70 yards apart, packing a potentially powerful sledge-hammer-like blow. Taking the front would be Brigadier Willis A. Gorman's brigade, followed by Brigadier General Napoleon Jackson Tecumseh Dana's brigade and Brigadier General Oliver O. Howard's brigade of Philadelphians. This forceful maneuver was not without risk; the stubby lines of Sedgwick's division were extremely vulnerable to flank attack, should they ever face the misfortune of becoming exposed. As his men moved off, Sedgwick's only available support was French's division, following 20 minutes, behind only to veer off course to the southwest, after losing sight of the rest of Sumner's men, leaving the flanks of the attacking force wide open.

Moving across the grotesque forms of the dead and wounded, Sedgwick's division pressed on towards the West Woods just north of the Dunker Church. The men of the newer regiments bit their lips and gritted their teeth as their eyes gazed upon the terrible aftermath of battle and anticipated the grim fate that awaited them. Some, just couldn't take the pressure and performed what veterans called the "cannon quick step," fleeing for the rear. Unfortunately for the Federals, they provided a welcome new target for Stuart's Horse Artillery, which had been giving the Federals hell all day. Anthony W. McDermott of the 69th Pennsylvania in Howard's brigade noted of the fire,

> The range of the Confederate artillery upon our lines was most accurate and destructive; every conceivable article of destruction that could be used was hurled against us—solid shot, shell, spherical case, grape and canister and judging by the tearing sound through the air, the general

opinion was that railroad iron, nails, etc, were belched from the cannon's mouth, so that our men jocularly claim that whole blacksmith's shops were discharged from their guns against us.

Noticing that the men of his 19th Massachusetts regiment were becoming increasingly unnerved by the shelling, Colonel Edward W. Hinks put his troops through the manual of arms drill in full view of the Confederate guns. Though a rather odd maneuver, it had the desired effect of restoring the mens' confidence, allowing them to push on.

Riding up front with their men were Sedgwick and Sumner, willing to undergo whatever horror their men might experience. The only opposition to the onslaught were the thin battered commands of Jackson's wing which seemed hardly able to put up much opposition in the face of Sedgwick's 5400 bearing down on them. However, help was on the way; McLaws had finally arrived from Harper's Ferry at sunrise and was even now advancing to support the left. As the Federal left flank and center were as yet not seriously engaged that morning, Lee decided to dispatch George T. Anderson's brigade to Jackson at 0730 while sending orders for General Walker's division, posted below the Rohrbach Bridge, to head north to join the fight on the left. He arrived there sometime around 0900. These commands were moving up from the south, just as the unknowing Sumner was

George S. Greene whose division was able to make significant headway at Antietam.

The Young Napoleon, George McClellan, rides the line of battle at Antietam to encourage his troops.

Edwin Vose Sumner (1797-1863)

A robust 64 when the Civil War broke out, Edwin V. Sumner was one of the oldest general officers serving in the field operations of the Union Army. Ever since he received a commission as a second lieutenant in 1819 with the regular infantry, Sumner remained with the military, serving with the cavalry on the western frontier. Achieving the rank of lieutenant colonel for gallantry in the Mexican American War, Sumner was placed in charge of Fort Leavanworth and later commanded a campaign against the Cheyenne Indians in the 1850s.

After the War Between the States commenced, the old veteran took command of the II Corps of the Army of the Potomac and attained the rank of major general after action in McClellan's Peninsular Campaign. A tough fighter, Sumner was nicknamed "Bull" or "Bull Head" due to his roar-

ing voice and a soldiers' legend that musket balls bounced off his impregnable skull. Unfortunately, Antietam proved to be Sumner's undoing when he launched an assault with Sedgwick's division without protecting his flanks and allowed the Confederates to trap the force in a murderous pocket of fire. Following the failed attack, the general lost his nerve and refused to allow Franklin's corps to launch a counter attack against the depleted Rebel left, a drive that might have won the day for the Federals.

After the Battle of Fredericksburg, stung by criticism of his ability, the handling of his corps at Sharpsburg and tried by the pressures of field command, Sumner asked to be removed to a less stressful post. Given the Department of Missouri, the old soldier died of pneumonia before he could assume his new position.

---

entering and passing through the West Woods. Meanwhile, the remaining Confederates fell back before the oncoming enemy, setting up a last ditch defense beyond the West Wood, firing away from behind the cover of a farm house and haystacks. Realizing the desperation of the moment, Early, commanding the only other organized force in the area, redressed his lines of 900 Butternuts to launch an attack.

While the Federals occupied their time with the meager force ahead of them, McLaws' and Walker's divisions with G.T. Anderson's brigade had arrived just at the right time, facing the right position where they could hurt Sumner and Sedgwick the most, on their exposed left flank. While one brigade managed to get lost, the Rebel reinforcements after much confusion set up with Anderson and Kershaw on the right, Barksdale in the center, and Semmes on the left with Brigadier General Robert Ransom's brigade in support. Joined by Early, their advance upon the unsuspecting Federals was easily concealed behind the trees, gulleys, and limestone outcroppings of the West Wood. While Sumner stopped to talk with Lieutenant Colonel John W. Kimball of the 15th Massachusetts, a shocked major gave a shout of alarm, "See the Rebels!" Sumner turned to the Federal left to

see the imminent danger, only to exclaim, "My God! We must get out of this." All of a sudden the woods on Sedgwick's left exploded in a destructive blast of Confederate musketry; the 72nd Pennsylvania on Howard's left totally disintegrated under the fire. Continuing the merciless blaze of musketry, minnie balls flew as thick as "hail stones," according to a Yank. Shots fired from the Confederate front lines tore through the troops in Sedgwick's first line, doubling their effectiveness when they slew men in the rear ranks as well. Shattered by the attack, many stunned regiments collapsed as troops began to desert their positions, fleeing in panic. As the enemy swept into the rear of Howard, the only avenue of escape was to the north. When a mob of soldiers came out of the woods, Pelham's guns took aim and opened up on those hapless individuals.

For those who attempted to stay, the situation in the West Woods became increasingly untenable. The front under Gorman now found itself preoccupied with applied pressure from Early's and Colonel Andrew Grigsby's men, with some of the enemy coming to within a distance of 15 yards to unleash their fire on the uneasy Federal line. Despite the intense salvos of musketry, Federal commanders continued to stay with their men to try to bring some kind of order to the growing chaos. While attempting to wheel his men around, Sedgwick was hit by a bullet, but refused to leave, only to have another knock him off his mount. It took a third one to finally force him to leave the fight. Dana himself was also wounded, but adamantly refused to abandon his men in their time of need. At this point the noise of the musketry was becoming so deafening that even Bull Sumner's voice could not be heard over the din. Howard recalled his commander's difficulty in attempting to give orders over the racket in his official report, "The noise of the musketry and artillery was so great that I judged more by the gestures of the general (Sumner) as to the disposition he wished me to make than by the orders that reached my ears." Originally, the men of Howard's brigade mistakenly thought Sumner had ordered a charge and immediately fixed their bayonets, cheering wildly, only to be told by the general, "Back, boys, for God's sake, move back! You are in a bad fix!" As the predicament gradually worsened, the first two lines attempted to weather the fire, while the brigade of Philadelphians in the rear fell apart, retreating from the terrible slaughter. In Dana's brigade, the men of the 59th New York managed to pull together to return fire, but through a tragic mishap unleashed a fusillade into the backs of the 15th Massachusetts right in front of them. Despite this unfortunate occurrence, the 15th fought on, the men loading and firing as if "on dress parade" as one member noted.

Inevitably, with the Rebels enveloping the Federals in a terrible pocket of destructive fire, blasting away on Sedgwick's front, left and rear, Sumner realized the division could not hold this position in the West Woods much longer, and ordered a complete withdrawal. Some units managed the retreat in order, with the 20th Massachusetts putting their rifles to their shoulders, and marching away at a ordinary pace. Under heavy fire, what was left of the routed command quickly fled for the cover of the North Woods, sweeping up some of Hooker's men near the Poffenberger farm in the retreat. While falling back, detachments from Gorman's and Dana's brigades attempted to make a last ditch stand, only to be thrown back by the victorious Rebels of Early's, McLaws', and Anderson's commands. A defensive line was finally organized along the Poffenberger farm with the men of the I, II, and XII Corps before the North Woods throwing the enemy back with musketry and canister. Stumbling into the deadly fire of a Federal battery, one soldier of the 17th Mississippi recalled, "The grapeshot, shrapnel, and what not puttered around us so that if it had been raining we would have all gotten wet"

Within the short 15 minutes of the engagement, 2100 of Sedgwick's men had fallen in the West Wood; many were hit before they were able to fire an angry shot in reply. Among the regimental casualties, the 15th Massachusetts and 42nd New York lost roughly half of their men, while the 19th Massachusetts lost all its field officers amongst its own heavy toll. Upon the field between the East and West Woods, a total of 12,000 men lay either dead or wounded carpeting the once peaceful farm land with blue, grey, butternut and crimson.

Meanwhile, Greene's men, replenished with ammunition, continued to hold their position before the Dunker Church coming under a heavy attack from Kershaw's South Carolinians, forcing back the 125th Pennsylvania the West Woods. After the demoralized remnants of Kershaw's command fell back, another Confederate charge was led by Colonel Van H. Manning, commanding a brigade from Walker's division, at 1000. The move was viciously repulsed as the Federals, concealed behind a hill, lured the enemy into close range. Dangerously massed up before the rise, the Rebel brigade lay down, attempting to return fire while suffering heavily from the rifle blasts of the Yankees. Major Orrin Greene of the 7th Ohio reported, " . . . we poured fire into their advancing columns volley after volley. So terrific was the fire of our men that the enemy fell like grass before the mower; so deadly was the fire that the enemy retired in great disorder, they not being able to rally their retreating forces." Manning himself was wounded in the attack, passing command to Colonel E.D. Hall as a retreat was called. Taking advantage of his success, Greene pursued the Southerners "like hounds after frightened deer," as Major George L. Wood of the 7th Ohio put it, breaking into the West Woods, providing the Federals with a threatening salient within the Rebel line. If these Yankees received reinforcements in time, the Army of Northern Virginia could be torn in two, ensuring that the sacrifice of the thousands of men lost earlier in the morning would not be in vain. However, the battle was finally shifting away from the Confederate left at its most desperate moment, to the south where a few Rebel brigades lay entrenched in a sunken road.

While Sedgwick's division of the II Corps was horribly wrecked in the West Wood, French's

John Brown Gordon (1832-1904)

With no prior military experience when the War Between the States broke out, John Brown Gordon controlled Lee's II Corps, which comprised half of the foot troops of the Army of Northern Virginia at the end of the conflict. Born in Upson City, Georgia, Walker led an undistinguished academic career, dropping out of the University of Georgia. Undaunted, he started a career in law, but attained success developing mines in his native state. In the ranks of Confederate service, after initially serving as a captain in a company known as the Racoon Roughs, Gordon rose through the ranks in the Army of Northern Virginia. At Antietam, he hit five times and was severely wounded while commanding the 6th Alabama Regiment at the Sunken Road.

Though almost losing an arm to amputation, Gordon recovered from his injuries to return to the field, where he was promoted to the rank of brigadier general and served in the Wilderness and accompanied Jubal Early on his assault against Washington in 1864. Following the war, Gordon energetically took to politics, being elected to the U.S. Senate three times. His rather overly romantic *Reminiscences of the Civil War* serve as essential reading for Civil War historians.

division bore down on the Rebels before the Mumma farmhouse, attempting to go into support of Greene's men near the Dunker Church. With Brigadier General Max Weber's brigade on the left, a brigade of green regiments under Colonel Dwight Morris in the center, and Brigadier General Nathan Kimball on the right, French's advance would take him against the Confederate center under Harvey Hill, originally consisting of Garland's, Colquitt's, Rode's, Ripley's and G.B. Anderson's brigades. The units found protection in a road to the northeast of Sharpsburg, which was carved into the earth by erosion and use. However, during the ensuing struggle on the left, all but Rode's and Anderson's brigades had gone to help Jackson.

Skirmishers on the front lines feeling out the position of the enemy.

Commander of the first assault on the Sunken Road, William H. French.

After fighting against the I and XII Corps, the mangled remnants of Garland's, Anderson's and Colquitt's brigades returned to the center, setting up to the left of the main line in the Sunken Road, being later joined by Walker's division and Ripley's brigade bringing the Confederate numbers to 2500. To impress upon the soldiers in the center the importance of their position, Lee rode up to tell his men to hold at all costs, to which Colonel John B. Gordon of the 6th Alabama in Colquitt's brigade replied, "These men are going to stay here General, till the sun goes down or victory is won." The Colonel was to recall later, "Alas! many of the brave fellows are there now."

Passing the burning remains of the Mumma house, set on fire by Hill's men to preclude its use by Federal sharpshooters, French's 5,700 men continued on to the Roulette farm, where they came under fire from Confederate skirmishers fighting a delaying action. While driving the enemy from the field, the 132nd Pennsylvania suffered the cruel misfortune of being near a hive of bees, struck by a piece of Rebel roundshot; the regiment was thrown into a panic by a swarm of the stinging insects. After getting the 132nd sorted out and calmed down, the Federals advanced over a rise before the Sunken Road. Entrenched behind a breast work of fence rails were Hill's men, with muskets ready, patiently waiting the order to fire. With Weber's brigade of Delawareans, New Yorkers, and

Remnants of Sedgwick's fateful advance into the West Woods.

General Lee Loses His Temper

While engaged in supervising his forces during the immense conflagration at Sharpsburg, General Robert E. Lee stumbled upon one of his soldiers straggling from the ranks. Not only had the contemptible individual deserted his comrades in their hour of need, but he had also violated the orders prohibiting foraging as he was attempting to drag a pig he had killed back to camp. Heatedly incensed by this shameful spectacle, Lee had the man arrested on the spot and ordered him to be turned over to General Jackson to face immediate execution. Receiving the unfortunate skulker in the thick of battle, Jackson decided the man could hardly be killed when his lines were so outnumbered and so hard pressed. Instead of fulfilling Lee's order, Stonewall had the man armed with a musket and sent him forward to where the fighting was thickest. Though a straggler and a thief, the soldier gave a good account of himself, surviving the battle after displaying

much gallantry. Evidently escaping his death sentence, the Confederate became known as the man who lost his pig, but "saved his bacon."

Confederate cavalrymen attempt to deter stragglers from fleeing the ranks at Antietam.

Marylanders taking the lead, the Federals ascended the ridge and came in sight of the Rebel line. Weber dressed his brigade into four ranks and gave the order to surge forth. Despite the violent intentions of the Yankees, Colonel Gordon took the time to admire their advance, "It was a thrilling spectacle. . . . Their gleaming bayonets flashed like burnished silver in the sunlight. With the precision of step and perfect alignment of a holiday parade, this magnificent array moved to the charge, every step keeping in time to the tap of the deep sounding drum." Though ready to unleash a volley, Colonel F.M. Parker of the 30th North Carolina restrained his men, telling them not to fire until they could see the belts of the Yankees' cartridge boxes. Gordon himself had his troops wait until they could almost make out the eagles on the buttons of the enemy's uniforms. After continuously taking aim at the approaching line, finally a devastating volley ripped into Weber's brigade at the close range of 100 yards. Colonel E. A. Osbourne of the 4th North Carolina in G.B. Anderson's brigade remembered, "Instantly the air was filled with the cries of the wounded and

dying and the shouts of brave officers, trying to hold their men, who recoiled at the awful and stunning shock so unexpectedly received." At first the Union line attempted to stand and fire, taking a horrible punishment while doing so. Next, bayonets were fixed and a charge attempted, but the enemy fire proved too powerful, shattering the attempt. Falling back to the cover of the ridge, soldiers began to return Rebel shots fast and fiercely with one soldier recalling, "I fired as fast as I could load, causing the barrel of my rifle to become so hot that it burnt me when I touched it." In their first few moments in combat, Weber's brigade had lost a dreadful toll of some 500 men. When Morris' rookies came up to support Weber, the 14th Connecticut panicked and fired into the backs of their comrades. While the 14th Connecticut collapsed under the intense pressure, the 108th New York and 130th Pennsylvania managed to get in line before the blaze of musketry from Sunken Road. Covered with soot from black powder and smoke, these Yankees appeared like apparitions from the depths of Hades, and caused the Rebels to call out, "Go back there,

you black devils.''

Seeing the Federals falling fast, Anderson attempted to launch a counterattack, which withered to a halt under the tremendous fusillades of the Union troops. On the Confederate left, Rodes also tried to drive the Yankees from the field, only to meet the same fate as Anderson's men. While taking up the regimental colors of the 108th New York, Lieutenant William W. Bloss was wounded when a minnie ball crushed the bridge of his nose and almost suffocated him with coagulated blood. He ran to the rear, yelling out to some of his men, ''For God's sake . . . jam a straw up my nose, I am strangling.'' At first, his compatriots attempted to apply the procedure delicately, only to have the officer grab the straw and shove it fiercely up his nostrils to save his life.. Receiving word from Sumner that he was in dire straits and required French to engage the enemy as vigorously as

One of the defenders of the Sunken Road or Bloody Lane, John B. Gordon of the 6th Alabama.

The burning house of Samuel Mumma set afire by Confederates to prevent it from becoming a haven for Yankee snipers.

possible, the division commander responded by sending in his last brigade.

Relieving Weber's and Morris' men was Kimball's brigade, filing out on the crest before the Rebel line. His attempts to storm the Sunken road met the same terrific musketry as his fellows, managing to do little more than increase the casualty lists. With Kimball's command wasting away, French's division was becoming increasingly spent on the bloody ridge; the troops were ordered to lie down to protect themselves. Firing just over the crest, soldiers would retreat to reload in safety behind the hill before going back up to fire another shot. An incautious Yank ignored such safe tactics, pluckily sitting on a boulder firing away in full view of the Confederate line. Looking back to his compatriots, he yelled, "Come over here men, you can see 'em better." Despite the destructive musketry on both sides, some Federals managed to take Lieutenant Colonel J.M. Newton, commander of the 6th Georgia, into Kimball's lines. Mortally wounded, he told his captors, "God bless you, boys, you are very kind." Turning his thoughts to his men, dead or dying in the Sunken Road, Newton lamented, "You

have killed all my brave boys; they are there in the road." Looking over into the Confederate lines, they could see the trench filling up with human casualties. Standing within the carnage, Gordon noticed a father mortally wounded lying by his son, killed in the fighting. Despite his loss, the parent turned to his commander calling out, "Here we are. My boy is dead, and I shall go soon; but it is all right."

In hurling the strength of his division against the Sunken Road, French had lost 1,750 men, a casualty loss of over 30 percent. Fortunately for French, help was on the way in the form of Israel Richardson's division. Finally getting his 4,000 men across the Antietam at 1030, Richardson put Brigadier General Thomas F. Meagher's brigade on the right alongside John C. Caldwell's brigade on the left. Following up in support was Colonel John R. Brooke's brigade. The Confederates were reinforced as well, with Richard Anderson's division, containing 3,400 men, going into the cornfield of Henry Piper's

Stragglers, wounded, and debris around the Mumma House after the focus of the battle shifted to the nearby Sunken Road.

farm behind the Sunken Road.

To relieve French's line, running low on men and ammunition, Richardson sent in his pet unit, Meagher's Irish Brigade, to go up against the Rebel position. Taking the crest with its emerald banners waving defiantly in the air, the unit let loose a volley that, in the words of one Irishman, "made the hills ring far and wide," only to receive in turn a galling blast of fire which brigade Historian D.P. Conyngham called "the severest and most deadly ever witnessed before." Seeing an emerald banner fall to the ground, Meagher called for a charge yelling out, "Boys, raise the colors, and follow me!" The Irish Brigade drove towards the Confederate line before being forced to a halt by the Rebels' incessant deadly blaze of torrential gunfire that had blunted earlier Federal assaults. Though taking heavy casualties themselves, Rodes and Anderson's men refused to budge from their defenses once again defying the foe while dealing him a heavy cost.

While Meagher himself had his horse shot out from under him and had to be carried to safety, the Irishmen stayed on the field blazing away until their muskets were so hot that officers reported "the rammers were leaping out of the pipes at every discharge." As ammunition ran

Ruin of the Mumma House. Unfortunately, as the Confederates destroyed the house the Mummas would not receive compensation from the Federal government for their loss.

low, men were sent to collect cartridges from the dead and wounded lying nearby. The Confederates were inflicting a deadly toll: the 63rd and 69th New York recorded losing half of their men, with the latter regiment losing 70 out of the 72 who had recently joined the unit. In all, at least 550 Irishmen had fallen. Meanwhile, Caldwell's brigade had managed to threaten the Rebel right flank only to be called back in order to save Meagher's hard pressed Irishmen.

Leading the 5th New Hampshire into the battle, Colonel Edward C. Cross gave his men a few terse words of encouragement before they went in, "Men, you're about to engage in battle. You have never disgraced your state; I hope you won't this time. If any man runs, I want the file closers to shoot him; if they don't, I shall myself. That's all I have to say." As Caldwell's troops took the crest, Federal shells directed at Rebel guns screamed over their heads. At the same time, Rebel cannoneers responded with vicious blasts of solid shot, tearing up the ground and blasting the Union line. One soldier from New Hampshire falling wounded called out to Cross, "Oh, God I'm wounded," to which the unsympathetic colonel replied, "Its the fortunes of war, my young man. It's the fortunes of war." Staying in the front lines, General Richardson was seen ambling about looking for a certain general missing from the field. When told the object of his search was hiding behind a haystack, the General roared,

The Fighting Irish of the Army of the Potomac

During the great Irish potato famine of the 1840s, multitudes of the sons and daughters of the Emerald Isle sought to escape the poverty and deprivation of their homeland to seek a better life in America. Flocking primarily to the industrial North in search of opportunity, a number of these individuals joined the Union Army when the Civil War broke out in 1861. A whole brigade was comprised solely of Irishmen, consisting of the 63rd, 69th, and 88th New York, thus called the Irish Brigade. The unit's trademark was its magnificent array of flowing green battle flags endowed with golden harps and shamrocks, proudly confirming the heritage of these soldiers in blue. Unlike the other glory units of the war such as the Iron Brigade and the Stonewall Brigade, the Irish Brigade remained unique throughout the entire war.

Serving in almost every major engagement in the Eastern Theatre, the unit was most famous for its gallant charges at Antietam, Fredericksburg and Gettysburg. At Sharpsburg on 17 September, the Irishmen bravely assaulted the Confederate line in the Sunken Road, failing to take the position, but inflicting heavy casualties on the enemy. At Fredericksburg, another desperate charge was led against the Confederate positions entrenched behind a stone wall at Marye's Heights, the brigade losing 545 men out of 1400. By Gettysburg, the Brigade was a mere shadow of itself in former days having lost hundreds of men in combat. The ranks of the 63rd, 69th and 88th New York were so depleted that the regiments were consolidated into two companies each. On the second day of the battle, the brigade helped brace Sykes' lines by charging Longstreet's Confederates in the wheatfield on Meade's left.

Following the end of the war, a very depleted Irish Brigade with its green banners in tatters, made a grand march through the capital before it was mustered out of the service. The

illustrious service of the unit has made it one of the most famous of all brigades in American military history.

"God damn the field officers!"

After maintaining a strong defense, the command structure in the Sunken Road was beginning to deteriorate, as officers fell before the intense Federal fire. While getting his men into position, Richard Anderson fell wounded, leaving the command of his division to fall upon the uncertain shoulders of Brigadier General Richard Pryor. As Caldwell went into position, Pryor had only managed to get one of his brigades into the Sunken Road. When he sent his own brigade into the line there, troubles increased, as the lack of room forced some Confederates to spill out of the road and lose its cover. Standing among his Alabamians, John Gordon was hit five times. Receiving his final wound in the jugular, the General fell face forward into his hat. Had the head piece not been pierced by a bullet, the colonel might have met a gruesome death, drowning in his own blood, which poured out from his neck wound.

By 1200, the Confederate line was finally beginning to collapse, not only from the heavy toll of casualties, but also from some severe misunderstandings between the commanders in the field. In attempting to extricate his troops to solve the crowding problem in the Sunken Road, Colonel Carnot Possey, commanding Featherston's brigade of Richard Anderson's division, pulled his men out, only to set off calls of a retreat, and forced Pryor's and Wright's brigades to break for the rear. Taking command of the 6th Alabama after Gordon fell, Lieutenant Colonel J.N. Lightfoot approached Rodes to request his regiment be removed from the line, his men being subjected to severe fire where there wasn't much cover. Rodes gave him permission to take his men to a more defensible position. Lightfoot returned to his command, immediately pulling them out of the Sunken Road. When asked by his compatriots if the whole brigade was being ordered back, he mistakenly and disastrously answered yes. As the rest of Rodes' troops retreated from their positions, Colonel Francis Barlow, commanding both the 61st and 64th New York, charged into the road, getting an enfilading fire on the rest of the line, forcing the rest of the enemy to run, and capturing 300 prisoners. Despite being forced to retreat, an ornery Rebel lagged behind the rest of his comrades, firing shot after shot until running out of ammunition. With the Rebel command collapsing, the Federals advanced forward to finally take the Sunken Road. Bluecoat T.F. Debugh Galwey with French's men

Another skilled fighting general lost during the Antietam campaign, Israel Richardson.

recalled, "It seemed like merely a hop, skip, and jump till we were at the lane, and into it, the Confederates breaking away in haste. . . . " Arriving where the Rebels had blocked the legions of the Union Army for so long, Livermore of the 5th New Hampshire recalled, "In this road lay so many dead rebels that they formed a line which one might have walked upon as far as I could see, many of whom had been killed by the most horrible wounds of shot and shell, and they just lay there as they had been killed apparently, amid the blood which was soaking in the earth." One Confederate who was lying wounded in the road had ample evidence of the terrible fire his command had been under, reportedly telling his captors, "When I fell, I had one bullet in me, now I have five."

French advances on the Roulette Farm as the
Federals descend upon the Sunken Road.

As hundreds fall either dead or wounded, French's
and Richardson's divisions fight to take control.

All of a sudden, disaster now threatened the Confederate center. Finding his troops routed, Rodes attempted to rally his troops to create some sort of defense against the advancing Federals, only managing to get some 150 men to join him. To bring a halt to the Federal advance, Longstreet brought up guns to shell the oncoming enemy. Throwing in M.D. Miller's battery of the Washington Artillery, the cannoneers opened up with a deadly barrage of canister. As Yankee riflemen began to pick off the gunners, Longstreet ordered his own staff to join the fight; they took over a piece, loading and firing it against the enemy, while Longstreet stood holding the reins of their horses, giving direction and advice. To increase the damage on the enemy, Miller loaded his cannons with double shots of canister, the guns recoiling almost a foot after each deadly burst. The fire was fearful, as one soldier recalled in the Piper Cornfield as the Confederate cannons "poured into the standing corn stalks such a pelting storm of grape that each explosion seemed like a rushing mighty wind and driving hail. It was sour office now to hold the position gained . . . the boys protected themselves by hugging the soil. It was not surprising how readily they stuck their noses in the dirt." Unable to take any more, the Yankees fell back to the Sunken Road.

Organizing a detachment of troops from various regiments, Hill sent them forward against the Federal line. Awaiting them amongst others was Colonel Cross and his 5th New Hampshire. The Southerners bravely approached to within close quarters of the Federal line in the Sunken Road. Seeing a color bearer, a call went up to shoot the man holding the flag; a blaze of musketry went up after which the bearer and his banner was nowhere to be seen. Sticking with his men in the thick of combat, Cross (a veteran of clashes with Indians on the frontier), with a red bandanna tied around his forehead and his face streaked with blood, called out, "Put on the war paint!" to which soldiers wiped their faces with the torn ends of cartridge paper. Then the Colonel called out, "Give 'em the war whoop!" The effect of this highly unusual exercise bolstered the morale of the New Hampshire soldiers with shouts of "Fire! Fire! Fire faster!" going up and down the line. Caught up in the excitement, Lieutenant Livermore grabbed a rifle to fire off a few rounds himself. Noticing his subordinate's bravado, Cross cautioned him,

The Sunken Road more than 20 years after blood flowed freely there.

Richardson's left in the desperate conflagration before bloody lane.

"Mr Livermore, tend to your company." With the 81st Pennsylvania coming over to enfilade the left flank of the Confederate onslaught, the Southerners could take no more, falling back through the Piper farm. Still desiring to hit the Yankee line, Hill himself grabbed a musket to personally lead 200 men in a counterattack which had no chance of success. Despite the huge threat to the Confederate line, this enormous amount of activity was enough to make the Yankees think twice about continuing onwards.

Realizing that desperate times called for desperate measures, Longstreet called for a charge against flank to drive back the enemy. Raising 675 men from Cobb's brigade, the Third Arkansas and 27th North Carolina, this force was sent in under Colonel John R. Cooke, engaging Greene's forces around the Dunker Church. Patiently waiting reinforcements and getting only a few men from Gordon's command, the division believed Sedgwick's command to be in the West Woods. This speculation caused a nasty surprise when Ransom's men joined the fray, surprising the Federals on the right.

With his flank turned, Greene fell back from his advantageous position in the Confederate line. At this moment, Cooke was ordered to launch his attack. In the advance the color bearer of the 27th North Carolina was running ahead of the rest of the command. When Cooke ordered him to slow down, the soldier replied, "Colonel, I can't let that Arkansas fellow get ahead of me." Seeing two guns going to Greene's assistance, he sent his screaming men in their direction, shooting down almost every horse and half of the men working the battery. Riding among the troops came an unknown Confederate officer, obviously drunk, who called out, "Come on, boys, I'm leading this charge!" Disgusted by the spectacle, Lieutenant Colonel R.W. Singletary shouted at him, "You are a liar sir! We lead our own charges!" Overtaking some of Greene's men, the Yankees surrendered, but Cooke's Rebels had no time to collect the weapons of the enemy; leaving armed captives in the rear, the Confederates pressed forward. Moving on the right flank of the Sunken Road and Richardson's division, Cooke made a nuisance of himself before Kimball threw his brigade in the way. Both forces met at a distance of 200 yards; in one instance a Rebel got close enough to the guns of the 1st Rhode Island Artillery only to have his head bashed in by a Yankee wielding a musket as a club. The blow was so great, that the unfortunate Southerner's brains "splattered" a nearby gun and "were baked as quickly as if they had been dropped on a hot stove," according to

gunner Thomas M. Aldrich. One of his comrades, with a morbid sense of curiosity scraped the mess off the gun to keep as a souvenir.

Finding themselves increasingly hard pressed, low on ammunition and with no hope of receiving any reinforcements, the Rebels were forced to retreat. While falling back, the Confederate troops were peppered by fire from the Federals they had left behind earlier as captives. Taking position on the Hagerstown Turnpike the depleted and exhausted regiments of Cooke awaited the renewal of the battle.

When the Federal advance stalled, Richardson was searching for some artillery to get it going again. While pausing to take a drink, he was struck by a Rebel shell fragment from which he would die weeks later. Despite the loss of Richardson, the Confederate line remained ripe for the attack. Some 2,500 Southerners had fallen attempting to hold the Sunken Road and repel the Union advance; those who

Photograph taken on the day of the Battle of Antietam. Smoke from the fighting on the right billows across a field where a battery waits to go into action.

Some of the hundreds that lost their lives in the defense of Bloody Lane.

of a few men, not more than forty in all, the brigade had completely disappeared." Colonel R.T. Bennet in command of G.B. Anderson's brigade, recalled, "Masses of Confederate troops in great confusion were seen; portions of Anderson's division broke beyond the power of rallying after five minutes' stay." Certainly, now was the time to drive a mighty blow through the Confederate lines, an attack which could surely shatter Lee's army and force it to flee to the banks of the Potomac where it could be captured or cut apart as it tried to cross into Virginia.

Watching the great conflict from across the Antietam at the Pry House, McClellan and some of his subordinates lacked the nerve to act with remained standing occupied a thin line, anxiously awaiting the next move on the part of the Federals. Taking stock of his own command, Rodes wrote, "I found that with the exception the decisiveness that the situation demanded of them. McClellan was not lacking in troops.

Franklin's corps had arrived in the vicinity of the battle around 0900. It had not been engaged, save one brigade, which still left a good 10,000 men on hand. The V Corps had likewise seen little action, and offered some 6,600 men to throw into the fray. By the end of the Sunken Road fight at 1300, McClellan had at least 16,600 men to renew the contest against the weak and shattered wings of Jackson and Longstreet. Perhaps at no time before or since in the war did the Federals have such an opportunity to crush Lee and his army. After his two divisions were sent to bolster Sumner, Franklin seemed to have regained his nerve after the Crampton's Gap debacle and was in favor of an advance. On coming upon the leader of the II Corps, Franklin found him "much depressed," claiming his troops, totally exhausted, could not take up the fight. Hearing of Franklin's plans of attack, Sumner demanded the general stay in position for if the IV Corps was wrecked the entire right wing of the army would be in danger. Believing

Ambrose Everett Burnside (1824-1881)

Born into a Southern family from South Carolina transplanted to Indiana, Burnside initially was employed as a tailor before winning an appointment to West Point at age 19. After leaving the army in 1853, Burnside sought a fortune from the patent and production a breech loading carbine of his own design, only to have the venture fail when the government refused to purchase the weapon. Later, the army purchased 55,000 Burnside carbines for its armies during the Civil War. Fortunately in the meantime, Burnside's good friend and future commander, George Briton McClellan, found employment for him with the Illinois Central Railroad until war broke out in 1861. After commanding a brigade at First Bull Run, Burnside won a successful campaign leading the IX Corps on the North Carolina coast in a time when Federals were scrounging for military victories, which brought him to the attention of President Lincoln. Though being offered command of the Army of the Potomac, Burnside

refused, partly because he recognized his own limitations and also because he preferred to serve under McClellan until the old chums had a falling out during the Battle of Antietam. On 7 November, Burnside accepted Lincoln's request to relieve "Little Mac."

Unfortunately, the bewhiskered general's lack of ability was openly evident in a disastrous attack on the Confederate Army at Fredericksburg, which caused the loss of 13,000 troops while inflicting less than half as many fatalities on the enemy.

Relieved of command after attempting to blame his subordinates for his own failures, Burnside was given command of the Department of the Ohio where he engaged in a forceful effort to stamp out sedition, arrested the Copperhead politician Clement L. Vallandigham and suppressed the pro-Southern *Chicago Times*. After defeating James Longstreet at Knoxville, Tennessee, Burnside returned to the East and command of the IX Corps where he mishandled the attack on the Petersburg Crater. With his military reputation irrevocably tarnished, he finally resigned his commission shortly after the end of the ear managing to win a successful career in politics with three terms as governor of Rhode Island and a seat in the U.S. Senate.

William B. Franklin (1823-1903)

A Pennsylvanian by birth, William B. Franklin distinguished himself by graduating first in his class at West Point in 1843, outperforming classmate Ulysses S. Grant. From the Academy, Franklin achieved an illustrious military career which included surveying the Great Lakes, participating in the search for a southern pass through the Rockies with the Corps of Topographical Engineers, served with distinction in the Mexican American War, and even supervising the construction of the dome of the capitol Building in Washington, D.C.. Holding the rank of brigadier general of the Volunteers when the Civil War broke out, he participated in the disaster at First Bull Run, commanding a brigade of Massachusetts troops in Heintzelman's division. When the Army of the Potomac was organized, Franklin worked his way into the clique of the unit's commander, George Brinton McClellan and received command of the VI Corps.

At Crampton's Gap during the An-

tietam Campaign, Franklin displayed a singular lack of imagination in engaging the small Confederate force. Though managing to seize the pass, he halted before a reorganized enemy line which dwarfed his command. Later at Antietam, he regained his fighting nerve only to be held back by Sumner who had wasted his II Corps on the Confederates earlier in the day. Taking command of a grand division in Burnside's reorganized Army of the Potomac, Franklin was among those blamed by that general for his crippling loss at Fredericksburg. Exculpated from this accusation by a court of inquiry, Franklin returned to corps command to serve in the Department of the Gulf during Nathaniel Banks' ill fated Red River Campaign. Struck down by a wound in battle, Franklin did not return to the field during the last days of the war.

Resigning his commission, the former soldier returned to a successful career in engineering while attaining the posts of presidential elector and com-

missioner general for the Paris Exposition.

an aggressive move would be successful, Franklin petitioned McClellan who arrived on the scene to take an account of the situation himself. Listening to Sumner's fears, McClellan's own fears and penchant for caution swelled within him. Instead of the battered Confederate force that actually existed ahead of him, he saw only the mighty host lying in wait to spring upon his army. The attack would not be launched.

Still, McClellan would be offered another chance to change his mind. Brigadier General George Sykes of Porter's division, across the Antietam near the Sunken Road, had learned from one of his soldiers that the Confederate line there was merely a weak shell ripe for a crushing blow. Approaching McClellan for permission to make an attack to be supported by the rest of the V Corps, the plan was effectively scrapped when Porter supposedly informed his commander, "Remember, General, I command the last reserve of the last army of the Republic." Such words were enough to dissuade the Young Napoleon from living up to his name-

sake. So far, McClellan had managed to squander his fortune with the lost order, his successes on the battlefield, and subsequently the lives of his men. If the battle was to be won, the men participating in the battle to the south under Burnside would have to accomplish it.

While the Federal commander with the massive forces at his command refused to use them, Robert E. Lee and Stonewall Jackson, with hardly any spare troops at hand, were trying to accomplish the impossible: a counterattack against the Army of the Potomac. To determine the feasibility of an attack, Jackson sent a soldier up a high tree to take a look at the enemy's position. When asked how many troops he saw in the area the Rebel replied, "Whooee, oceans of them." Shortly after 1230 General John Walker approached Jackson, Stonewall told him Stuart was busy gathering a force of 4000 to 5000 troops for a flanking maneuver against the Federal right, saying, "We shall drive McClellan into the Potomac." With orders to support the maneuver, Walker gathered up what troops he could. He waited until 1530 for the sound of

Stuart's attack, then met with Jackson who informed him the Cavalry commander had found the Federal right anchored on the banks of the Potomac. Saddened by the failure of his operation, Jackson merely mused, "It is a great pity,—we should have driven McClellan into the Potomac."

CHAPTER IX

BURNSIDE'S BRIDGE
17 September, 1862

Throughout the day in the Cornfield, in the East Woods, in the West Woods, and in the Sunken Road, McClellan's efforts to crack Lee's line had met disappointing defeat after disappointing defeat. Yet the most tragic and discouraging fight was about to begin to the south at the Rohrbach Bridge, soon to be known forever more as Burnside's Bridge.

A half mile away from the Eastern side of the stream on the cultivated fields of the Henry Rohrbach farm lay the 12,500 men of the IX Corps under Ambrose Burnside and Jacob Cox. Earlier in the morning, the Confederate forces opposing this mighty host consisted of the divisions of D.R. Jones and John Walker. However, by 0900 Walker's division and G.T. Anderson's Brigade from Jones divison had been pulled out of line to assist the beleaguered Confederate left and center, leaving a paltry force of 3000 men to contest any advance made by the enemy. With the troops that remained, Jones held a line extending from the Boonsboro Pike, leading out of the center of Sharpsburg to the Harper's Ferry Road. Garnett's Brigade was on the left followed by the brigades of Jenkins (under Colonel Joseph Walker), Drayton and Kemper. Brigadier Robert Toombs was ordered to place his brigade in an advanced position on the bluffs overlooking the Rohrbach Bridge with 400 men of the 2nd and 20th Georgia regiments under Colonel Henry L. Benning. These troopers from the Peach State found themselves blessed with extremely good cover behind the abundance of rocks and trees about the site they were to defend. From behind this protective shelter, they could draw a deadly bead on any Yankees running through the open ground across the stream for the bridge. To guard Benning's flank,

The man whom Burnside's Bridge was named after, Ambrose Burnside. His leadership in the assault against Lee's right cost hundreds of lives.

the 50th Georgia from Drayton's brigade was sent south of the bridge to hamper enemy attempts to cross the creek. Adding to the potency of the entire force were five powerful batteries stationed behind the main line.

All combined, only 520 Georgians faced off against the 12,500 men of the primarily veteran IX Corps should it attempt a crossing, making

159

the contest appear to be somewhat one sided. Unfortunately for Burnside's Bluecoats, the Federal left was faced with a plague of severe command crises, cruelly hampering any advantages maintained in manpower. This collapse of effective leadership essentially stemmed from the growing differences between McClellan and his subordinate, the bewhiskered Burnside. Though up to now both men had been good friends, affectionately using the nicknames of "Mac" and "Burn," their relationship had recently come under some strain after the battle of South Mountain. Annoyed by Burnside's sluggish march in the pursuit of the Confederate Army on the 15th, McClellan had this curt dispatch criticizing his subordinates actions and demanding a prompt explanation for his failure to follow orders.

While stung by this condemnation, Burnside found himself disturbed by McClellan's organization of the Army of the Potomac on the field of battle. Following South Mountain, Little Mac had dispensed with his use of wing formations, relegating wing commanders Burnside, Sumner, and Franklin to the sole control of their respective corps without really informing them of this action. While the latter two generals seemed to acknowledge the move without any real concern, Burnside refused to believe himself to be anything less than a wing commander, wielding the power of two corps, the I and IX. Thus, when McClellan's battle plans removed Hooker from Burnside's control, placing him on the opposite flank of the army, his old friend Burn became incensed, regarding the act as the equivalent of an embarrassing demotion which he would not accept. Despite having half of his wing taken away from him, the general refused to reduce his rank by accepting the mere command of the IX Corps. This situation produced a debilitating effect on the command structure of the IX Corps; now all orders emanating from the General Commanding during the battle would have to go through the lengthy process of being forwarded through Burnside and then passed along to Cox who would put them into effect.

Combined with ill effects of the misunderstandings and ill feelings between McClellan and Burnside among the leadership of the IX Corps was the discomforting fact that the role the unit was assigned to play in the battle was never really well defined. Conflicting statements on the part of the general commanding seem to suggest his intentions for Burnside's and Cox's men were somewhat vague. In his

Commander of the Confederate right flank, David R. Jones.

official report of 15 October 1862, McClellan's plans seemed to include a mere diversionary thrust across the Rohrbach Bridge to deter the Rebels from reinforcing the flank assailed by the Union right. In 1863, McClellan contradicted by claiming Burnside was to launch a major attack. Whether a diversion or a main attack, the men of the IX Corps were unaware of any real design for them and were likewise oblivious of the situation confronting their comrades in the north; they would be fighting out of sync with the attacks launched there.

Of course the greatest obstacle of all facing the Federal troops was the splendidly crafted triple-arched stone bridge—some 125 feet long and twelve feet wide—much too narrow for an advancing corps—which they would have to cross to attack the Confederate right. The Federals would have to advance in a close column allowing their flanks to be exposed to a murderous enfilading fire from the well protected Georgians on the bluffs and entrenched in rifle pits behind breastworks across the creek. Evidently, despite the tremendous disadvantages facing any attempt to advance over the bridge, neither

Robert Augustus Toombs (1810-1885)

One of the South's political generals, Robert Toombs hailed from Wilkes County, Georgia, and ironically graduated from New York's Union College in 1828 to enter a career in law. He attained both wealth and eminence in his native state, and almost won the presidency of the Confederate States of America but was defeated by Mississippian Jefferson C. Davis. As Secretary of State in the early days of the Confederacy, Toombs inaugurated a stormy relationship with government leader by opposing an attack on Fort Sumter. Unhappy with his position in Davis' cabinet, Toombs resigned to take to the battlefield as a brigadier general commanding a brigade of Georgians in Longstreet's division. Managing to win the ill favor of his commanding officer, the cantankerous

Georgian was put under arrest for a short period in August of 1862 for neglect of duty. After returning to com-

mand a short time later, Toombs confided to his wife he would resign his commission after the next great battle, which turned out to be Antietam. There, he maintained a stubborn resistance against IX Corps at Burnside's Bridge, holding up the Federal advance against Lee's right flank for three hours. Staying with the army until March 1863, Toombs finally resigned after failing to receive a promotion to major General. He returned to public life, and became the gadfly of the Confederate government, serving as a major critic of Davis' policies. After briefly returning to military service to fight under Johnston, Toombs fled the country after the war, only to return two years later, once again engaging in Georgia politics though not taking any real office.

Where a handful of Georgians impeded the progress of some 12,000 Yankees, Burnside's Bridge.

Burnside, perhaps too miffed at McClellan to take the trouble, nor any serious Federal commander, gave any credence to the possibility of fording the stream itself. A native of the area, Kyd Douglas of Jackson's staff, seemed to think the Antietam was easily passable, as he claimed of the bridge and the stream, "It was no pass of Thermopylae. Go and look at it and tell me if you don't think Burnside and his corps might have executed a hop, skip, and a jump and landed on the other side. One thing is for certain, they might have waded it that day without getting their waste belts wet in any place."

As dawn broke on the 17th, the men of the IX Corps found themselves cursed by the conflicting egos of their commanders and orders, which left their mission uncertain at best; mistakes that would leave a heavy cost in lives. For most of the early morning hours, cannon on both sides merely shelled enemy positions and launched some counter battery fire. One soldier recalled that despite the tremendous amount of racket caused by the artillery, the cannonade had a drowsing effect, lulling one to sleep. The night before, McClellan had written Burnside that he was to remain in waiting until the necessary orders were given to begin the assault across the bridge. At 0910, just as Sumner rushed Sedgwick's division for its fatal engagement into the West Wood, an order to "carry the bridge, then gain possession of the heights beyond, and to advance along their crest upon Sharpsburg and its rear" was sent on to the headquarters of the IX Corps. Once the move was under way, McClellan gave assurances of reinforcements to support the attack. Reaching Burnside sometime around 1000, the commander passed along the orders to Cox who went on to supervise the assault.

View from the Confederate position across from Burnside's Bridge. The Rebel's almost unobstructed field of fire allowed them to slaughter Yankees as they attempted to storm across the bridge.

The Fighting Man's Friend

Probably no other Federal general in the war commanded more respect and admiration from his men than did George Brinton McClellan. In organizing and leading the Army of the Potomac, he had the knack for inspiring troops even after leading them to defeat at the Peninsula and wasting their lives at Antietam. One singular instance between McClellan and one of his soldiers displays the general's uncanny aptitude for winning the devotion of his troops.

After the Battle of South Mountain, a corporal of the Iron Brigade was bringing prisoners to the rear to turn them over to the proper authorities. Directed to a house where McClellan had set up his headquarters, the soldier was searching for someone to take his captives when he stumbled into a room where an officer was seated, writing at a desk. When the man looked up, the stunned Federal found himself in the presence of none other than George Brinton McClellan. No doubt irritated by the sudden intrusion, the general demanded, "What do you want?" Taken aback, the corporal could only reply, "I have some prisoners, General, I am ordered to turn them over to you." "Who are you and where do you come from?" asked McClellan gruffly to which the corporal gave his name and command. "Ah,

you belong to Gibbon's brigade. You had some heavy fighting," the McClellan remarked, his irritation over the interruption gradually slipping away. "Yes, sir, but I think we gave them as good as they sent." "Indeed you did," McClellan said, "You made a splendid fight." The corporal found the time to relax a tad, at least enough to boldly venture, "Well, General, that's the way we boys calculate to fight under a general like you." Greatly impressed

and enlivened by the statement, McClellan rose from his seat to shake the soldier's hand, saying proudly, "My man, if I can get that kind of feeling amongst the men of this army, I can whip Lee with no trouble at all!"

That night the corporal returned to his command with a story that quickly spread through the ranks; McClellan had shaken the hand of an enlisted man and complimented him on a fight.

As the advance was organized, Crook's and Sturgis' brigades took the lead, with the 11th Connecticut, under Colonel H.W. Kingsbury, thrown out as skirmishers to feel the enemy's position. Once a foothold was gained on the other side of the Antietam, Sam Sturgis' Second Division was to plunge over the bridge to exploit the success. Meanwhile, Rodman and the rest of the Kanawha Division were to head south in the attempt to cross the Antietam at the ford downstream discovered by Federal engineers, and move north to link up with the rest of the corps to drive on Sharpsburg.

Once the operation was under way, it quickly degenerated into a laughable fiasco of the worst magnitude. In trying to get into position to charge the bridge, Crook managed to lose his sense of direction, reaching the banks of the

stream some 400 yards north of the Rohrbach Bridge. There the brigade took cover to engage in a sharp firefight with the enemy on the other side of the creek. Tied down in the skirmish, Crook reported back to Cox that he was too heavily occupied to attempt to bear down upon the bridge. Meanwhile, the 11th Connecticut suffered severely from the well-placed shots of the enemy, losing their commander after he was hit four times by minnie balls. Taking his company to the banks of the stream, Captain John D. Griswold led his men into the water to wade across to the other side, only to see them cut apart in the attempt. Griswold himself was mortally wounded, managing only enough final strength to drag himself to the western shore, where he collapsed dead. To the south, Rodman's men found the designated ford, but discovered the bluffs on their side made crossing impossible. Learning from local citizens the location of another possible point of fording the stream, to the south, the division set off to find it, delaying the flanking maneuver against Toombs' men.

With the first attempt a failure, the mission to take the bridge fell upon Sturgis' division, with Brigadier James Nagle's brigade leading the attack, supported by Ferrero's brigade. Noticing the 48th Pennsylvania having problems getting into position in one of Rohrbach cornfields, Sturgis harshly berated the regiment's commander, "God damn you to hell, sir, don't you understand the English language? I ordered you to advance in line and support the 2nd Maryland, and what in hell are you doing flanking around in this corn . . . ?"

With the 2nd Maryland and 6th New Hampshire in the lead, supported by the 9th New Hampshire and the 48th Pennsylvania, Nagle's

Federals fixed bayonets and charged down Rohrersville Road with Federal musketry and cannon fire attempting to silence Georgian volleys. Despite the heavy bombardment, the Southerners leveled blast after blast of minie balls, canister, shot and shell into the ranks. One of the 48th Pennsylvania's ranks recalled, "Instantly the hills blazed with musketry. There were broad sheets of flame from the wall upon the crest, where the cannon, double shotted, poured streams of canister upon the narrow passage. The head of the column melted in an instant." When a large piece of railroad iron flew across the stream from a Confederate gun, a German officer exclaimed, "Mein Gott, we shall have a blacksmith's shop to come next." As they bore down on the bridge, the Yankee

The two 51sts, the 51st Pennsylvania and 51st New York, make their way across Burnside's Bridge in the face of heavy fire.

Clara Harlowe Barton

With the tremendous number of casualties resulting from the Civil War, leaders on both sides found themselves at a loss to provide proper care for wounded soldiers. Early in the conflict, a clerk in the patent office, Clara Barton, with no prior medical experience, sought to meet this concern. Shocked by the lack of medical supplies and treatment available for the wounded on the field of battle and during their removal to hospitals, Barton inaugurated efforts to collect bandages and food for casualties by advertising in the newspaper the *Worcester Spy*. After caring for her dying father in the winter of 1862, she committed herself to following the campaigns of the Army of the Potomac to administer aid to the wounded and dying on the battlefield.

Arriving at the Battle of Antietam, Barton provided surgeons with desperately needed bandages and anesthetics. Tending to the wounded in the field, she was nearly a casualty herself when a bullet pierced her sleeve and killed the soldier she was attending. Though hardly acquainted with the art of surgery, Barton later used a pocket-knife at a soldiers request to remove a musket ball from his cheek and ease the pain from his wound.

While continuing her humane services throughout the war, Barton expanded her duties to include the creation of a program to locate soldiers missing in action. Lincoln himself gave personal approval to the plan giving her the title of ''General Correspondent of the Friends of Paroled Prisoners.''

In this post, she interviewed freed prisoners to locate those soldiers not accounted for in battle who might be held in Southern jails. Her duties also included scouring newspapers to find names of lost troops in the lists of the discharged from hospitals, service and enemy prisons.

Following the war, Barton continued to champion the cause of health care, her efforts culminating in the establishment of the American Red Cross.

---

regiments simply could not bare the cruel fire. Men ran for whatever cover they could find. Seeing his command starting to crack, Duryea called out, ''What the hell are you doing there? Straighten that line! Forward!'' His attempts to keep his men moving were to no avail; the entire attack collapsed; the Federals had suffered heavy casualties, with the 2nd Maryland losing 44 percent of its numbers, with no real advantages won.

Over at the Pry House, McClellan was becoming increasingly impatient with his old friend; it was already past 1200 and the IX Corps still remained on the eastern bank of the Antietam. To speed things up, the general commanding dispatched his Inspector General, Colonel Delos B. Sackett, to ensure the bridge was taken. While McClellan was venting his frustrations, Burnside was becoming increasingly distraught by his commander's complaints. When Sackett arrived, the general told him, ''McClellan appears to think I am not trying my best to carry this bridge; you are the third or fourth one who has been to me this morning with similar orders.'' Burnside then ordered Cox to make another attempt to take the bridge, who entrusted Ferrero's brigade with the deadly mission. In deciding to have the 51st Pennsylvania and 51st New York lead the advance, Ferrero attempted to encourage his men, crying out, ''It is General Burnside's special request that the two 51sts lead take that bridge. Will you do it?'' From the ranks of the Pennsylvanians one soldier inquired ''Will you give us our whiskey, Colonel, if we take it.''

The subject of drink and the 51st Pennsylvania was a notorious one, but Ferrero was willing to make a promise, ''Yes, by God you shall all have as much as you want if you take that bridge. I don't mean the whole brigade, but you two regiments shall have as much as you want, if it is in the commissary or I have to send to New York to get it, and pay for it out of my private purse; that is if I live to see you through it. Will you take it?'' To this statement the troops let out a harmonious ''Yes!''

At 1230, the 670 men of the twin 51sts launched their spectacular crusade to win their whiskey. Instead of charging down the Rohrersville Road exposed to enemy fire, Ferrero's men took to the hill above the ridge and with a shout began their 300 yard charge to the bridge, some shouting, "Remember Reno!" Immediately coming under the violent blasts of deadly case shot and canister as well as the bullets from snipers, the Federals could not take the punishment. Instead of rushing the bridge, the regiments slipped to either side with the New Yorkers taking cover behind a wood fence to the left of the bridge, while the Pennsylvanians rushed behind a stone wall on the right to fire from there.

Despite their defiant stand against the Yankees, Toombs' soldiers were finding their position untenable. After firing away for three hours, their ammunition was running low, while the Federal fieldpieces across the way were taking a heavy toll, unleashing a furious storm of grapeshot and canister. The 2nd Georgia had already lost 50 percent of its men with most of the field officers of the brigade falling either dead or wounded. Commanding the regiment, Lieutenant Colonel William R. Holmes fell after being wounded several times by bullets with three more men going down after attempting to recover his body. Despite their fine cover, Rebel sharpshooters were themselves losing heavily from well placed discharges from their Federal counterparts. Worse still, the Yankees to the north and south of the Bridge had finally managed to cross the creek and were bearing down on Toombs' command.

Zouaves of the 9th New York in their desperate charge against Lee's right.

After a few hours of searching, Rodman had finally found Snavely's Ford two miles downstream, crossed the water and was coming up to assail the right flank of the Georgians. To the north, Crook's men had also managed to find a crossing, putting them on the western banks of the Antietam; they moved to the southwest to join the rest of the corps. Successfully delaying the advance of the IX Corps for three hours, Toombs began to retreat to the main Confederate line. Seeing the Rebels begin to fall back, Colonel Robert Potter of the 51st New York threw his men across the bridge followed by the Pennsylvanians. Swarming over the narrow esplanade, the ranks of the charging mass of troopers so jammed the bridge that a halt had to be called. Jumping up on the ledge of the bridge, Colonel Potter urged his men on, swearing all the while. Colonel John R. Hartranft of the 51st Pennsylvania, exhausted from the drive, called out to his troops, "Come on, boys, for I can't haloo anymore" Once across, the Federals sent a few volleys into the ranks of the remaining enemy, driving the rest of the Confederates away from the bluffs. At about 1300, Cox and Burnside finally claimed the bridge, having lost 550 troops in the costly venture.

In attempting to continue their drive across the bridge toward Sharpsburg, the Federal commanders found themselves plagued by more colossal mishaps. His men both exhausted and low on ammunition, Sturgis brought his brigade to a halt on the bluffs across the stream, so reinforcements and the ammunition trains could be brought up. This entire process was to delay any further Union advance until 1500, wasting precious hours, as the narrow bridge became jammed with the traffic of soldiers, ammunition wagons, and artillery.

To once again impress the necessity of speed upon Burnside, another of McClellan's staff officers, Colonel Thomas M. Key, arrived with a dispatch from the General Commanding with orders to get the attack going again at once. The message also included a secret mandate to relieve Burnside, turning his command over to Major General George W. Morell, if an advance wasn't launched immediately. None the less, the drive of the IX Corps wasn't to continue until two hours after the bridge was carried. During the respite, soldiers from both sides engaged in picket fire as cannons dumped shots on inviting targets. At one point, some Federals attempted to light fires to boil coffee, forgetting the resulting smoke would alert Confederate gunners to their position. All of a sudden the unfortunate Yankees came under a heavy shelling.

At this fateful moment, Lieutenant Colonel Thomas S. Bell in his excitement over the day's fight, joyfully slapped a private on the back saying, "We did it for them this time, my boy," and he was instantaneously killed by a piece of shrapnel catching him in the temple. His lifeless body fell to the side and rolled to the bank of the Antietam. While sitting on the low wall of the bridge, Colonel Ferrero had a close call when a shell exploded 15 inches away from him, tearing away at some masonry while blowing a mule to "atoms."

Meanwhile, the Confederate infantry patiently waited the Federal attack, preparing for the worst. After climbing a church steeple in Sharpsburg to get a birds eye view of the battlefield, Private Alexander Hunter of the 17th Virginia reported to his commander, Colonel Montgomery D. Corse, telling him solemnly, "We are lost Colonel; we haven't a single reserve." "Is it possible?" The colonel replied, only to be told it was a fact as Hunter had not seen a single Rebel to support the present line. Ruminating over his perilous situation, Corse "clenched his teeth like a bulldog," but he and his men stood firmly resolved to hold their position. Hunter recalled, " . . . as the news ran along the line, each man knew we had to stay there and, if needs be, die there."

Finally, at 1500, Cox gave the command to renew the offensive, with Rodman's division advancing on the left and Wilcox's division on the right supported by Sturgis' division and the Kanawha Division. Seeing the vast numbers of Yankees surging across the broken ground of ravines and hallows, D.R. Jones' men waited in battle line, taking whatever defensive ground they could find behind rises and stone and rail fences. Taking the right of Rodman's advance, Colonel Benjamin C. Christ led his Yankees, supported by Crook, up the Rohrersville Road. Before them, just in front of the town of Sharpsburg, was a plateau containing a cemetery, where a host of Rebel artillery was pounding the approaching enemy with a fantastic cannonade. Contesting Christ's advance was Colonel F.W. McMaster's command of 100 men of the 17th Georgia and Holcombe's Legion of South Carolinians supporting Jenkin's sharpshooters. The 79th New York drove the enemy back through the farm belonging to John Otto to an apple orchard, where McMaster's embattled Butternuts were joined by Garnett's and Jenkins' brigades. Finding the left under Welsh and his supports lagging behind, Christ's men paused to wait for them, suffering terrible fire from the Rebel batteries in their front. These Federals did receive some assistance from the 2nd and 10th U.S. Infantry under Captain John S. Poland of Sykes division, who drove back the extreme Confederate left under Garnett. Finally, Welsh's brigade fought its way up to the left of Christ to join the pitched struggle. A massive firefight resulted before the orchard, with the Federals bringing up artillery to shell the Rebel line before driving them off with a mighty charge. Though his command was cut in half, McMaster stubbornly continued to hold out on the field, retiring to a stone house and mill which were converted into forts. Within this strong position, the Confederates fought off the Yankees until forced to withdraw when the enemy stormed the buildings with bayonets. Federal guns were now turned upon their Rebel counterparts on the cemetery hill, blasting away until the enemy could take no more and was also forced to withdraw. The Federals were able to ascend the high ground before Sharpsburg only to have their advance halted due to lack of ammunition. Still, a important point had been gained from which to launch an attack that could effectively flank Lee's right, endangering the entire Confederate army.

At the same time, Rodman's division was closing in on the Rebels from the south with Colonel Harrison C. Fairchild's brigade on the right and Colonel Edward Harland's First Brigade taking the left. On the advance, the Federals were struck by a horrid sight: the charred bodies of wounded Rebels who had been laid on beds of straw only to be burned to death when their resting place caught fire from exploding shells or musketry.

While Fairchild's brigade was getting into position, the Yankees came under a merciless bombardment from the Southern guns before them. J.H.E. Whitney of the 9th New York remembered the enemy missiles falling on the ranks of his comrades, " . . . many of the shells striking in front of them and ricocheting over their heads before exploding; others, more unfortunately, striking and bursting in the ranks, killing and wounding half a dozen men at each discharge." A shot exploding in the ranks of the color guard of the 9th New York took three men down while a corporal standing nearby was sent tumbling head over heels down a hill. In the midst of the terrific barrage, Lieutenant Colonel Edward A. Kimball of the 9th New York could be seen chomping at the bit, eager to put his troops in motion. Finally, Rodman arrived to answer the colonel's anxieties, yelling out,

"First Brigade! Forward!"

Taking the advance, the 9th New York, a Zouave regiment, was ordered forth to storm the Wise's Rebel battery, supported by Drayton's and Kemper's men, located on a far off ridge, inaugurating one of the most spectacular infantry charges in the entire Civil War. All of a sudden, the regiment leapt up into the hot fire of canister and started off on a long and bloody crusade across the fields of Sharpsburg, scores of men falling under a tornado of fire while the survivors pressed forward chanting their war cry, "Zoo,zoo,zoo." Looking back over the trail of their advance, Whitney recalled, "As far back as they could see, the track of the regiment was strewn with the slain who dotted the earth as so many footsteps of blood to the victory they were striving for."

After finding cover in a ravine, the troops halted for a while to gain a short respite from the deadly fusillades of the enemy and to reform the already depleted ranks. Among the troops, Kimball exultantly congratulated his 9th New York, shouting out, "Bully Ninth! Bully Ninth! I'm proud of you!" Already 200 men had been left behind after falling dead or wounded in the bloody charge. Still taking some casualties from Rebel guns, many Yankees fell victim to deadly missiles as the Confederate cannoneers adjusted their aim. As David L. Martin of the 9th recalled,

The battery . . . whose shots at first went over our heads had depressed its guns so as to shave the surface of the ground. Its fire was beginning to tell. I remember looking behind and seeing an officer riding diagonally across the field—a most inviting target—instinctively bending his head down over his horse's neck, as though he was riding through the driving rain. While my eye was on him I saw, between me and him, a rolled overcoat with its straps on bound into the air and fall among the furrows. One of the enemy's grapeshot had plowed a groove in the skull of a young fellow and cut his overcoat from his shoulders. He never stirred from his position, but lay there face downward—a dreadful spectacle. A moment after, I heard a man cursing a comrade from lying on him heavily. He was cursing a dying man. As the range grew better, the firing became more rapid, the situation desperate and more exasperating to the last degree. Human nature was on the rack, and there burst from it the most vehement, terrible swearing I ever heard.

While under cover, Whitney recalled this grisly scene:

. . . behind company H, lay a man wounded in the most frightful manner. The lower portion of his jaw had been carried away, and the torn fragments that remained, together with his tongue, clotted with gore, hung down upon his breast. He sustained himself with one hand while with the other he proudly waved his fez in the air, an action that interpreted the language of his heart—"fallen not conquered."

"See that!" exclaimed Lieutenant Colonel Kimball, pointing excitedly with his sword, "Isn't that enough to make you fight?"

The men looked at each other, and the tears that then mingled, and which the hot and hissing shell could not staunch, seemed red and sympathetic with blood.

After the New Yorkers rose up to resume the charge, the Rebels continued to lay down a most devastating fire as David Martin recalled, "In a second the air was full of the hiss of bullets and the hurtle of grapeshot. The mental strain was so great that I saw a singular effect mentioned, I think, in the life of Goethe on a similar occasion-the whole landscape turned slightly red." Finally as they closed on the ranks of Drayton's and Kemper's men, taking cover behind a stone wall, orders were given to approach within "whispering distance" of the Rebels and then to give them "a hot fire of 'minie'" followed by a charge with bayonets.

Awaiting the Federals, Private Hunter of the 14th Virginia and his comrades placed their rifles on the lower rail of the post and rail fence before them, gritting their teeth while their hearts pounded, waiting for the enemy charge to come. Recalling the scene, Hunter wrote,

Colonel Corse gave but one order- "Don't fire, men until I give the word." As we lay there with our eyes ranging along the musket barrels, our fingers on the triggers, we saw the gilt eagles of the flagpoles emerge above the top of the hill, followed by the flags drooping on the staffs, then the tops of the blue caps appeared, and next a line of the fiercest eyes ever looked upon. The shouts of their officers were heard, urging their men forward. Less brave, less seasoned troops would have faltered before the array of deadly tubes leveled at them, and at the recumbent line, silent, motionless and terrible, but if there was any giving away we did not see it.

Approaching to within 50 yards of the Confederate line, the wall literally bristling with musketry, the Federals held their fire until one Confederate poked his head up above cover, providing too inviting a target for the Yankees to pass up. All of a sudden the gaudy lines of the Zouaves let loose a torrential blaze of gunshots, sending thirteen bullets alone into the brain of that unfortunate Southerner whose curiosity had gotten the better of him. The rifles of the 9th New York continued to vomit forth such burning fire that, in Whitney's words,

"there was scarcely a hole in the wall that was not pierced, and a finger could not be raised above it without fear of amputation." Rushing towards the wall, the color bearer of the New York regiment fell to the ground from an enemy shot with the banner going onto another carrier who was shot down as well. After yet another flag bearer was shot down, a youth took up the standard, only to have his body riddled with bullets. In the advance a total of eight men had held the colors only to fall dead or wounded. With the rest of the brigade up, the Yankees led a mighty charge, storming the Confederate position, forcing the outnumbered Confederates to flee towards Sharpsburg. Confederate John Dooley of the 1st Virginia wrote of his retreat:

Oh, how I ran! or tried to run through the high corn for my heavy belt and cartridge box and musket kept me to half my speed. I was afraid of being struck in the back, and I frequently turned half around in running, so as to avoid if possible so disgraceful a wound.

The highwater mark of the drive by Kimball's men of the 9th New York. In the distance is the town of Sharpsburg.

At this moment, it again appeared that the entire Confederate army was doomed: most of Jones' division was broken and already Sharpsburg was filled with stragglers, men who had had enough of battle and were trying to seek some safety in the homes of the town. As Federal shells landed in the vicinity, the troops panicked and sought whatever cover available to shield themselves from the deadly cannonade. Attempting to organize some force to block the Yankees, Lee rode amongst this discouraged mass of Butternuts encouraging them to take up their arms and return to the fight. While Hunter passed some time with his Yankee captors in the rear ranks, one Federal pointed to the vicinity of the battle to say, "It's all up with you, Johnnie; look there." Hunter wrote of the mighty contest before him, "Long lines of blue were coming like the surging billows of the ocean. The Bluecoats were wild with excitement, and their measured hurrah, so different from our piercing yell, rose above the thunder of their batteries beyond the bridge. I thought the guard was right, that it was all up with us, and the whole army would be captured." All that now stood in the way of Burnside and victory was Robert Toombs tired and depleted brigade, replenished with ammunition, standing defiantly in the face of the advance of Harland's brigade on the far left of the Union attack. Due to a mishap, the only regiment to get word to move against the Confederates was the 8th New Hampshire, taking a lead far in advance of

the rest of the brigade.

While the Army of Northern Virginia seemed to be entering its darkest hour, a column of troops was seen moving up from the south. Lee directed Lieutenant John Ramsay to look off in the distance to discover whose troops they might be; he replied they were flying Confederate banners. Lee looked on, knowing the day would be saved, saying confidently, "It is A.P. Hill's men from Harper's Ferry." Indeed it was; the valiant Powell Hill had driven his men at a furious pace, covering some seventeen miles in the remarkable time of eight hours. Riding among his 3,300 troops and urging them on was the General himself, sometimes unmercifully dealing blows with the flat of his sword to speed stragglers on their way. When Hill arrived on the field, he realized the importance of getting his troops into battle to stem the Yankee tide. Instead of attempting to organize an attack, he threw his brigades piecemeal against the oncoming hordes of Yankees.

Unconscious of the new threat coming in from the south, the 8th Connecticut advanced against a newly arrived a battery of Captain D.G. McIntosh of the Pee Dee artillery located in a cornfield. J.L Napier of the battery recalled that the enemy was as thick as "Pharoah's locusts" and about their approach under the battery's fire, "The guns began firing double charges of canister; there was a large U.S. flag just in front of the left gun at which our fire was directed. It was shot down three times when the enemy stopped and laid down. The flag was stuck apparently in the ground and remained flying for a few moments when it was shot down again and we saw it no more." Still, the Connecticut regiment pressed forward, closing in on the battery until the gunners were forced to flee for their lives. Yet before they abandoned their guns, McIntosh's men dealt harshly with the Federals pouring double shotted canister into their ranks, and making the enemy pay harshly for its victory. The next day, 48 Bluecoats were found in a heap where the cannons had discharged their final deadly shots. Despite their initial enthusiasm over their victory, these Yankees of the Nutmeg State were shocked to learn they were without supports and enemy

Almost but not quite. Federals of the IX Corps almost succeeded in breaking Lee's line when they reached the Lutheran Church in Sharpsburg. Their exultation would have been short lived as A.P. Hill's Light Division arrived to drive them back.

Slaughter of the 7th Maine

There was one more attack made by the Federals near the Sunken Road on 17 September; an ill advised charge which did nothing, but add to the legion of dead and wounded that was already lying on the field from the fight earlier in the day. In response to a battery commander's complaints of Confederate snipers on the Piper Farm near the Hagerstown Road, Colonel William H. Irwin rode to Major Thomas W. Hyde of the 7th Maine, and ordered, "Major Hyde, take your regiment and drive the enemy away from those trees and buildings." Seeing his commander shamefully inebriated, Hyde declared, "Colonel, I have seen a large force of rebels go in there, I should think two brigades." "Are you afraid to go, sir?" chided Irwin who repeated the command. Acquiescing, Hyde said, "Give the order so the regiment can hear it and we are ready, sir." After Irwin did so, the 7th Maine prepared to launch its attack sometime around 1700.

Before moving off, Hyde had the two young boys carrying the marking guidons sent to the rear; the lads pretended to do so, but returned for the advance. In the attack one would fall

dead from a bullet while the other lost his arm. As the Federals approached the enemy lines, they passed over the Sunken Road, still packed with the dead, dying and wounded. Stopping in the cornfield to redress their lines, the Yankees from Maine surged forth towards the Hagerstown Road. Some regiments of Brigadier General W.T.H. Brooks' Brigade wanted to join the charge, but their commander responded, "You will never see that regiment again." Trying to support these troops, a battery behind them tried to shoot over the heads of the Maine men in the advancing line but dropped a shot into their ranks which knocked out four men. Moving faster now, the Federals came under fire from a Rebel line behind a stonewall along the Hagerstown Road. Driving the Rebels through the Piper Farm, Hyde could see his command was outnumbered by the Southerners, but pressed on none-the-less. At a rail fence, as a sergeant was attempted to pull down an opening for the major's horse, an enemy shell caught his haversack, throwing hardtack into the air and bringing a moment of humor to the increasingly grim situation.

Pressing against the Confederates, the Maine boys found themselves trapped in a horrendous pocket of fire. When a shot pierce the arm of the flag bearer, Corporal Harry Campbell, the dismounted Hyde called out to him, "Take the other hand, Harry." After hearing Campbell give another cry, the major turned to take up the colors, only to find himself ahead of his regiment which was rapidly retreating. Seeing the Rebels approaching close enough to read the word "Manassas" on one of their battle flags, the officer fled. Attempting to get away, Hyde was almost surrounded when a cry went up from his men, "Rally, boys, to save the Major." With the Yankees surging forth once more to save their commander, the Rebels were forced back allowing Hyde to take his men back to Union ranks. As the Maine troops returned, their comrades raised hats while shouting mighty cheers. Hyde was to recall later, "When we knew our efforts were resultant from no plans or design at headquarters, but were from an inspiration of John Barleycorn in our commander alone, I wished I had been old enough or distinguished enough to disobey orders."

troops were bearing down on them.

Though the advance of Hill's troops from the south had been detected and signalmen had apparently flagged the news to Burnside's headquarters, nothing was done to effectively meet the attack allowing the Confederate force to bear down on the unknowing Federal left. Informed of the Rebel attack from his own sources, Rodman was on his way to warn Fairchild when he was struck down and killed by a Rebel bullet.

Hill's initial target would be Harland's Brigade. Coming under fire from Archer's and Toombs' men in the front and left the 8th Connecticut fell into retreat. The rookie 4th Rhode Island, only in the ranks for three weeks and the 16th Connecticut regiments found themselves in a fire fight in a cornfield with veteran Rebels of Gregg's brigade. Their inexperience was displayed markedly as the green Yankees stumbled around ineffectively, confused even fur-

ther by the Southerner's Federal blue uniforms they had captured at Harper's Ferry. During the fight, Gregg fell from his horse apparently wounded by a Yankee shell. As he was being carried from the field on a stretcher, one of his bearers exclaimed, General, you aren't wounded, you are only bruised." Realizing the truth of the statement, Gregg leapt off the stretcher and returned to the fight.

Believing a charge might be in order, Colonel William H. P. Steere of the 4th Rhode Island petitioned the commander of the 16th Connecticut to support an advance by his regiment. A messenger returned with a refusal saying, "We must depend on ourselves." Before enemy supports could arrive to stem the tide, Gregg managed to touch the flank of the Yankee brigade, sending it sprawling back to the bridge on the double quick. With his left crumbling, Cox had his entire command withdraw. Attempting to make a stand at a stone wall near the Otto cornfield, Ewing's Ohioans made the mistake of confusing the enemy approaching them to be Federals in Yankee blue. A few volleys from Gregg's, Archer's and Pender's brigades shattered the charade sending the Northern brigade fleeing off to join the rest of the Federals heading towards the bridge.

Enjoying a congenial smoke with his captors, Hunter took in a view of the Confederate onslaught and the subsequent Federal retreat:

> The air was filled with bursting shells, as if a dozen batteries had opened at once from the direction of Sharpsburg, and while we stood gazing we saw emerging from a cornfield a long line of gray, musket barrels scintillating in the rays of the declining sun and the Southern battle flags gleaming redly against the dark background. . . . From the long line of gray a purplish mist broke, pierced by a bright gleam here and there, and the noise of the volley sounded like the whir of machinery. . . . The triumphant advance, the jubilant shouts, the stirring beat of the drums, the mad, eager rush of the forces in blue were stayed, and back they came without order or formation, and we joined the hurrying throng, not stopping until we reached the valley near the bridge.

With Burnside's Federals loosing the gains which had cost them so much in both time and blood, the battle against the Confederate right ended by mutual consent. The failed drive towards Sharpsburg had cost the Yankees 2350 men in killed and wounded, while the Confederates lost some 1000 men, with Hill only suffering scant loss of 63 men. Some of the troops of the IX Corps, especially those who had fought on the right with Wilcox, felt cheated of victory, being called back when victory had been so close. Bitterly, Whitney wrote of the retreat, "Triumph was to be limited to results scarcely more gratifying than those of defeat. Those who had lost their limbs and spilled their blood to gain success must lie upon the field still bleeding, hungry, thirsty, and dying by hundreds, because their General was too cowardly to close with the enemy and save them from a terrible fate." Indeed had Burnside or Cox been more aggressive, they might have been able to drive the exhausted Confederate line, still outnumbering the Confederates on the right by at least two to one even after he was reinforced by Hill. Additional reinforcements lay near the Middle Bridge to support a possible attack in the form of the V Corps. However, on September 17th, neither Burnside, Porter, nor McClellan were about to think in terms of pressing forward to victory, choosing rather to halt and make the best of the small gains they had made.

By 1630, the battle drew to a conclusion for Wednesday, 17 September 1862. All told, the Army of the Potomac had lost 2,108 men dead, 9,540 wounded and 753 missing, a total of 12,401 casualties, a quarter of the strength of the entire army. On the other side, Lee had lost 1,546 dead, 7752 wounded, and 1018 missing, an aggregate loss of 10,318 men fallen, leaving 31% of the men as casualties. Altogether, 22,719 Americans fell on the fields of Sharpsburg on that single September day, a record that has not been exceeded by any of this nations battles before or since.

On both sides those who could sought what rest possible in the midst of the dead and wounded. Historian of Kershaw's brigade recalled:

> It may be easily imagined that both armies were glad enough to fall upon the ground and rest after such a day of blood and carnage, with the smoke, dust, and weltering heat of the day. Before the sound of the last gun had died away in the distance one hundred thousand men were stretched upon the ground fast asleep, while near a third of that number were sleeping their last sleep or suffering the effects of fearful wounds.

A Yankee concurred with such sentiments writing, "The men were physically exhausted, hungry and but a few had food, thirsty and without water, sad at heart-for comrades who had been killed or wounded . . . " Two Federal soldiers headed for a inviting pile of straw to rest upon. When told there was a dead body lying beneath it, the Federals merely collapsed on the bed, using the body of the corpse as a pillow. The soldiers who could seek a pleasant rest were the lucky ones as multitudes of others lay upon the field awaiting assistance which in some cases would not arrive in time.

Miserable and horrifying scene on the Antietam battlefield on the night of 17 September 1862.

CHAPTER X

LEE RETREATS
18 September - November, 1862

The battle of 17 September had ended and night cloaked the blood soaked Maryland countryside, the darkness broken by the multitudes of men lying on the field, their wounds still unbound, their blood seeping out upon the farmland. Of the night, Lieutenant Colonel Francis W. Palfrey of the 20th Massachusetts had this to say, "The blessed night came, and brought with it sleep and forgetfulness and refreshment to many; but the murmur of the night wind, breathing over fields of wheat and clover, was mingled with the groans of countless sufferers of both armies. Who can tell, who can even imagine, the horrors of such a night, while the unconscious stars shone above, and the unconscious river went rippling by?"

Despite the massive carnage of the day's hideously sanguinary battle, both sides prepared for a possible continuance of the further effusion of blood. On the morrow, McClellan would seemingly hold all the cards; he still overwhelmed the Confederate army in manpower. Better still, despite numerous setbacks on the field of battle, the Union would maintain the initiative as the enemy was in no condition to make an attack. Claiming such advantages, McClellan merely had to take up the fight once more and drive the Army of Northern Virginia into the Potomac. Faced with such odds, one would likewise suspect that Lee would be preparing to withdraw his army to safety in Virginia, for weak ranks could hardly weather another day of full battle. Despite all appearances, neither McClellan nor Lee had decided to act within the limits of reason.

At Federal Headquarters, the Young Napoleon had already decided to plan with extreme caution. He was satisfied with the very limited

gains his army had made on the field: in the north the ground from the Antietam to the Hagerstown Turnpike and the Rohrbach Bridge in the south. While his possession over this territory was meaningless except as a springboard to launch another attack, McClellan decided against risking anything at all to achieve total victory, postponing the renewal of the offensive until reinforcements arrived. The next day, he would give orders for his troops to hold in their positions, but not to attack. Antietam veteran and historian Francis Palfrey described the general's decision thus, "General McClellan decided not to renew the attack on the 18th. It is hardly worthwhile to state his reasons. . . . The fault was in the man. There was force enough at his command either day, had he seen fit to use it." In refusing to take up the initiative, McClellan essentially ignored the fact that he had most

Confederates slain before the Dunker Church.

Camp followers and soldiers prowling the battle-field the night after the fight in search of treasure and supplies.

Former members of Jackson's foot cavalry, mutilated by the fierce fire in and around the Hagerstown Road, "patiently" await burial.

Hospitals at Antietam

Throughout the abysmal conflict, barns, houses, and all other available buildings were converted into hospitals as thousands of wounded men were brought in from the lines to be attended by surgeons. Those who could be taken care of frequently faced amputation as the only means to care for their wounds.

The scene of the field hospital must have been a horror to behold. Active throughout the day, doctors were literally covered in blood as they went about their gruesome tasks. Limbs cut from patients were thrown into large piles or stacked like cordwood. Throughout the hospitals men could be heard wailing miserably over their fate and from their pain. Parched with thirst, they cried for water and those fortunate enough to receive a canteen quickly guzzled its contents. Others, thinking of loved ones at home, cried out. "Why was this war begun? Lord have mercy on my dear family. Must I die and never see them again?"

There were many singular experiences forever lingered in minds of the soldiers that witnessed them. Vauntier of the 88th Pennsylvania recalled seeing comrade Lorenzo Wilson arrive in a field hospital with his leg almost entirely shot off except for a thin layer of skin holding it together. When asked about his condition he replied, "Boys I've got it." In a Confederate hospital, a Southern gunner was brought in with a terrible leg wound. Though the attending surgeon wanted to amputate the limb, the cannoneer just pointed at a pistol at his side, saying defiantly, "You see that? It will not be taken off while I can pull a trigger." A rookie lieutenant of the 35th Massachusetts, was treated for his wounds and when he learned he was to recover, exclaimed, "Oh isn't this rich! Only

a month away from home and back there again with wounds; got in a big battle, and victory; and all the girls running after me, and all the fellows envious." Captain James A. Martin, who had fled from the battlefield at Second Manassas, said after losing his leg at Antietam, "Now when I get back to Baltimore, if anybody says I was a coward, I can tell them that if they were willing to go where I was and stay as long as I did, they may call me a coward...." Alas he would not get the chance, dying a month later in Frederick. Brought off the field by their enemy, some Confederates invariably found themselves in Union field hospitals. After one member of the 14th Indiana had his leg removed, he was placed near a Rebel who was complaining the Yankee doctors were ignoring the Southern wounded. The Hoosier morbidly recalled that when the soldier was placed on the amputating table "he was treated as the others when the time came." A member of the 9th Massachusetts recalled this scene which occurred shortly after the battle:

A boy, about fourteen years old was one day undergoing the process of amputation. He lay upon the stage, dressed in his rebel uniform, his face pale, and his large blue eyes gazing wonderingly around. His injured leg was stretched before the surgeons, who were carefully feeling it about the wound—a black break the size of a nickel cent. A sign from one of the doctors, and the instruments were brought and placed upon a large box that once contained army clothes, but now was partly filled with bandages besmeared with blood. The surgeon selected one of the instruments; a cloth was held before the nostrils of the white-faced boy; the surgeon began his work. The skin of the white leg was cut; in a little while the bone was off, the skin laid over, the bandages applied, and the whole bound carefully up. "It is finished," said the doctor, as he wiped the blood off from his hands. He said truly; the work was finished. The boy was dead.

of two whole Federal corps, the V and VI, that had yet to see a full taste of combat on the field before Sharpsburg. Furthermore, 6,000 men of Couch's division were rejoining the army; while another 6,600 more troops were on the way up from Frederick after being dispatched from Washington three days earlier. Added with the remains of the four corps that had taken up the fight on the 17th, McClellan could count on over 60,000 men to take up the battle should he desire to do so: a powerful legion by any standards. Unfortunately, the general could not bring himself to use the forces at his command; he believed his army to be fought out, in need of both reinforcements and supplies.

On the opposite side of the field, Lee was gathering his field officers to get an overview of the situation that faced him and his men. Upon receiving each commander, he asked, "General, how is it on your part of the line?" Harvey Hill replied his troops had barely held and would not be able to do much against the overwhelming numbers of the Federals on the next day. When Stonewall was asked about the condition of his troops, he said that his losses had been excessive with many of his field officers being shot down. Approached for his report, Hood plainly stated that he had no division. Upon hearing this, Lee shouted excitedly, "Great God, General Hood, where is the splendid division you had this morning?" The Kentuckian replied, "They are lying on the field where you sent them, sir; but few have straggled. My division has been almost wiped out." Longstreet arrived at the meeting late, stopping in Sharpsburg to help a family put out a fire in their burning house. Fearing Old Pete might have been wounded, Lee was relieved to see him, excitedly placing his hands on the general's shoulders, exclaiming in hearty relief, "Here is my old war horse at last." When asked how his

Dead of the Sunken Road. Thomas Livermore wrote that during the battle,"In this road lay so many Rebels that they formed a line which one may have walked upon as far as I could see...."

troops were holding up, Longstreet replied that his men had suffered severely and he only had enough strength to throw up a picket line. Most of the officers of the Army of Northern Virginia were of the opinion that the command could take no more punishment and would have to be withdrawn across the Potomac. On this advice Lee merely turned to his commanders and delivered a shocking address, "Gentlemen, we will not cross the Potomac to-night. You will go to your respective commands, strengthen your lines, send two officers from each brigade toward the ford to collect your stragglers, and get them up. Many others have already come up. I have had the proper steps taken to collect all the men who are in the rear. If McClellan wants to fight in the morning, I will give him battle again." With the stragglers collected, the Army of Northern Virginia could only boast some 28,000 men on the field. Out of pride and perhaps a little contempt for his enemy, despite suffering 13,000 casualties with no reserve available, Lee would wait for McClellan to renew the battle.

When the sun rose on Thursday 18 September, except for a smattering of picket fire, neither side made a move. It was as though both

Bodies of D.H. Hill's men lie amongst the rails which composed the breastworks before the position they sought to defend. Unfortunately for these unfortunate fellows, it did not provide them with enough protection.

sides made an agreement, as one Texan said, "I'll let you alone if you let me alone." Between both stationary armies lay the somber evidence of the earlier day's battle. In the various accounts of the Battle of Antietam, the terrible visage of the aftermath of this nation's bloodiest day seems to have dominated soldiers' views of the fight at Sharpsburg. Writing in regimental histories and reminiscences, soldiers recalled the horror they saw. One of Franklin's Yankees wrote,

> The scene on the battle-field was past description. The mangled forms of our own comrades lay stretched upon the ground, side by side with those of the rebels. On almost every rod of ground over one hundred acres, the dead and wounded, some clad in the Union blue and some in confederate gray, were lying. A ghastly sight, presenting all the horrible features of death which are to be seen on such a field. At one point in our own front, for more than half a mile, the rebels lay so thickly as almost to touch one another. On the field where Hooker's men had won and lost the field, the dead and dying were scattered thickly amongst the broken cornstalks, their eyes protruding and their faces blackened by the sun. Wherever the lines of battle had surged too and fro, these vestiges of the terrible work were left. In the edge of the (West) wood, where the rebels had made a stand against Hooker's advancing divisions, the bodies lay in perfect line, as though they had fallen while on dress parade. Further to the left there was a narrow road, not more than fifteen feet wide, with fences on either side. Here a regiment of rebels was posted; when our batteries getting an enfilading fire upon them, and the infantry at the same time opening a murderous fire, the regiment was literally destroyed; not more than twenty of their number escaping. Their bodies filled the narrow road. Some were shot while attempting to get over the fence; and their remains hung on the boards. A more fearful picture than we saw here, could not be conceived.

Frederick L. Hitchcock of the 132nd Pennsylvania recorded,

> The lines of battle of both armies were not only marked by the presence of the dead, but by a vast variety of army equipage, such as blankets, canteens, haversacks, guns, gun-slings, bayonets, ramrods, some whole, others broken,-verily a besom of destruction had done its work faithfully here. Dead horses were everywhere here, and the stench from them and the human dead was horrible. "Uncle" Billy Sherman has said, "War is hell!" yet this definition, with all that imagination can picture, fails to reveal all its bloody horrors.
>
> The positions of some of the dead were very striking. One poor fellow lay face down on a partially fallen stone wall, with one arm and foot extended, as if in the act of crawling over. His position attracted our attention, and we found his body literally riddled with bullets-there must have been hundreds-and most of them shot into him after he was dead, for they showed no marks of blood. Probably the poor fellow had been wounded in trying to reach shelter behind that wall, was spotted in the act by our men, and killed right there, and became thereafter a target for every new man that saw him. Another man lay, still clasping his musket, which he was evidently in the act of loading when a bullet pierced his heart, literally flooding his gun with his life's blood, a ghastly testimonial to his heroic sacrifice.

The Miller cornfield, that had played host to continuous charge after charge, countercharge after countercharge, was now a grotesque charnel house containing the vast numbers of men who had fallen there. A gunner of the 1st Rhode Island wrote of the scene there:

A group of Confederate wounded on the field after the battle. Crude tents, with muskets used as tent poles, provide some protection from the elements.

Drawings such as this one, as well as photographs, brought the grim reality of the cost of Civil War back to the home front.

Citizens come to view the grim harvest of the war effort as vultures descend to feed on bodies.

The dead were found in all imaginable positions and often horribly mangled. One Confederate had been killed while climbing over a fence, his body remaining in such a position that it might have readily have been taken for that of a live man; another was struck while tearing a cartridge, the charge still remaining between his stiffened fingers; the head of another was taken off by a cannon ball; while a manly-looking Union soldier apparently had no wound anywhere, but closer inspection showed that a ball had entered one ear, coming out of the other. It was simply horrible to look upon these heaps and windrows of festering bodies that once contained the spirits of the best soldiers of the two armies. The cornfield near which the 88th (Pennsylvania) stood was a veritable field of blood, being almost covered with gore, shreds of hair, bones, and brains . . . the men soon sickened at these repulsive sights, few going more than once over the field.

The historian of the 60th New York wrote of the forms the dead after being struck by rigormortus,

I noticed one rebel with five shots through his head. He was kneeling on one knee, his gun lying on his left hand as though he had been in the act of taking aim. When I saw him he had probably been dead some 12 hours, but other dead lay against him so he had not fallen from the position he was in when shot. Others were in a sitting posture; some were lying on their side, as if asleep; some where lying on their backs, with their arms outstretched, and fingers spread, as if they were clutching or keeping off a foe. Where the artillery had swept them with grape and canister, their line of battle could be traced by the dead bodies that lay on it-sometimes as far as the eye could see.

Lying out in the heat of the day, the bodies became swollen, bloated and turned sickeningly black. A Federal on the field of battle said of the spectacle, "Nearly all (the dead) lay with their faces up and eyes wide open presenting a spectacle to make one shudder. . . . Their limbs and bodies were so enlarged that their clothing seemed ready to burst." Throughout the previous night and even during the day, individuals with little moral qualms scoured the dead for trophies and booty. Many bodies could be seen with their shoes removed and their pockets turned inside out, robbed of items they would no longer have a use for. One Yankee brought in a piece of paper found on the body of a Confederate. It contained the tracing of the hand of an infant, a child born while the new father was away at war. Below the tracing were the words from his wife, "If you want to kiss the baby you must kiss this hand." For some of the rookie troops, the fields of Sharpsburg presented their first introduction to the grim realities of war, as Alfred S. Roe of the 10th Massachusetts noted: " . . . what an introduction to the embryo soldier that terrible field of Antietam must have been! Had he cherished any delusive fancy as to the romance of the war, the rapidly swelling corpses of lately active thinking men must have reduced him to the hard pan with sickening haste."

As Thursday passed away, enemy troops sniped at one another, setting up crude breastworks of dead bodies for protection. In front of the Federal lines near the Sunken Road, Yankees were forced to listen to the never end-ing cries of the dead and wounded of both sides before them. Determined to assist the wounded, one Federal attempted to ease the suffering of one of the enemy's fallen, braving the picket fire to crawl out between the lines to give a Southerner a drink of water. In other parts of the field, an informal truce existed for troops to collect bodies, bury the wounded, and even discuss recent events with the enemy. While one Federal was scouring the field for wounded friends needing assistance, he chanced upon a lieutenant from the Louisiana Tigers, searching the field for his dead brother. With tears in his eyes, the Southerner pointed to the bodies of his deceased comrades to say, "Most of my men lie there." After carrying on a short conversation, both men parted company, expressing the hope they would not be forced to meet on the battlefield the next day.

Fortunately for the troops of both sides there would be no renewal of the fight on the 19th either. Realizing McClellan reinforced would be almost invincible, Lee finally decided to pull his troops across the Potomac on the night of the 18th, crossing at the Boteler's Ford and moving on to Martinsburg, Virginia in the Shenadoah Valley. During the movement, a band struck up the tune of "Maryland, My Maryland" only to meet the protests and catcalls of their comrades, openly displaying their bitterness over their adventures and treatment in the Free State. While the survivors of the 1st Texas passed by the 6th North Carolina, a soldier of the Lone Star State called out good naturedly "Hallou, fellers! Have you a good supply of tar on your heels this morning?" Evidently the North Carolinians

were not in the mood for such jokes. "Yes," came a sour reply, "and it's a real pity you'uns didn't come over and borrow a little the other day; it mout have saved that flag o' your'n." In the early morning hours of the 19th, Walker reported to Lee that only a few ambulances and a battery lay upon the Maryland side of the Potomac, the general commanding let out a great sigh of relief: "Thank God!" Undaunted by the setbacks of his campaign in the Maryland, Lee was still pondering the possibility of returning to the offensive by crossing back over the Potomac at Williamsport up to the west. However, he had only to look at his army to see that the almost continuous fighting and marching since Cedar Mountain had completely worn his men out.

With his enemy on the run, McClellan took his time in launching a pursuit. In character, he claimed his army to be too worn out and his supplies too depleted to make an advance. Thus, most of his troops sat idle while others went about burying the dead and collecting the wounded still on the field.

While part of the army remained at Sharpsburg to attend to the remnants of the battle on the 19th, Fitz John-Porter made a weak attempt at a crossing of the Potomac, sending the 1st U.S. Sharpshooters supported by the 4th Michigan into Virginia. Encountering fire from two Confederate brigades and part of Pendleton's Reserve Artillery, the Federals forced the Con-

Though enemies in battle, Confederates and Federals agree to a truce to collect wounded comrades and bury the dead.

federates back and took four of their guns as trophies. After the fight, Porter recalled his force that night preparing for a stronger attack the next day. Upon seeing the captured guns, Griffin, whose battery had been cut up at the first great battle of the war, exclaimed, "I've recaptured one of my old guns that was lost at Bull Run." Reporting back to Lee, Pendleton made out the situation to be worse than it actually was, claiming he had lost all the guns of the Reserve Artillery to the enemy. Far worse than this information was the possibility that the Federals might be attempting to force a crossing to catch up with the ragged Army of Northern Virginia while it was on the retreat and most vulnerable to attack. To meet this threat, Lee dispatched A.P. Hill with his Light Division to force the Federals back into Maryland. The next morning the Confederates slammed into three Federal brigades sent across the river by Porter. Caldwell said of the picturesque Confederate advance:

> Our whole first line of three brigades moved as one man, as steadily, coolly, deliberately as if on the drill ground. . . . What a spectacle it must have been to the enemy! . . . the same men who had marched nearly five hundred miles in Virginia and Maryland, in rags, on insufficient food, and many of them without a shoe to their feet; the same men, who had, but the day before, been withdrawn before the treble number of Federals; these same men turned upon them, unconfused by moral appearances, unterrified by the formidable array of artillery and infantry, and sternly moved through thunder and slaughter to the last death-clinch!

As the increasingly hard pressed Yankees fell back, the 118th Pennsylvania was cut apart when it didn't receive the orders to retreat after its commander had fallen. Finding themselves alone against an enemy division and armed with defective Belgian muskets, the only thing the Pennsylvanians could do was to flee in panic. Wading across the ford, they made inviting targets for Confederate soldiers who poured a deadly fire into the retreating mass. Porter's artillery on the Maryland side of the Potomac attempted to cover the retreat, blasting away at the opposite bank. Caldwell said of the cannonade, "The roar of the pieces, and howl and explosion of the shells, was awful. Sometimes a shell burst right in the ranks tearing and mangling all around it." One Rebel was literally thrown into the air by one mighty explosion. This little adventure on the part of Porter had cost his corps 363 men killed, wounded, and missing. Of these, 269 were from the 118th Pennsylvania. The Federals had found the Reb-

els still maintained a formidable bite. After learning their lesson, they would not cross the Potomac in force for some time.

As the final days of September passed McClellan still refused to budge from Antietam, as he gathered supplies and reinforcements to strengthen his army before engaging in any attempt to return to Virginia to engage Lee. His hesitancy endeared him to no one in the Federal capital with Lincoln and Halleck both eagerly pressing him to move quickly and return to the offensive. On 1 October, Lincoln himself paid a visit to the general in an attempt to get the Army of the Potomac to budge. While he thought he had won assurances from Little Mac to move sometime soon, the army remained on the Maryland side of the Potomac. Almost a week after Lincoln's visit, Halleck sent a dispatch to McClellan, ordering him to take to the offensive, while promising 30,000 reinforcements to ease the general's crippling fears that he could do nothing substantial while outnumbered by the enemy. Still, as in the Peninsula, the general called for more supplies, more troops and wasted more time.

McClellan's failure to do much of anything allowed Lee to bring his army back up to strength, taking in most of the stragglers he had lost going into Maryland, as well as new recruits. By October 10th, his army was rejuvenated to a total strength of over 64,000 men. The inactivity of Lee's opponent allowed Stuart to launch one of his famous raids, crossing over the Potomac into Maryland and Pennsylvania, causing hundreds of thousands of dollars in property damage and completely evading all attempts to capture him.

Lincoln's growing impatience slowly worked its way into his dispatches to the stalling McClellan. When the general complained the horses of his cavalry were fatigued, the president sent this biting rebuke, "Will you pardon me for asking what the horses of your army have done since the battle of Antietam that fatigues anything."

Lincoln was hardly amused by Stuart's costly and embarrassing theatrics or McClellan's failure to even appear active; increasingly he came to the conclusion that if the Union was going to win the war, McClellan would have to go. Finally, over a full month after the battle, McClellan declared his intention to return to Virginia on 26 October; though he actually put his troops on the move a week later. Giving the general one last chance to redeem himself, the President would remove the Young Napoleon from his position if he allowed Lee to solidly plant itself between the Army of the Potomac and the Confederate capital. Unfortunately, McClellan's stalled offensive allowed Lee to dispatch Longstreet to Culpeper to impede the Federal advance. Enough was enough. On November 5th, an emissary was sent to the Army of the Potomac to dismiss the general commanding and turn the reins of control over to Burnside. To leaders in Washington this move contained some risk. McClellan might refuse to step down, causing a major crisis; there was no certainty as to what the army might receive the action. While visiting the general, Lincoln had actually called the Army of the Potomac "McClellan's bodyguard." Further, Lincoln's choice to head the army, Burnside, had already rejected the offer to command the army twice before and might do so again. Fortunately for the Republic, the transition went smoothly, Burnside, perhaps still smarting from his treatment by his old friend during Antietam, accepted the position. Thus ended the great struggle that was the Antietam Campaign.

While final confrontation between Lee and McClellan at Antietam was effectively a draw, both sides had reasons to claim victory. While the final culmination of the campaign was not the triumph the Confederacy needed to win the war, Southerners had some reason to be satis-

Relieved from command, McClellan turns over the Army of the Potomac to his old friend Ambrose Burnside.

fied with the outcome. Militarily, the campaign had been waged with Lee's customary masterful skill; the battle of Manassas demonstrated his own genius as well as that of his subordinates. The greatest success of September of 1862 came with the entire capture of the Federal garrison of Harper's Ferry with only a slight loss of life. No doubt, Lee might have accomplished a great deal more had not a copy of Special Orders 191 been found. Once he found out, McClellan was on the move, Lee moved with the necessary speed to save his army from destruction. Assisted by Harvey Hill's stalwart defense at Turner's Gap, and Jackson's and A.P. Hill's speed, as well as Federal sluggishness, he managed to have enough of his army up on the field for the fight near the banks of the Antietam. In supervising the battle, Lee and his lieutenants once again demonstrated their outstanding brilliance, shifting troops where needed to blunt the thrusts of his adversary. In the cases where they didn't have organized reinforcement s available, lines were scraped up and thrown into the fray. Though hard pressed throughout the battle, the generals and men had refuse to quit and retreat. However, they had reached the limits of their endurance and without reinforcements they could do no more but retreat.

In falling back to Virginia, Lee lost the influence his movements might have had if a victory had been won on 17 September. Though supposedly loyal to the South, Maryland had not arisen to join the Confederate cause or even provide Lee with much in the way of manpower and supplies. Worst still, the campaign did little

to weaken the resolve of the war effort of the North. Perhaps the most important result the battle was to have for the South was to force the political powers in Great Britain to give the possibility of Confederate recognition second thoughts. After learning of the outcome of Antietam, Prime Minister Palmerston wrote to Russell about recognition, telling him, "the whole matter is full of difficulty, and can only be cleared up by some more decided events between the contending armies." Thus, despite victoriously repulsing the thrusts of a numerically superior enemy with admirable skill, Lee and the Confederacy lost the Antietam Campaign when it returned to Virginia.

Despite the inconclusiveness of the battle of Antietam, McClellan perceived the campaign and battle as a great victory won through his own skill, the bravery of his men and the grace of God. Indeed, he had some reason to be jubilant. Pulling the army together after months of disappointing and humiliating defeats, McClellan had restored the army, taking it to the field to do battle with Lee and managing to force him back into Virginia. While the general could be content with that, he had betrayed his men and himself by failing to take advantage of the tremendous opportunities given to him. After dismal Peninsular Campaign, he was granted a gift which few military leaders ever attain after great defeats. a second chance. Taking the field against Lee in Maryland, his fortunes were increased when fate bestowed upon him Special Orders 191. Despite such incredible luck, the general squandered all the breaks given to him. In failing to get his troops on the road the evening of the 13th immediately after receiving the orders, in failing to attack on the 15th and the 16th, he practically gave away all the advantages the orders had given him. Still, there were many chances for Little Mac to redeem himself. Despite his sloppy coordination of the battle, had he committed the full strength of his army, using Franklin and Porter on Wednesday the 17th or the following day, he might have been able to bring the battle to a decisive conclusion. However, the faults plaguing the commander, his fear of the enemy strength and the inability of bring himself to commit his army decisively, brought his downfall. McClellan had often proven himself an able general. He had created

the Army of the Potomac, he had organized great campaigns, his plans of battle were sound; the will behind them was too weak to achieve a real victory.

While the Antietam Campaign was a failure for McClellan, Lincoln managed to salvage a victory out of the inconclusive battle. With the war dragging on into 1862, and victory nowhere in the foreseeable future, the president desired to infuse a revolutionary sentiment to reinvigorate the Federal war effort. By summer of that year, he decided emancipation of slavery was just the element needed: it would undercut the basis of the South's economic and social structure, would give the North a semblance of moral superiority over its adversary by taking up the cause of human freedom, and force European nations to seriously consider the unpopularity of allying with a faction that supported slavery. On 2 July, Lincoln read a preliminary proclamation before his cabinet and asked for the opinions of his advisor. Of them all, Secretary of State Seward gave the most sagacious advice, telling the President to wait until the Union forces won a real victory before issuing the decree; in a moment of defeat, it would waste the political capital of the gesture, making it seem as though the Federal Government was making the move in desperation rather than strength. Antietam wasn't much of a victory, but after the failures of the Peninsula and Second Bull Run, Lincoln would take what he could get. On 22 September, the Emancipation Proclamation was issued, promising to free all slaves in those states still in rebellion against the Union after 1 January 1862. In doing so, the proclamation and the entire Antietam Campaign itself, meant the damning scourge of the institution of slavery was to inevitably and finally meet its extinction in this republic. However, for Emancipation to succeed, the South would have to be subdued and that would take three more years of gruelling warfare and tens of thousands of lives. As Vauntier was to conclude, "The gist of the matter is that the war could only be ended by the hardest kind of fighting, that war means blood and death and desolation, and that when the big captain took the helm he sailed over seas of blood to victory and peace."

GUIDE FOR THE INTERESTED LAYMAN
Recommended Reading

Probably the best study of Antietam or of any Civil War battle, for that matter, is Stephen W. Sears *Landscape Turned Red* (New York: 1983) which was instrumental in the preparation of this work. Two other books by Mr. Sears deal with McClellan, giving the reader an incomparable examination of the personality of this controversial figure: his biography of the general, *George B. McClellan: The Young Napoleon* (New York: 1988) and a collection of Little Mac's letters, *The Civil War Papers of George B. McClellan* (New York: 1989). Other studies of the battle include James V. Murfin's somewhat garbled account, *The Gleam of Bayonets*

(New York: 1965) and Edward J. Stackpole's, *From Cedar Mountain to Antietam* (Harrisburg: 1959). A clear understanding of the Virginia phase of the Antietam Campaign can be garnered from Dennis B Kelly's article in *Great Battles of the Civil War* (New York: 1989). As to the Confederate capture of Harper's Ferry, read Dennis E. Frye's "Stonewall Attacks!-The Siege of Harper's Ferry" in Volume V, Issue 1 of the *Blue & Gray Magazine*, which also includes a tour of the area. Of the soldiers accounts, John D. Vauntier's *The 88th Pennsylvania Regiment in the War for Union* (New York: 1894) is one of the best regimental histories avail-

able, giving an impressive description of the somewhat confusing Battle of Second Manassas. On the Confederate side, J.F.J Caldwell's *The History of a Brigade of South Carolinians* (Philadelphia: 1866) offers a moving description of the fighting at Second Bull Run. As to the Maryland Campaign, Frederick L. Hitchcock's *War From the Inside* (Philadelphia: 1904) tells of the horrible fighting before the Sunken Road. *John Dooley: Confederate Soldier* (Georgetown: 1945) relates the tribulations of the ranks in the Army of Northern Virginia throughout their movements in Maryland. Other sources used for this work are:

Manuscripts

Antietam Collection. Dartmouth College Library, Hanover N.H.
George B. McClellan Papers. Manuscript Division, Library of Congress.

Books

Abraham Lincoln: The War Years. Carl Sandburg. (New York: 1939).
Advance and Retreat. John B. Hood. (Philadelphia: 1880).
The American Iliad. Ed. by Otto Eisenchmil and Ralph Newman (New Jersey (New York: 1947).
The Antietam and the Fredericksburg. Francis C. Palfrey. (New York 1882).
A.P. Hill: The Story of a Confederate Warrior. James I. Robertson. (New York: 1987).
The Army Under Pope. John C. Ropes. (New York, 1882).
"Battery D, First Rhode Island Light Artillery, at the Battle of Antietam, September, 1762." J. Albert Monroe.
Battle in the Civil War. Paddy Griffith. (Nottinghamshire, Great Britain: 1986).

Battlefields of the Civil War. (New York, 1980).
Battles and Leaders of the Civil War. Eds. Robert U. Johnson and Clarence C. Buel. 4 vols. (New York: 1866-67).
The Blue and the Gray. Ed. by Henry S. Commanger. (New York: 1950).
Brook Farm to Cedar Mountain. George H. Gordon. (Boston: 1885).
Bruce Catton's Civil War. Bruce Catton. (New York, 1984).
Campaigns in Virginia, Maryland, and Pennsylvania 1862-1863. (Boston 1903).
Chronicles of 21st Regiment New York State Volunteers. (Buffalo: 1887).
The Civil War: A Narrative. Shelby Foote. (New York: 1958).
Civil War Quarterly. Vol. IX, June 1987.
A Complete Military History and Record of the 108th New York Volunteers from 1862-64. George Washburn (Rochester, N.Y. 1894).
Confederates and Federals at War. H.C.B. Rogers. (New York, 1983).
Days and Events. Thomas C. Livermore. (Boston: 1920).
Disaster, Struggle, Triumph. Arabella M. Wilson. (Albany: 1870).
A Federal Surgeon at Sharpsburg. Ed. by James I. Robertson, Jr. Civil War History. June, 1960. Vol 6, # 2.

Four Years with the Army of the Potomac. Regis De Trobriand. (Boston: 1889).
Four Years with the Stonewall Brigade. John O. Casler (Guthrie Ok.: 1893)
The 48th in the War. Oliver C. Bosbeyshell. (Philadelphia: 1869).
From Bull Run to Chancellorsville. Newton M. Curtis. (New York: 1906).
"A High Private's Account of the Battle of Sharpsburg." *Southern Society Historical Papers*, XII. (1884).
Historical Times Illustrated Encyclopedia of the Civil War. Ed. by Patricia Faust. (New York: 1986).
Histories of Several Regiments and Battalions from North Carolina in the Great War, 1861-1865. 5 vols. (Raleigh: 1901).
History of the Bucktails. Howard Thomson (Philadelphia: 1905).
History of the Eleventh Regiment Ohio Volunteer Infantry. (Dayton, Ohio: 1866).
History of the 51st Regiment of Pennsylvania Volunteers. (Philadelphia: 1869).
History of the 45th Regiment. Ed. by Allen D. Albert. (Williamsport Pa: 1912).
History of Kershaw's Brigade. D. Augustus Dickert. (Newberry, S.C.: 1899).
History of the 9th Regiment Volunteer Infantry. Daniel G. MacNamara. (Boston: 1889).
History of the 19th Regiment Massachusetts Volunteer Infantry. (Salem: 1906).

History of the 124th Regiment Pennsylvania Volunteers. Robert M. Green. (Philadelphia: 1907).

A History of the II Army Corps in the Army of the Potomac. Francis A. Walker. (New York: 1886).

History of the 17th Virginia Infantry. George Wise. (Baltimore: 1870).

History of 60th New York State Volunteers. Richard Elly. (Philadelphia: 1864).

History of the 29th Regiment of Massachusetts Volunteer Infantry in the Late War of the Rebellion. William H. Osborne. (Boston: 1877).

Hood's Texas Brigade. J.B. Polley. (New York, 1910) Infantry in the Civil War. (Clinton Mass.).

I Rode with Stonewall. H.B. McClellan. (Boston: 1885).

The Irish Ninth. M.H. MacNamara (Boston 1867).

The Iron Brigade. Alan T. Nolan. (Berrier Springs. Mich. 1983).

Lee's Lieutenants. Douglas S. Freeman (3 vols., New York: 1971)

The Life of Billy Yank. Bell I. Wiley. (Baton Rouge, 1987).

The Life of Johnny Reb. Bell I. Wiley. (Baton Rouge, 1987).

Lincoln and the Civil War in the Diaries and Letters of John Hay. John Hay. Ed. by Tyler Dennet. (New York: 1939).

Memoirs of the Confederate War for Independence. Heros Von Borcke. (2 vols. New York: 1938).

"Marylanders and the Invasion of 1862." Richard R Duncan. *Battles Lost and Won.* Ed. by John T. Hubbard (Westport, Conn: 1975).

McClellan's Own Story. George Briton McClellan. (New York: 1870).

Memoirs of Robert E. Lee. A.L. Long. (Secaucus, N.J., 1983).

One of Jackson's Foot Cavalry. John H. Worsham. (Jackson Tenn.: 1964).

Personal Recollections of the Civil War. John Gibbon. (New York: 1928).

The Photographic History of the Civil War. (New York, 1911).

Rebellion Record: A Diary of American Events. 11 vols. Frank Moore. (New York: 1861-1863).

Recollections of a Confederate Staff Officer. G. Moxly Sorrel. (Jackson, Tenn.: 1958).

Preserve the Union. Thomas M. Aldrich. (Providence, Rhode Island: 1904).

Stories of Our Soldiers (Boston: 1893).

The Story of a Cannoneer Under Stonewall Jackson. Edward A. Moore. (Lynchburg, Va: 1910).

The Story of a Confederate Boy in the Civil War. David E. Johnston. (Portland: 1914).

The Story of the 15th Regiment Massachusetts Volunteers. Andrew F. Ford.

The Story of the 48th. Joseph Gould. (Philadelphia: 1908)

The 10th Regiment Massachusetts Volunteer. Alfred S. Roe (Boston: 1909).

Terrible Swift Sword. Bruce Catton. (New York: 1963).

Three Years in the Army. Charles E. Davis Jr. (Boston: 1894).

Three Years in the VI Corps. George T. Stephens. (New York: 1870).

Three Years with Company K. Austin C. Stearns. Ed. by Arthur A. Kent. (Cranbury N.J.: 1976)

The "Ulster Guard" and the War of the Rebellion. Theodore B. Gates. (New York: 1879).

Under Five Commanders. Jacob H Cole (Patterson, N.J.: 1906).

Uniforms of the American Civil War. Philip Haythornthwaite. (Poole, Great Britain, 1975).

The Virginia Campaign of 1862 Under General Pope. Ed. by Theodore F. Dwight. (New York: 1891)

A Virginia Yankee in the Civil War: The Diaries of David H. Strother. David H. Strother. Ed. by Cecil D. Eby. (Chapel Hill, N.C.: 1961)

War of the Rebellion: A Compilation of the Official Records of the Union and Confederate Armies. (70 Volumes, Washington: 1880-1901)

War Years with Jeb Stuart. W.W. Blackford. (New York: 1945).

The Battlefield

Located outside the small town of Sharpsburg is the Antietam National Battlefield comprising 810 acres of the original 12 square miles of the battlefield. Though the area has changed somewhat since the battle was fought so many years ago (the East and West woods have been cut away considerably since the war), the remnants of the Sunken Road and the site of Burnside's Bridge allow one to gain a good impression about how the battle was fought.

The easiest way to reach the field is by car, but the more energetic Civil War buff might choose to bike or hike the towpath of the Chesapeake and Ohio Canal leading from Georgetown through southern Maryland, following the majestic Potomac River. There are campsites every five miles along the route which leads right to Harper's Ferry and an area rich in the history of the Antietam Campaign and of this nation. From Harper's Ferry, reaching the battle field is not difficult, but requires both time and effort. Maps are available from American Youth Hostels. An instrumental companion to any tour of the battle field is Dr. Jay Luvaas' and Colonel Harold W. Nelson's *U.S Army War College Guide to the Battle of Antietam* (Carlisle, Pa: 1987), which was also instrumental in the preparation of this work.

Fictional Literature

Numerous lyrics have been written about the Antietam Campaign by soldiers and romantic poets, but none have gained the prominence of J.C. Whittier's dubious "Barbara Frietchie." Some fictional accounts of the battle itself are *Old Fusee* or *The Cannoneers Last Shot* published in 1883 and Donald J Sobol's *The Last Dispatch; A Story of Antietam.*

Simulation Games

Two games dealing with the Battle of Antietam are *A Gleam of Bayonets* published by TSR and the newer *In Their Quiet Fields*, published by The Gamers.

An outstanding rendition of the fight at Turner's Gap is *South Mountain*, published by West End Games.